THE BUSINESS CARD BOOK

What Your Business Card Reveals about You... And How to Fix It

Foreword by Mark S. A. Smith

Dr. Lynella Grant

Off the Page PRESS

THE BUSINESS CARD BOOK
What Your Business Card Reveals about You...
And How to Fix It

Copyright ©Lynella Grant, 1998
ISBN 1-888739-50-9; Softcover
ISBN 1-888739-51-7; Hardcover

Publisher: Off the Page Press
P.O. Box 1269, Scottsdale AZ 85252
(602) 874-0050
fax (602) 970-3925

Library of Congress Cataloging-in-Publication Data

Grant, Lynella, 1944 -
　　　The Business Card Book: What Your Business Card Reveals about You...and How to Fix It / Lynella Grant
　　　foreword by Mark S. A. Smith
　　　528 p. 32 cm.
　　　Includes biographical references and index
　　　ISBN 1-888739-50-9 (paper) ISBN 1-888739-51-7 (hard)
　　　1. Business Cards.　　　I. Title.
　　　HF5851.G7 1998
　　　741.6'85—dc21　　　97-18863
　　　　　　　　　　　　　CIP-REV

Typesetting: SageBrush Publications, Tempe, AZ
Cover: Foster & Foster, Fairfield, IA

To Order, see Ordering Information in the back
Or call 888-582-6402 for orders. All major credit cards accepted
Visit our Web Site: www.quick-and-painless.com
or our Fax on Demand: (888) 206-3056

Dedication

To the Entrepreneurial Spirit, which is
Ignited by Vision and Determination,
Driven by Ingenuity and
Sustained by Gumption, with
Diligent Attention to the Job at Hand;
Which Challenges us to
Achieve our Goals and
Improve whatever we touch—
By dint of our Resourcefulness

and

To Anyone Who is in Business,
who is, indeed, attempting to
grab onto a dream
and hang on until it succeeds—
whatever it may cost

How To Use This Book

> This book is designed to be easy to read and easy to find the information you need. Keep it on hand for future reference. Use only those parts you have time to consider now, and revisit it whenever a new card is needed.

Alternative methods to help you locate the specific information you need:

Treat this volume as a reference book not only for business cards, but also for your business identity. There is no need to read it from front to back. Choose the topics that interest you now; peruse other chapters later. It provides more information than you're likely to need at any one time, but consider it as part of your basic business library. You'll use it in different ways throughout your career. Each time you change jobs or reprint your cards, you'll find new reasons to consult it. Since more than half of the card-carrying population changes their card for some reason each year, you can be sure that you, too, will have a progression of cards throughout your working life.

Clearly, this book contains more than you ever thought you wanted to know about business cards. As initially written, the book confined itself to the non-verbal messages on cards. Inevitably, particular questions arose, such as which address to use or what type size works best. Before long, the desire to be comprehensive took over. Some card design elements are a matter of taste, but others reflect on your competence. The goal from the start has been to avoid blunders that undermine your image or credibility. Replace them with messages that make you seem dazzling and desirable.

It takes many "hats" to achieve a good business identity. You're not likely to have all those skills yourself, but **your judgment is required** to achieve the image that suits you best. Understanding all of the steps involved is the best way to obtain value and cooperation from the professionals you employ.

Unsure about your card?

If you want to receive a diagnosis of your card, send it to the Business Card Clinic®.

We can tell you what's healthy and what treatment is indicated. See page 479.

Graphic Table of Contents
Parts of a Business Card

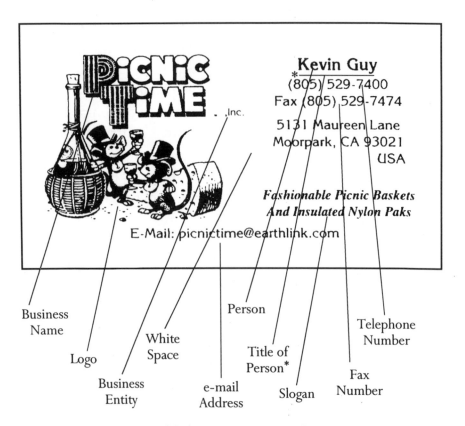

Location of Information

*   A title goes right under the name.

THE BUSINESS CARD BOOK

Extended Table of Contents

> Chapter **1**

> Chapter **2**

> Chapter **3**

Chapter **14**

Chapter **15**

Chapter **16**

Grab Their Attention

Mark S.A. Smith

Only a second that's all the time you get to make an impression on a prospective customer. And if you don't connect, they're gone probably forever. Your business card is a powerful part of your arsenal for building a lasting impression.

A well-crafted business card instantly tells your new contact who you are, what you do, and why they should pay attention to you. It communicates your status, experience, and ability to your new contact both consciously and subconsciously. It can brag about your position and accomplishments when it wouldn't be appropriate for you to do so. Your business card, done right, is a stand-alone advertisement that lets a prospective customer take the next step with confidence.

As a tactical weapon, business cards are easy to carry and leave a tangible reminder of your contact. You can exchange them for other people's business cards. It lets others easily pass on your information to others who can use your services. And without them, you'll never be able to enter those drawings for a free meal or the prize *du jour*. (Remember to bend the corners of your card to increase your odds of winning.) I see thousands of business cards a year. Unfortunately, most cards aren't well-crafted and it's really nobody's fault. There's 10,000 places where you can buy 1,000 business cards for $10.00. But you won't get help with the card's design. No one taught you how to design business cards. And if you use a designer, they've usually never been taught how to create powerful business cards either. Often the result is a beautifully designed card with nearly unreadable typography that doesn't communicate much more than can be found in a telephone book. The solution for crafting your powerful, prospect-grabbing, profit-building business card is in your hands. In this book, Lynella Grant has done all of the research, most of the thinking, and a lot of the work for you. Follow the step-by-step plan that she's created, and you'll craft a business card that's one in a million in being memorable and one in a thousand for getting the business you deserve.

Reach for this book every time you make a change in your business. Reach for this book every time you hire a new person to help you. And reach for this book every time you must write a small advertisement. Because, with this book you're going to learn how to sell you, your company, and your services with that little piece of cardboard we call a business card.

Mark S. A. Smith
Author, *Guerrilla Trade Show Selling*

Release the Power of Your Business Card

"Don't hire me!"

"I don't know what I'm doing."

"How can I tell you what I do, when I still haven't figured it out myself?"

If your potential customers ever heard you talk like that, you'd be out of business. Yet these kinds of statements are exactly what many businesses say about themselves everyday—without intending to.

A business card is a concise form of business communication. It is your stand-in when you aren't present—**the handshake you leave behind**. It is often all that your prospects have to remember you by. As with every other form of communication, much more information is transmitted than the mere words themselves. On one level, the card provides the printed words and graphic symbols you **intentionally** put there (the apparent message). However, on another level, numerous messages lurk between the lines. They provide the "body language" of your card (the hidden message). The combination of these elements creates impressions, emotional responses, and positive or negative reactions.

Business Cards Display the Business Personality

The business card reflects the personality and priorities of the business owner (even if there was professional design assistance). Since it is often an extension of the person(s) who started or runs the business, it is possible to discern aspects of the underlying personality and values.

A business card, however, does not always operate as an extension of a unique personality. The personal element is unlikely to be evident in such organizations as:

- Medium and large corporations
- Companies that result from merging several businesses into a composite organization
- Government entities and agencies
- Organizations operated by committees or boards
- Professions like law and medicine, where only minor variation in cards is permitted
- Churches, charities, and non-profit organizations

However, this information about business cards can still be useful, even for such organizations. They, too, have a message to communicate. That presents a riddle: How do you personalize the card of an impersonal organization?

Remember that all of your business advertisements, letterhead, cards, etc. operate as snapshots of your business. They reveal what your company feels is important. Too often, these are wasted opportunities—ones that could have been used to establish strong connections with the desired customer. Everything included in this book is designed to aid businesses in getting the most mileage from their communications.

Here's What You Want to Know About Me

Any business card should be able to answer four questions for the person receiving it:

1. What does your business do or offer?
2. Why should I remember you?
3. What sets you apart from your competitors?
4. How do I contact you? (phone, fax, address, etc.)

Most cards fail do to a good job of answering the first three questions, so there is little reason for a prospect to need the fourth.

Imagine instead having a business card as targeted as a heat-seeking missile, able to locate prospects and impress the dickens out of them so they rush right over to deposit their money in your hands. It's possible.

A Business Card is the Most Frequently Used Form of Business Promotion

In most cases your business card operates as a missed and mis-used opportunity. Fear not, for the chapters ahead provide all you need to use such opportunities to the max. Since your card is a snapshot of you, it should establish a positive and reassuring presence that makes your contact **want to do business with you**. When done well, it establishes a strong impression that communicates your true value.

A business card has power far beyond its puny size. As I mentioned earlier, it not only carries direct messages in words, but delivers subliminal messages as well—messages that are influential in the realms of feeling and desire. Such subliminal qualities are barely noticed, but attract or repel because they are reminders of intense prior experiences. These non-verbal emotional signals determine whether we have confidence in a business and will seek it out. Prospects respond to reassuring messages or "kiss you off"—all without a conscious thought.

But, you may protest, yours is a restaurant, a pool cleaning service, a real estate office, etc. The customer needs to **see what you do** before judging. "Surely, performance is more important than a little business card." True, but if you don't provide potential customers a reason to check you out, if you don't establish a bond of confidence with them, you will **never get a chance** to show that you can "Wow" them.

Your Card Makes a Statement About You

It may say:

- □ Negative things like "Don't hire me" or "I'm sloppy"
- □ You're so boring that you are totally forgettable, a virtual non-entity (Could you possibly be as dull as your card indicates?)
- □ I'm competent and know exactly what I'm doing

You can't afford to settle for anything less than the last option. If you've gone to the trouble to be in business, you need to use **all** your resources effectively. And make no mistake, your **business card can be the most effective marketing device you have!**

It may be the smallest representative of your business, but it is very powerful. By the time you've developed a card that really works for you, you will also have developed an effective strategy for all your business communications. You'll have achieved a winning card **and** a winning business.

Eliminate negative impressions like these:

- □ Indifference
- □ Inexperience
- □ Bad taste
- □ "Small Timer"
- □ Chintzy or under-funded
- □ You simply don't have a clue

Huh...What Was That You Said?

Everyone in business gives and receives hundreds of cards. Most of them fail to effectively market the businesses they represent— but **you can stand out in a more potent way**. In the chapters ahead, you'll learn how to avoid "gossiping" or non-descript cards that do so much mischief. You'll also learn many ways to make yours work for you—and work hard.

The primary emphasis of this book is on communication; design is secondary. Both are important, but the methods used to create your image on a card should be subordinate to the message you want to express.

This book has a single purpose—to make you really **notice** your business card and the image it establishes in the recipient's mind. Don't waste your opportunities to communicate directly and powerfully. As you become more aware, you will be better able to effectively deliver your own message. Discover ways to send both tangible and intangible messages that can further your success. Eliminate those signals that interfere with your goals. Soon, you will be able to recognize how well you are conveying the messages that you want—and be able to maximize them.

Learn how to:

- Develop a memorable card that makes you shine
- Send messages that will make your business succeed
- Eliminate impressions that unwittingly thwart your goals
- Look like a well-established operation, instead of a starter-upper
- Become aware of the influence of non-verbal messages
- Attract the kind of customers or clients you seek

Go Back To the Beginning

Don't overlook your reason for being in business: earning a profit doing what you like to do. A strong, consistent, positive impression increases sales and customer satisfaction, which, in turn, also improves your earnings. After you connect with your customers, and earn their confidence, you gain all the benefits resulting from their loyalty. No, your card cannot do all that alone—but it plays a starring role in that all-important step where their confidence in your business needs to be established—the famous and indelible "first impression."

A business card can indicate how healthy or successful a business is, based on confidence-building cues woven into its design. It reveals the presence of a marketing strategy, and shows how well the business has differentiated itself from its competitors. Such visual refinements take time and systematic effort, usually demonstrating that the business has gotten beyond the basics.

You're Not "Just Another Pretty Face"

Don't be fooled by appearances! This book is not just about getting a pretty, clever, or eye-catching card. Those are certainly desirable objectives, but not nearly enough. Your goal should not be skin deep, to just "look good." Instead, the card should reveal qualities that are an *inherent* aspect of your business, that kindle a desire to do business with you. Do you know which underlying qualities are your greatest strengths—the ones your customers most value about you? First identify them; then display them. If these benefits are not evident, your card is only doing part of its job.

Remember to Remember

What do you hope the business contact you just met will remember about you? This is probably the single most important question to ask **before** creating your card. Do you want them to remember you—or do you want them to remember your business card? This is not a trick question: Is it you *or* your card?

The primary reason you give that card is to **HELP THEM REMEMBER YOU!** Later, the sight of that card should bring you and the experience of meeting you instantly to mind. Every element on your card, (including how, where, and why they received it) should assist you to achieve that goal.

THE LIFE'S WORK OF YOUR BUSINESS CARD IS TO MAKE *YOU* MEMORABLE AND DESIRABLE.

Both you and the card must work together to create a strong, positive, and consistent impression.

Eliminate Ten Common Business Card Mistakes

- ☐ Does not clearly define what you do or sell
- ☐ Does not make you memorable (in a good way)
- ☐ Indicates unflattering things about you—like you're tacky or cheap
- ☐ Does not generate additional business
- ☐ Creates a muddled or cluttered impression
- ☐ Omits essential information, or is filled with non-essential information
- ☐ Looks out of date, or has information that no longer applies
- ☐ Is hard to read or confusing to the eye
- ☐ Lacks a point of interest, image, or theme
- ☐ Scrambles messages with inconsistent design elements

Be aware of what your business card says about you behind your back. The more business cards you pass out, the more you rely on them to represent you and the services you provide. They are your silent ambassadors.

Sharpen Your Eye

Each time someone presents you with his card, its details are speaking to you. Train your eye to "read" more of that information. Awareness makes you more discerning, more attuned to the layers of messages and technical fine points incorporated in every business card. With practice, your eye becomes more skilled at recognizing the meanings.

Even before reading the rest of this book, you've probably altered your reactions to business cards (including your own). You will react differently simply by knowing there is much more printed there than "meets the eye." The more you notice, the better you become at discerning those meanings and spotting subtle messages.

The "design" determines the overall impression given by a card. Since business cards are so small, every part needs to be in scale and to fit together harmoniously (like a melody). The total design and tone of your card indicate whether you are daring or conservative, refined or crude, careful or sloppy, etc. Such impressions have a powerful influence on those who recognize their meaning.

"I've Got a Business to Run"

You could be wondering whether you really want to bother thinking about a business card, when there are so many more important and pressing things demanding your attention. Cards are often considered frills, better left for someone else to deal with.

It's hard to argue with that logic, except to say that success in anything depends on the ability to tell what is important from what isn't. Your business day is consumed by choices, and your business survival depends on the quality of such decisions. A business card reflects core business decisions, such as your location, business name, image, and positioning. When such decisions have been well thought through, they can more easily be translated into an effective card and a coherent marketing program. Given how much a card reveals about the business's priorities, can you afford to ignore it?

Customarily, a small business goes though several stages regarding its choice of business cards:

1. Quick print standard options—the generic "printer's special"

2. Initial efforts to customize a card and image, usually as a do-it-yourself effort, with varying degrees of success

3. Design professional hired to tailor an image that shows "you have arrived"

Businesses often make the mistake of waiting until they are successful to develop their successful image. That is not necessary or wise. By using the advice in the chapters ahead, you can **appear to be successful** much earlier. Then your card **leads you** toward your goals, rather than tagging along behind.

You can design a great image and effective card for peanuts or spend too much for a card that does a poor job of promoting you. A small amount of money can buy a lot of image. When carefully done, your business card is able to provide value far out of proportion to its cost. The more important consideration is what your present card is costing you in sales and lost opportunities. Can you afford the one you're using now? Can you afford to delay replacing a mediocre visual identity?

WHY I WROTE THIS BOOK
The Author

It's hard being interested in a wide variety of things, because you appear to be unfocused. However, five years ago I ascertained the core element common to my diverse skills and careers—my fascination with pushing beyond the mundane. In that spirit, I adopted the name, The Problem D'Solver®, and through practice have cultivated the capacity to see the unfamiliar in the commonplace. A business card is a perfect example of an object that everyone sees but few really notice. As I started to **pay attention** to business cards, they had more and more to say to me.

To back up, I was born in Alaska when it was barely civilized, so possess a frontier mentality. I thrive on figuring out what lies ahead. Once initial challenges have been confronted and subdued, I'm inclined to move on. Along the way, I've passed through some fascinating careers:

- Attorney
- Commissioner of Indian Affairs for the State of Arizona
- Psychologist
- Personnel Director
- Real Estate Salesman (first licensed at 16)
- Statistician and Research Designer
- Author

- ☐ College Teacher
- ☐ Manufacturer
- ☐ Professional Speaker
- ☐ Inventor
- ☐ Professional Cook

My cards often reflected my own state of confusion or clarity. Through my varied careers, I've had many different kinds of business cards. The process of mentally working out my card would compel me to figure out what was really happening with my business. When I was unclear about the business goals or priorities, the card would show it. At the point when I had achieved a sharpened focus, I could easily figure out (and visualize) what my card should say. The effort to create an effective card would help me to "invent myself."

By the time I next reprinted them, it would be apparent how my perception of the business had grown a bit. This process was not unique to me. You've probably noticed something similar in your own business development. A business card needs to change as the business changes. **Your card should evolve in tandem with the business growth.**

Use Your Card to Define Yourself

In my legal practice, I have assisted in many start-ups, and advised businesses at various stages of maturity. Since I am a thoroughly addicted (and unrepentant) entrepreneur, I have also encountered many small business "creative types," who were struggling to make their ventures fly. It seemed apparent to me that there is a maturity curve for every business. Just as a baby crawls before walking, and does both before requesting the keys to the family car, a business faces different issues and priorities at the beginning than it encounters in later stages. It is often possible to tell from looking at a card whether a business person has mastered various business skills.

Often a card would create images or invoke feelings not directly related to the printed words. At first this perplexed me; however, after careful observation, I began to understand the value of the "unprinted word." A card characteristically reflects some aspects of the owner's personality and reveals a unique flair and vision. Once I recognized business cards as indicators of a business's stage of development, it was a small step to notice other messages as well: positioning, a coherent marketing strategy, company identity, taste, etc.

Such observations led me to seek out more information. Although there are some design-oriented books on the subject, there is relatively little available about business cards themselves. Here was a universal object that hasn't had sufficient attention—what an oversight! This book fills that need and shows how to get the benefits that a powerful card can provide.

I'm fully persuaded that **a business card is the most discounted and unappreciated business asset.** Just observe how many products exist to help create impressive resumes. We should care as much about our business cards as we do about our resumes. You can make this tiny, overlooked object become a force for driving your business or employment strategy. Usually, we ignore something because it's small and unimportant. But, though small, your card **is** important. Harness its untapped potency to achieve your goals.

Consider Problems as Valuable Resources

Anything that appears to be a problem is a demand for fresh thinking!

I chose the name "The Problem D'Solver®" because I think of problems as assets! Problems can be mined for massive rewards—once you stop avoiding them. Put another way, a problem is a door you have not yet opened—but you're ready to. When even a problem can be treated as an asset of your business, then what isn't? Fresh thinking brings to light unnoticed business opportunities, and unnoticed resources and abilities. The possibilities are endless.

In order to get the benefit from a problem, you must first **be aware of it**. Then you must **desire a solution** enough to deal with it. After a person decides that something needs to be fixed, figuring out what to do about it is not that difficult. Eliminate problems with your card so you can **communicate what you intend with power and style**. In the process, you address many business choices indirectly related to your card. But once you think about them, your business will reap many tangible and intangible benefits. Developing a potent business card also propels you toward a more productive business operation.

INFORMATION IN THIS BOOK
Note to the Reader

This book is written to assist everyone involved in business, so "you" refers to the owner(s), representatives, and employees of the business. No gender disrespect is intended in using pronouns or examples. Being in business is a big enough challenge, whatever your gender.

As with any advice, select what works for you in your particular situation. Every card you see is instructive, showing what works well or what doesn't. When in doubt about your own card, discuss it with your printer or a person who is more knowledgeable in graphic design. And really, your best feedback comes from your customers. If you ask them and then observe and listen, they will guide you to create a card that **makes them want you**.

The Cards Shown in the Book

Business cards have been extensively used to illustrate the written text. Although a few have been created to explain specific points of interest, most are real-life examples from existing businesses. Each was chosen for its ability to illustrate a point or a way of displaying information. They are not being held up as perfect examples, but each of them has something that makes it stand out.

They collectively illustrate the fact that a card can "work" for a wide variety of reasons. These cards also demonstrate the infinite variations permitted within the business card format and encourage you to experiment with different effects for your own "masterpiece."

This book does not hold up any real-life cards as bad examples. You have plenty of those already in your own card files. Most of the cards shown are a mixture of strong and weak parts—yet, the overall effect is still positive. These cards prove that **even a single element can make a card stand out as special.**

Many exquisite cards are very colorful, but unfortunately, this is a black and white book. Colors, paper textures, and special effects (like embossing and foils) do not show up with black ink. Consequently, only cards that reproduce in black and shades of gray were selected. Noteworthy features on many of the selected cards have been lost. Also, some high-impact visual effects are not represented here because they could not be transferred to these pages.

The cards used were selected to be illustrations only. Some of the businesses represented no longer exist, or the information shown on the cards may be out of date. In almost every case, we have secured permission before including a card. Use these examples as models, but two considerations are always paramount: your taste and deciding what works for you. Ignore anything in the chapters ahead that doesn't serve or apply to you.

MY PROMISE TO YOU THE READER

- ☐ You will never look at a business card in the same way again
- ☐ You will gain the power to communicate your message directly and powerfully
- ☐ You'll stand out in a very appealing way
- ☐ What you do to develop your business card will provide benefits in other aspects of your business and your life

Section I

The Body Language of Your Card—Discover Your Silent Ambassador

Express Your Business Personality through Body Language

An equally appropriate title for this book could have been *The Body Language of Your Business Card*. Body language is the nonverbal way people communicate through gestures, posture and facial expression. These symbolic gestures accompany every interaction and convey even more information than the spoken language. In efforts to persuade, symbols are more trustworthy and influential than words. The card displays those ever-present tidbits of imagery that express the bearer's personality.

Once someone reads your card, they feel they know something about you and your business. They have a sense that they know a bit about you personally. When they choose your business, they are responding, in part, to the character they feel then know. For example, you may meet someone and sense that they are open and accessible, or that someone else is cold and distant. Such perceptions determine whom you seek out. The same is true in business, and demonstrates why some businesses really are more attractive. Such engaging traits are revealed through the images on a person's business card—and they *do* influence us.

Hit Your Communications Bullseye

The business card is a highly condensed form of communication. You score a bullseye when you **deliver what you have to** say (your arrow) **to the person it's intended for** (your target). Business success depends on how consistently you "hit the mark." Your card is a crucial part of that effort. It is one of the ways you maximize your resources, and reveals whether you're hitting or missing the illusive bullseye.

You can have more than one target, more than one group you serve, but you should make distinctly different, carefully focused efforts to reach each of them. If you try to satisfy everyone, you often satisfy no one very well. **The public doesn't buy; individual people do.** Though a purchase may be dictated by company policy, the personality factor will always play a role in the buying decision. In some cases, it acts as the only factor. Decide how you want to express your business personality so that you achieve your future goals—a successful and prosperous operation.

Section Table of Contents

Chapter 1

Create Potent Impressions that Establish Your Identity

"Doctor, My Card's Not Feeling Well"

You go to the doctor's office because you're feeling ill. He takes some blood, puts a drop on a slide and looks at it through a microscope. From that little sample he is able to determine much about your state of health. He uses the sample to evaluate the infinite physical processes taking place in your body. Each test measures elements that show which physical processes are normal and which are out of order. The resulting diagnosis is not mysterious, only a matter of interpreting the evidence.

A business card works in much the same way. It is a little "sample" of your business. Many things can be diagnosed about the state of your business health by a careful examination of your card. It reveals signs of health or weakness, progress or decline. Anyone making the effort can read those telltale signs. Most people "read" some of the signs, though they may not realize it on a conscious level. Such signs influence how they perceive you and your company.

Consider any negative messages on your card as symptoms of an underlying malady. Once a weakness is diagnosed, a cure can be found. Often, the disorder is simply a sign of neglect. Just as a fever indicates an underlying medical condition, true recovery results from curing the cause, rather than the symptom (the fever). You don't want to just create a pretty card (no fever), but to produce a card that reflects a healthy and well-run enterprise.

Your Card Establishes Your Identity

Your card is your billboard, an advertisement for you, the company, and its products and services. Think of it as the **handshake you leave behind**. It establishes the business identity and attempts to garner the respect of all who receive it. It communicates to your prospect on a variety of levels, so try to deliver a coherent message. Expense is seldom a hurdle in achieving an effective card; the hurdle is discovering, and expressing the identity of the enterprise. Your card should set you apart, while making it plain what you and your company do. As a friend commented, "An undefined business card is not worth reading."

Polish Your Business Image

Almost everyone in business is aware of the importance of establishing a good professional image. They buy high-quality professional attire, take care in their personal grooming; and invest in a well-decorated office at a good location. Yet, how often the carefully crafted image is undermined by inattention to detail. Telltale signs of indifference or ignorance often leave the opposite impression than the one intended. Your card is one of those details. Yet, if it is well done, it signals that you know what you're doing and are, indeed, professional.

Every business has an image, whether or not there has been any attempt to create one. The image could appear as a ragbag of assorted pieces or as a coordinated effort reflecting the presence of a plan. Like a wardrobe, a consistent tone and feeling sends one kind of message, while a mish-mash of unrelated pieces sends another message. Identify your strongest and most unique messages. Emphasize them and consistently promote them. Resist diluting or confusing your message. After all, your unique image is an important and valuable business asset.

Signs of a Good Business Image

- **Gets noticed** immediately
- Creates a **positive impression**
- Makes an impression that is **remembered**
- **Distinguishes** and sets the business apart
- Sends a **clear message**
- Leads to sales or some **benefit for the business**
- **Attracts interest** and catches the eye
- Shows **relevance** to the receiver

Brown ink on white stock; business name is brown and tan wood pattern, reflecting the wood products

Marketing includes all the things you do to come to the attention of those who buy what you offer. But never forget, *you* **are your most important product**. You are what sets your business apart from your competition. Deciding what you want your card to communicate will certainly affect the resulting card or the responses it provokes. You have a greater chance to increase sales, referrals, name recognition, etc. **if you have carefully defined your goal** and set specific ways to measure how close you've come. Think of all the ways that you could secure more business. That which is most unique or important about your business should be evident from your card—or how do you expect the potential buyers to initially find it out?

ARIZONA
WOLF TRAP
PROGRAM

Children Learning Through
the Arts

Frances E. Cohen
Regional Director

202 E. Earll Drive, Suite 140
Phoenix, AZ 85012
(602) 266-5976
FAX (602) 274-8952

Lilac blocks and blue type on white stock; are children's toys and show range of artistic activities for children

Go Fishing for Customers

Consider the card or any promotional piece as "bait." Each type of bait attracts a different kind of fish. You want a card that increases your visibility while attracting customers who want what you have to offer. Evaluate the bait you are using relative to what are you fishing for; then consider what you are actually catching. So, the real question is: **What is working for you and attracts customers to your business?**

Plan your sales tools from the customer's perspective. Consider what *they* like and care about, what they want to buy. A designer developed the package for a product to be sold in discount stores. The package was beautiful, but the product did not sell very well. Later, they re-packed the same product in a cheap-looking package, which sold at the same price. Sales immediately increased. The purchasers at such stores were price sensitive and felt that fancy packaging indicated a higher price. They treated the more generic package like a bargain because it looked like one.

Send a clear message, based on your knowledge of your customer's needs. Think about why **you're the one the customers should choose**, and communicate those benefits. As you find ways to address *their* needs and concerns, your "fishing trip" will be a success.

BOOKSTORE-
COFFEE HOUSE

BUY, SELL & TRADE
NEW & USED
BOOKS & RECORDS

The **Artful Dodger's**

FEED 'N READ

OLD KAHULUI STORE   871-2677
55 KAAHUMANU AVE, KAHULUI, MAUI 96732

Black print on mustard stock

Courtesy the Business Card Archives

Make the Most of Your Card

Developing a suitable card is a matter of finding a balance between creative expression and good taste. Good design, coupled with quality stock, denotes taste and importance. A cheap and tacky looking card puts you at a disadvantage, for anyone who looks at your card with distaste won't be eager to do business with you.

A picture is worth at least one thousand words. Like a photograph, the card provides a picture—an impression of you (and you don't get to use anywhere near a thousand words to convey it). First, define the business identity; then use words and images to capture some aspect of it as **your visual identity**. Your card is saying: "Here are my standards." Then the buying public decides whether or not they approve by voting with their dollars.

A business card may be little, but it performs some hefty functions that are necessary for business success. Think of them as the **three P's**:

- □ **Packaging** the business in a tangible, recognizable and transferable form—**image**
- □ **Positioning** the business and establishing its niche—**marketing**
- □ **Publicity**—getting the word out

Ten Reasons Why Your Business Card Is Your Best Promotional Device

- □ **First** (and sometimes only) promotional material—printed as soon as the business starts
- □ **Cheapest** advertisement—a boxful goes a long, long way!
- □ **Wide targeted distribution**—mostly given face to face
- □ Sets **business style** and format—echoed on stationery and products
- □ **Basic** sales tool; uncomplicated and flexible
- □ Most **frequently used** marketing tool for small businesses
- □ **Generates more business** and referrals than any other form of advertising (for many types of businesses)
- □ **Versatile**—easy, quick and inexpensive to tailor for different markets or purposes
- □ **Expected**—an established business practice
- □ Creates **name recognition**; personalizes you, and builds credibility

On a business card, the space restrictions are daunting. This little piece of paper is all you get to work with. Even if you use the back or a fold-over card, the space limitations can be intimidating, but never impossible.

actual size
3 1/2 inches x 2 inches (88 mm. x 52 mm.)
(always state the horizontal measurement first)

A horizontal card, also called landscape orientation

actual size
2 inches x 3 1/2 inches
(52 mm. x 88 mm.)

A vertical card, also called portrait orientation

(602) 966-3139

THE SHOE MILL

"SHOES FOR ALL WALKS OF LIFE"

398 S. Mill. #100 • Tempe. AZ 85281

Shoe Mill in purple, rest of card in forest green on white stock, shows all the people served; also pun in slogan

When you pass out a card, you want to **promote** your business and **reach** out to those who could benefit from what you do. But you are also attempting to connect with them in ways that encourages them to **want to do business with you**. Although a business card is simple, it is designed to both personalize and market you. While it doesn't provide a complete picture, it plays a necessary role.

Consider the image a card creates about you in the minds of others. Whether that image is professional or amateur, capable or inept, successful or struggling, you will be treated as though it's accurate. Knowing how to impart the images you want provides you a competitive advantage.

Harness the Power of Attraction

If you connect with people emotionally, they will **look for ways to do business with you**. Their money and actions inevitably follow their wants. Back up the initial impression with performance and reliable products that further reinforce their reasons for seeking you out in the first place. That's what makes them stick with you. Unless they **prefer you specifically**, you're just one of the many options to chose from. In that case, factors like price become more important, and you are constantly competing for business.

Your objective is to be perceived as having that "special something" customers want. What you choose to highlight about your business will appeal to some people, but not others. Test the impact of your image or slogan specifically on the **kinds of people you're courting**. Your customers can be enticed by highlighting those features that matters to them; not all prospects will be interested in the same benefits. Many people don't like sentimentality, yet that may be exactly the right note for the kind of product you sell. For example, men will respond positively to different images than women. Catering to your buyer's preferences is vital.

Photograph of football game in brown duo-tone and screened fans; print in black; sense of old souvenirs

Courtesy the Business Card Archives

Example of a rough-and-tumble, masculine-type card

Dark red print on a dusty rose stock

Example of soft, frilly, feminine-type card

Positioning Is in the Mind of the Prospect

Nido Qubein, a well-known business speaker, points out, "It's not enough to be good at what we do. The right people have to know that we're good at what we do. They also have to be convinced that what we do will help them meet their objectives or solve their problems, and that we can do it better than anyone else to whom they might turn. They won't come to this conviction unless we become good at marketing our expertise."[1] In order to create a relationship with your ideal customer, they have to become aware of **tangible benefits you can provide for them**.

Positioning is the key to effective marketing. "Positioning is creating and maintaining precisely the right perception **in the mind** of people who can buy our professional services. It's not what you or I think we can do that counts. It's what our clients perceive and act upon that counts."[2] Decide **precisely** how you want your business to be perceived, and then develop the messages that reinforce that impression.

Positioning is impossible without a clear understanding of **who your ideal customer is**. You must establish your ability to solve their major concerns. Draw upon your unique personal and business resources to meet their needs in ways that no one else can. You will know you have successfully positioned yourself when others think of you as having no competition. In your prospect's mind you have become the first and only choice.

What the Customer Really Wants From You Is You

Demographics tell about characteristics of groups, but **groups rarely buy or do business**. Individuals do—whether for themselves or as part of their employment. As you **relate to people one at a time**, you will gradually establish your desired image in the minds of many.

Customers are buying much more than products and services. They are buying your:

- Style and personality
- Reputation and values
- Appearance

- Decor and ambiance
- Services and expertise
- Aromas of the business (like baking bread, flowers or even ink fumes)
- Packaging
- Status of what is offered
- Staff and customer service
- Acceptance by the community

The "flavor" of your business is something that sets you apart from your competitors. How do you suppose potential customers are able to decide what they want from you unless they are aware of your business's personality? It is human nature to buy "personality" before deciding to buy anything else.

Credibility is indispensable for business health. Central to establishing your good name is creating an impression of honesty and integrity. People prefer to do business with someone they trust, so a good reputation is priceless. Don't ever put it at risk by engaging in borderline ethical practices. Reinforce values like integrity, reliability and consistency at every opportunity. Your customers will love you for it.

Establishing a reputation requires even more long-term effort than establishing an image, and the two are not necessarily the same. A good reputation is neither quick nor easy to come by, and it must be worked on constantly. "Once it's broken, it can't be mended," as the refrain goes, so it's wiser to "maintain" than repair it. Always remember, a reputation is not established just for outsiders, but permeates the way the entire organization operates. It should be consistently demonstrated with every contact—from employees, to suppliers, to customers. No amount of "spin control" can undo all the harm caused by lack of integrity or slipshod methods.

Target Your Card as You Target Your Market

Since the only benefits that matter are those that matter to your potential clients, learn as much as possible about their priorities and desires. Two benefits are better than one, because buying is a complex decision. Different people are looking for different things to satisfy different requirements. As you take those preferences into account, you will serve your clients better and keep them longer.

If possible, provide both rational and emotional benefits because they reinforce each other. Rational and emotional approaches appeal to different personality types. Concrete benefits or images help you to seem less abstract, making you appear to be more "real." A graphic image that makes the company or product tangible is even more important for businesses that sell services or provide intangible products, such as advice.

Rational decisions demand concrete evidence. (See Chapter 4 on ways to bolster your benefits.) And that becomes even more important as the buyer's education level or the price of the product(s) increases. Emotional benefits satisfy intangible desires for prestige, security, beauty, etc. They are much more compelling than the logical or need-driven benefits. However, some products, such as jewelry, are almost entirely impulse or emotionally driven.

A gallery of
beasts, books, and
handmade toys
celebrating
the spirit of the animals,
the old stories,
and the child within.

Open daily 12 noon to 7 p.m.
Between Spring and Broome Streets

THE
ENCHANTED
FOREST

85 MERCER STREET
SOHO, N.Y.C. 10012
(212) 925-6677

Black print on heavy cream-colored stock; it even feels enchanted

Courtesy the Business Card Archives

A card with an emotional appeal

Olive green and red logo with black type on beige recycled paper

JOANNE REASONER
Manager

OUTDOOR

POPULAR

OUTFITTERS

The Right Direction For Outdoor Gear.

1036 EAST BASELINE ROAD • TEMPE, AZ 85283
PHONE (602) 820-6362

A card with a rational appeal (even asserts its rightness)

Nowadays, everybody wants to find out what consumers like, want, or are looking to buy. A plethora of surveys, focus groups, and customer questionnaires permit marketers to hone in on illusive desires, that can be courted and catered to. When you know your customers' age, gender, education level, marital status, etc., you will be better able to find them and to serve them. Such knowledge gives you power. Knowing the mix of men or women in your customer base is invaluable. Men and women buy for different reasons, even when they buy the same product. The same can be said for any other demographic factor like age, race or income level. Consider whether these factors apply to the sale of all your products, or differ from product to product.

Mine your sales data for less-than-obvious connections. You don't need sophisticated computer analysis to find the gems of information in your own sales. Your cashiers or sale staff, undoubtedly, notice many relevant tidbits, if you can find a method to capture what they know. Look for ways to improve your business services and promotions by using such information.

Also, pay attention to your own purchases. You and your business are customers to other businesses, and buy a wide variety of products and services. You constantly select which businesses to patronize; you also decide which companies **don't deserve your business**. But do you ever pause to notice **what made you make**

such choices? Notice what little signals made you say: I want to buy here instead of there. I want this supplier, but not that one. If you start taking heed of your own selections, you'll discern reasons why some businesses do better than others. Such awareness helps you fine-tune the ways you deal with your own prospects and customers.

Create a Consistent Impression

Whenever you meet someone, you create an impression—actually a series of impressions. If it is an initial contact there is the famous "first impression" (that you never get a second chance to make). Any subsequent contacts with that person tend to re-confirm the opinion already held.

Think of a meeting with someone as though you are opening a file folder and entering miscellaneous information about them: name, gender, employer, age, nice smile, firm handshake, likes to water-ski, graduated from my *alma mater*, member of Toastmasters, looks married, etc. Everyone notices or files different information, depending on what matters to him. The chitchat back and forth, coupled with your observations, provides data for the entries.

By the time your conversation is over, you've had at least three reactions, all totally subjective (your personal opinion). Right or wrong, these impressions are likely to remain. Future action, if it occurs, is usually determined by this crucial initial contact. That is why your business card is so important! It plays a major role formulating first impressions.

Reactions on Initial Contact (like scales, showing a full range of responses)

- **Like—Don't Like**
  Overall positive or negative emotional reaction
- **Want To Know More—Don't Want To Know More**
  Considers business, social, other contexts; can have a different rating for each area

□ **Get More Information—Opinion Pending**
Curious or not, and if so, what about? Can be either
vague or specific issues, mild or pressing interest

The next contact you have with that person, you will "pull up
their file" (if your memory permits) and enter any new information.
You compare your recollection from prior times you met to what
you're encountering now. Match (click). Don't match (mild alarm
felt). You gather more information or double check for a logical
explanation—(warning flag). Or you might decide, who cares?
Forget them. It only takes a second; but in a sense, they live or die
in that second. Thumbs up; thumbs down. Of course, they're
evaluating you in the same way.

You want to trust your opinions about people. Because of what
psychologists call the halo effect, people interpret what they see
according to whether or not they like someone. A person will
habitually reconfirm a positive impression, once it has been made.
Any new information is interpreted as positive and consistent with
the established opinion (or negative, and still confirming, the initial
opinion). Therefore, it is extraordinarily difficult to change an
opinion once it is formed. Incompatible (not matching) information is ignored because it creates feelings of discomfort. On a barely
recognized level, you find yourself avoiding or conveniently forgetting a person who sends negative or inconsistent messages.

We can make strong and lasting impressions or weak and
negative ones in the same amount of time. Your business card helps
establish these impressions and serves to remind the receiver of his
feelings when you're not present. Thus, your card both establishes
and reinforces your image in a prospect's mind.

Silence the Slander in Your Midst

"You know, they don't have their act together—it's
pretty unprofessional."

"Something over there isn't 'quite right.'"

"It wouldn't surprise me to hear they're having some financial problems."

These are examples of hurting words, words that can do any business a lot of damage, words that would shock you if you heard them, words that would make you angry, words you wouldn't want repeated about you—or your business. Anyone spreading such gossip and slander should be sought out and silenced, if possible. No one would sit still for such treatment. By golly, you'd stop it! Yet the culprit is not some meddling busybody bent on doing you harm, nor a competitor eager to spread malice. The source could be your own business card, and you could be the unwitting accomplice who spreads a dubious message each time that you give one away.

The card you leave behind should serve as your silent ambassador. With a bit of careful attention, it could just as easily be spreading positive messages. First, you need to realize that you are sending multiple messages with your card and business documents. Unintended and unflattering messages are conveyed much too often. (See Chapter 2 on decoding messages.) But such slander can be silenced. Once you recognize it, putting a stop to such gossip is not that difficult.

Most People Notice One Out of Three Impressions

Even though you are constantly sending "silent messages," people receive only part of the "presentation." Studies have determined that a typical person receives more than 3,000 commercial messages each day. Everyone is flooded with them and filters out much of the sensory overload. If you don't want to be part of the visual clutter, you must maximize the impact of your message. Be prepared to consistently send and re-send your information in such a manner that it stands out from the collective mediocrity. It takes nine impressions to move a customer from indifference to commitment. Therefore, **repeat consistently; repeat consistently**.

Consider the people who will see and react to your card. Each of them may have different information needs and desires. Include information on your card to satisfy the different needs of various audiences. If one card won't satisfy all their requirements, provide several versions that provide the information that each of them uses.

For purposes of targeting your card, people may be conveniently grouped as

- Customers, those you have and those you are courting
- Suppliers
- Associated business people
- Social contacts

Know Your Competition

When designing your card, evaluate the competition.

- How you are **different** or better than the competition
- What they do or provide; how you can **improve upon it**
- How to **set yourself apart** and appeal to the desired customers

Distance yourself from competitors so that the distinctions between you are not blurred. Magnify those differences. Make it clear why customers should choose what you do over the others. Strive to be sufficiently different in your colors, logo, style, and overall image that you will not be confused with them.

Define your advantages. (See Chapter 4 for ways to bolster your uniqueness.) Stress distinctions between you and your competition, even if the differences are small. For example, every beauty shop does most of the same things with hair, yet the ambiance, music, prices and personality of the stylists appeal to different types of customers. Position yourself in the customers' minds. Even if your merchandise or service is essentially the same, emphasize differences that set you apart. These differences are exactly what should be revealed on your card whenever possible.

Try this experiment. Take several of your **competitors' cards**, and scratch out their names and write in your own. If the card still makes sense, you haven't yet established your unique identity. On the other hand, if your competitor could take your card, change the name and phone numbers, and still have an accurate card, you've failed to differentiate your business. The card should be revealing something unique to you, even if it is nothing more than your good taste.

Capitalize on What Your Competitors Are Overlooking

Pay attention to activities your competitors are not doing well. Capitalize on untapped opportunities.

- □ Specific **groups**, organizations, ages, genders, races, educational levels, etc. who are not being courted, served, or served well
- □ **Services** that are not provided
- □ **Limited** hours, house calls, weekends, deliveries, availability of financing, etc.
- □ **Completeness** of products or services
- □ **Speed** of response
- □ **Uniqueness** or specialization

You Gotta Be You

Even though your business card should target your market, it should also reflect your personality, along with that of your business. Provide a distinction no one else can offer. Then consider how best to combine your image and the customers' desires. Do your best to make the two inseparable. If you've designed well, any distinctions between you and what you sell will be blurred. When a potential customer thinks of you, an image of your product pops into mind and vice versa.

Both cards, black raised print on white stock

Look for ways to add personal contact in your business and correspondence. Break out of the institutional impersonality. Remind contacts you are a person and you see them as individuals. Handwriting sets a personal tone. Write on your cards as you give them away. On other occasions, send longer hand written notes; or use a software program called Personal Font, which looks just like your own penmanship. It customizes your own handwriting so it can be generated by the computer keyboard. (Additional information can be found in the Resource Section.) Also, anything handwritten is less likely to be tossed out by the person who sorts the correspondence.

Eight Ways to Enter the Mental Filing System

Whenever someone receives a business card, they briefly wonder whether it's worth keeping:

- As a link to a potential **customer** or client
- As a link to a **resource** or supplier
- As a link to a **colleague**
- For **social** or non-business reasons
- To use for **referring business**—to pass on to someone else
- Just because of something **likable**, unusual or useful about the person or their card
- To **update** information they already have; to be entered into the data base
- Reluctance to part with something, because "**you never know**"

If they can't find a reason to keep the card, it gets lost, or worse—**tossed**. Assuming the person is still interested, only then will she notice whether the information is clear and readable. Once again, she will decides if she has any interest in you, your business, or services. All this occurs in the few seconds when you exchange cards. Who knows how much (if any) of it will come to mind the next time she sees the card or needs what you provide. Find ways to "hook" the receiver to pay attention at the time the card is given. Remember, you are trying to convey a total image of yourself and your product(s) so it can be vividly recalled when needed.

Does Your Card Rate a Second Look?

It's easy to look at things without really seeing them. Who even **looks** at your card? Try this experiment with any business card.

1. Take a card and look at it intensely; take some time.
2. Pay attention to your own reactions while you stare at the card.
3. What do you notice at first glance? Consider the whole thing, the general impression.
4. Do you feel any emotions or sense any related images? Do any recollections arise?

5. Do you notice anything unusual (either good or bad) or especially familiar?

6. What sticks out? Is there anything that doesn't quite fit with the overall mood of the card? Do you feel attracted? repelled? indifferent?

7. Next, actually **read the information** on the card. Focus on each word and its meaning. By now, the first, second, and third reactions have already occurred. You have probably decided whether or not you care about what it says. You probably know whether or not the card is worthy of being kept. Repeat these procedures, testing your reactions to several other cards. Such efforts will help you refine the skills used to decode messages. (See Chapter 2 regarding the subtle messages on cards.) This exercise trains your eye to the nuances of a card.

8. Now, consider **your own card** and give it the same treatment. Be honest in your evaluation. Pretend you don't know yourself, and you are a potential customer. If you knew nothing about the business except what shows on the card, how eager would you be to seek you out?

Make 'em Take a Double Take

Aim for a double-take whenever you present your card. Usually, when someone is handed a card, she barely glances at it. Occasionally, several seconds later, something on the card triggers puzzlement. She looks again, and this time she really **sees the card**. Something else is going on as well. She is also responding to you and your message on a sensual, non-verbal level. Then she reads the words more carefully, to figure out why the first glance caught her attention. That's the double take. Now is the time to talk about the message on the card, to strengthen that connection to her. Become memorable. Develop a card that creates a double-take because that assures that the card is noticed.

As I said in the Introduction, I'm known as The Problem D'Solver® (dissolver), but many people misread my card as The

Problem Solver (sic). If they don't do a double-take or comment on the name, it's apparent they didn't catch the meaning, so I immediately explain the differences between **problem solving** and **problem dissolving**. (Problem solving is a temporary remedy, whereas, if a problem can be dissolved, it doesn't come back; you've outgrown it.) As a result of that discussion we're off to fruitful common ground.

Hot pink Planet Mirth, cheeks, mouth and halo, the rest in navy blue on glossy white stock

MobyDisc and tie in red; rest of the print in black on white stock

Vanilla Pudding Cards Don't Have Much Taste

The phrase, "vanilla pudding," describes something that is bland and lacking in flavor or personality. It embodies the one-size-fits-all, stick-to-the-middle-of-the-road, everyone-is-the-same approaches. Such a strategy is uniformly mediocre. The message is

"It's good enough," but good enough is not special; it is not unique; it is not memorable. It may be acceptable—but only barely. Is that really what you want? Acceptable? It may not offend, but it won't garner the response you are after. Some people won't notice or mind—but many will. Your card is not just a name and phone number—it's a representative of you.

```
ABC COMPANY

Joe Blow, Salesman
1234 Main Street    (111) 222-3456
Anywhere USA    Fax: (111) 222-3458
```

A vanilla pudding card—a business standard

Walk into almost any printer and say "I need business cards." The clerk pulls out the binder with severely limited options. Select from the offered choices of type, paper, color of ink, layout formats, etc. The process is much like ordering the lunch specials at a restaurant, except your choice will stick with you for years. Choose one from option A (card stock), one from option B (ink color), and so forth. The clerk totals up your charges, and several days later your mediocre, "good enough" cards are ready.

Many small business people do it that way—and that alone is sufficient argument against it. If that is how you decide what your card will look like, you've eliminated most of the options that produce a powerful impression, and Section II is full of them. Instead, your selection was dictated by the severely limited choices available. The "one size fits all" method rates high in simplicity, time saved and economy, but low on business image and uniqueness. By failing to give your business card serious attention, you achieve an image that is flat, uninteresting, and, in the end, self-defeating. Often, for the same amount of money, sometimes even less, you can have a stunning card that screams forethought and care. As Joel Weldon is famous for saying, "Figure out what everyone else is doing, and **don't do that**!" (emphasis added).

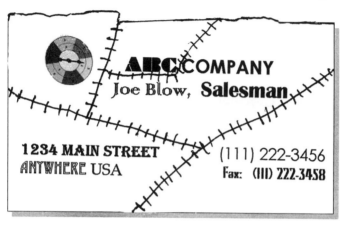

A Frankenstein card—parts stuck together, but they don't match

Don't Create Frankenstein Cards

The other extreme is a card that is patched together with things that simply don't fit. It isn't bland, but neither is it pleasing. The effect is somehow "wrong." Your personality is a broad scope of life experiences woven together to form a unique and coherent "you." This personality shows in your business identity, whether or not you mean for it to. A Frankenstein card simply is not integrated.

Frankenstein cards are a step ahead of vanilla pudding cards because an attempt is being made to develop a visual identity—but they are not there yet. These cards are "under construction;" they still need more refinement. Don't despair, these cards are on their way to becoming Prince Charming. Eliminate the "odd bits" and tweak till it clicks.

Abolish Common Business Card Blunders

- ☐ Off the rack—the standard prepackaged selections (vanilla pudding cards)
- ☐ Tacky and cheap—the basic model without any charm or options
- ☐ Too much packed on the card; difficult to read or comprehend
- ☐ Too many elements which are in conflict; over-designed or Frankenstein cards
- ☐ Missing critical information
- ☐ Grubby or marked up cards
- ☐ Scrambled messages with inconsistent elements
- ☐ Grammatical errors or typos

Such blunders convey negative impressions. They are usually signs of laziness, rather than a careful plan gone awry. The overall image is one of an amateur still trying to get his act together.

Add Spice and Something Nice

- ☐ **Humor**—funny, ironic, clever, a parody
- ☐ **Wit** or inspiration—thought-provoking, a play on words, or insightful
- ☐ **Eye-catching visuals**—puzzle, illusion, images that challenge
- ☐ **Useful**—informative, data, map, conversion charts, etc. (See Chapter 10 on reasons to keep cards around longer.)
- ☐ **Eccentric** or quirky flavor—though be careful that it makes positive associations
- ☐ **Unique**—based on something that really sets you apart, like a miniaturized product
- ☐ **Engage the senses**—sound, sight, smell, feel; makes the card physical

Some options work as fortuitously as good design. In each case, they make the card noteworthy and memorable—by making it unique.

BRUCE NOE, D.V.M.

2820 East University
Suite 104 Mesa, AZ 85213
(N.E. corner of University & Lindsay)

Weekdays   8-7
Saturdays   8-3

(602) 830-6810

Black print on blue parchment

Courtesy the Business Card Archives

Black print on white with intense blue eyes

Courtesy the Business Card Archives

Logo in red, type in black on white stock

Paws IV Publishing

Celeste Fenger
Marketing Coordinator

BOX 2364
HOMER, ALASKA 99603
907-235-7697
FAX 907-235-7698
1-800-807-7297
e-mail: pawsiv@ptialaska.net

Pink and green border; brown fox, black type on white stock

oh! my nappy hair

A salon & barbershop for
Women ▪ Men ▪ Children

Dredlocks · Perms · Braids · Weaves · Color · Cuts
and whatever else you desire

1607 - 2nd Ave.
Oakland, CA 94606
(510) 839-3877

805 S. La Brea
Los Angeles, CA 90036
(213) 939-3999

Strawberry border, blue dress, black print on white stock

Rainy Day
Publishing
DAVID LEGGETT
KIM LEGGETT

(888) 456-9326
(901) 755-8035
Fax (901) 755-2529

1740 GERMANTOWN PKWY.
SUITE 18
CORDOVA, TN 38018

Black print on heavy off-white stock

Remember the Rest of the Family

When considering the design of a card or a business image, please be aware that the card isn't an only child. It has siblings—letterhead, invoices, and brochures. There is a family resemblance, and each member reinforces the identity of the business. All documents need to be harmonious and reflect a common message. Consistency, elements of style, and a pleasing arrangement of parts are all important. When each element reinforces the others, the whole picture becomes much stronger. Always consider the rest of your business communication family when designing your card. Does it exist harmoniously with other company images? Does it send the same or a contradictory message?

Use consistent images and design in

- Letterhead, envelopes and labels
- Flyers, brochures, press kits, promotional materials, displays, training materials
- Invoices, statements, fax sheets, checks
- Packages and wrapping materials

Don't stop there—use your visual image everywhere, on everything. Put it on walls, uniforms, the outside of your building (so it can be read by a speeding vehicle), on signs, or anything you print. Make a statement; make it noticeable, and continue to reproduce it wherever and whenever possible. Show that you have developed an identity and that you are proud of it.

It is the consistent and persistent display of an image that eventually creates an identity in the minds of the public. It doesn't ever stop. Even though Coca-Cola is the most widely recognized symbol in the whole world (close your eyes and you "see" the red background and the white swirly script), the company still actively promotes and reinforces that image.

It isn't enough to be consistent, remember, your image also needs to be dynamic, relevant and memorable. You're striving to be noticed and show uniqueness in a way that makes a positive, easy-to-recognize and hard-to-forget statement.

It's Your Card and Your Choice

You may be a really wonderful, efficient, professional, hard-working businessperson, and all your clients know it, despite your having an ineffective card. If so, you probably had to work harder to overcome the deficiencies of your card to get those clients—you just didn't realize it. After all, you got their business, right? Of course you're right, but couldn't you have made better use of your time than working to overcome the less-than-ideal image? If that little, ubiquitous piece of cardboard is hurting your marketing efforts, it deserves your attention.

If you chose to ignore negative message(s) your business card might be sending, prepare to accept the results. But imagine how much better you could do without the handicap.

To Recap

Your visual identity is a vital business asset. Develop one that attracts those you want to serve, and then display it with flair. Your card is an important part of that identity; it helps to create a positive impression that sets you apart.

BUSINESS CARD LAWS

1. A business card is the smallest package your business comes in; make it as good as you and your business are.

2. A business card is a handshake you leave behind; create an impression they'll remember each time they see your card.

3. A business card is a team project, distilled from your vision, the designer's skill and the printer's craft, all arranged to speak in a meaningful way to your customer.

4. The life's work of your business card is to make *you* memorable and desirable. Both you and the card must work together to create a strong, positive, and consistent impression.

5. Use your card to build other's confidence about you and what you do.

6. Developing your card also helps you invent yourself and highlight what is unique about what you provide.

7. Your business card is part of a strategy to position yourself in the minds of customers and peers; it is effective when it makes them *want to do business with you*.

8. Effective cards are memorable because they are all too rare; invest the interest to make your card as interesting as you are.

9. Your card will become memorable if you involve both the emotions and the senses; give people a reason to care about you.

10. A business card can be your most effective marketing tool, but only if you get them into the hands of those who need what you offer.

11. There are many messages on a card besides the printed words. Eliminate those that undermine your desired image.

12. Your card should grow and evolve as the business changes.

©*Lynella Grant, 1998, The Business Card Book*

Chapter 2

Decode the Visible and Invisible Messages on Cards

"Read" Overlooked Messages

Doesn't the word "decoding" conjure up exotic images? In detective and spy thrillers the clues are there for anyone to see, but only the most alert can discern their meaning. Something appears to be one thing, but in reality, it is something else as well. Decoding actually involves developing a **method for interpreting what you** *already* **see**.

The ability to decode grows with discernment. You think you see something accurately. Then, before your eyes, it reveals more and more. Even more information becomes available to you once you are attuned to cultural and business nuances. Awareness of those other messages makes you a more effective businessperson. As you notice and respond to those clues, you will never look at a card in the same way again.

The ability to decode is not just for spies. Life works in much the same way. There are many things happening at the same time, each encrusted with meaning. Since you can't take it all in, you must choose what to pay attention to and what to ignore. The business card is just a very specific, tiny, tangible example of the ubiquitous presence of clues. Like the detective stories, the messages can be decoded by anyone who takes notice of them.

Decoding gives you more power. Once you notice and can identify something, you have power over it. What you choose to say on your card matters less than the fact that you are **aware** of (and hence can control) your impact. You are not blind to the influence of your business image on the people you seek as customers and clients.

Decipher Visible and Invisible Messages

A business card is usually a standard-sized (3½" x 2") light-weight, light-colored cardstock covered with printing. Those words and graphic symbols provide the card's **concrete messages**. Anyone looking at a card **reads** the same printed messages. Most people assume that the printing tells **all** a business card has to say—not true! Those obvious messages are just the starting point.

Of equal or greater importance are the **invisible** messages that *hitchhike* along. They operate like body language, sending abundant information without words. They reveal useful data like your degree of business savvy, how well you have your act together, and whether you have positioned yourself in your field.

Your card displays words and visual symbols. Symbols communicate intuitively and directly. If you have the right symbol, you evoke a full reaction, including sensory perception and associated positive memories. The advertising industry has made an art form out of establishing such connections. So should you.

Those invisible messages can be positive, negative, or a mix. Positive messages are reassuring ones like: well-established, quality organization, high status, educated, professional, reliable and knowledgeable. Messages like those do not occur without careful planning. Actually, most negative messages occur precisely because of the **lack of forethought**. Be alert for anything that detracts from your identity or message. It's doing your business harm.

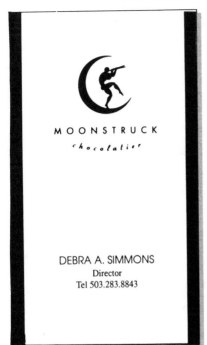

MOONSTRUCK
chocolatier

DEBRA A. SIMMONS
Director
Tel 503.283.8843

Moonstruck Chocolatier

Correspondence
6663 SW Beaverton-Hillsdale Hwy.
Ste. 194, Portland, OR 97225

Production Facility
7739 NE 21st
Portland, OR 97211
Tel 503.283.8843
Fax 503.283.8913

2-sided card, dark blue on heavy cream stock; vertical bleeds on each side of the front

Moonstruck Chocolatier

Everything about the card appeals to the senses and emotions:

- Engages the senses: touch, sight, hearing (the notes of the pipe), and, almost, taste
- Shows understated elegance in design and arrangement
- "Chocolatier" is uncommonly small and suggests upscale; also, suggests an emphasis on quality and image ahead of commerce
- The card looks and feels like high quality, so implies that the candy must be also

- Design is executed on heavy paper with a distinctive ink color, which is classy
- Bleeds on front unify the card and indicate a more expensive print job
- Classic image of Pan, the Greek god of forests and animals is playing his pipe super-imposed on another classic symbol, the crescent moon. Pan is delicately and gracefully poised, and you sense he is dancing; you can almost hear the notes summon you
- Images and card design suggest timelessness and a simpler life
- You're prepared to pay a premium price since everything says "expensive"
- Shows an extravagant use of white space

The front is all sensuous images; the back is very businesslike and shows there are two locations: one for business activities and the other for production.

The overall impression is of attraction, making you long to try the candy—in fact, my mouth is already watering.

Now that You Mention It...

Most of us are decoding messages to some extent already. Whenever I remark that there are non-verbal messages on a card, others respond, "Now that you mention it." They then relate something from their own experience, like "Once I saw their business card, I knew their request wouldn't be approved."

You often notice discrepancies between what people say and what they subsequently do. But when you think back, you realize you knew even before the disappointing experience that the person was unlikely to perform as he had promised. That is because you **perceived the discrepancies on a subconscious level**, where you felt something disquieting. You "knew" more than you rationally believed that you knew. When it's about a trivial thing, you hesitate to blow it out of proportion, but you still should give credence to that awareness. A sensed discrepancy simply means that the pieces don't fit for some reason—so you should not hesitate to figure out why. It could be a subtle warning of dishonesty, incompetence, or problems to come.

Kinds of Information Revealed by a Business Card
(and other business communications)

- Coherent **marketing strategy**
- **Customer orientation** or lack of one
- Level of **professionalism** and care
- Whether **well established** or positioned
- Approximate **size** of the business
- Evidence of **competence** and reliability
- **Stage** of business
- **Success** signs
- **Credibility** cues
- **Philosophy** or goals of the business

No card will show all of these factors, but some of these will always be indicated. However, you are going to interpret what you see on cards in a more systematic way. You can tailor your own information to send precisely the impression you intend. For example, you needn't look like a newly hatched business, but appear to be one that is well established.

Elaine Floyd
Author/Publisher

(314) 647-0400
FAX: (314) 647-1609

6614 Pernod Ave.
St. Louis, MO 63139

AM. ONLINE: NL News
COMPUSERVE: 72633,325

NEWSLETTER
r e s☺u r c e s

♦ *Marketing With Newsletters*
♦ *Making Money Writing Newsletters*
♦ *The Newsletter Editor's Desk Book*
♦ *Newsletter News & Resources*

Turquoise on vertical band of logo and on diamond bullets; the rest is black print on white stock

Newsletter Resources

▫ Card clearly identifies what is offered and who its market is through a bulleted list—newsletters about newsletters for those who do newsletters.

▫ Business is still quite small, since the author and publisher are the same, but that also suggests that there is personal attention for people who use the services.

▫ Combination of fonts in the logo (one word is all capital letters and the other one is all lower case letters) makes a visually interesting combination that does not take itself too seriously. The stack of newsletters is moving, not static, and the overall image is one of casual accessibility. You anticipate that the publications will also be practical and easy to read.

▫ Since this is a publication source for newsletters, the person is showing she knows something about layout and design. It is cordial, direct, and uncluttered.

- The electronic address shows that the business has an electronic presence, and probably is knowledgeable about using computers for newsletter design.
- Shows effective use of color; overall pleasing effect.

You feel encouraged to see their publications because they seem useful and inviting.

The only weakness is the word "Resource_s_" suggesting that it is one of many. An even stronger statement would be to call the business the Newsletter Resource (no "s") to state assertively that it is the *only* resource that you need.

The Receiver Is the Perceiver

Once it is printed, the card is unchanging. But one dynamic and critical (actually critical in both meanings) element is not on the card—the receiver. The card itself is coupled with the experience of receiving it. (See Chapter 12 about giving away your card.) **How someone responds to it is a crucial part of the card's message.** It establishes the emotional connection that will be recalled later.

Decoding a card takes into account the **reaction** evoked in the receiver. Make a habit of taking note of your own reactions to any card you receive. You already have a method for evaluating and responding to people, even if you haven't given it much conscious thought. As you take the time to carefully look at a card and the **way you received** it, you'll notice that more and more data becomes apparent to you. Look for the emotional and non-verbal messages borne on every card. When you simply haven't any interest in what it says, it leaves you feeling indifferent. Trust your own emotional reactions, and inquire further when you encounter contradictory messages.

Heed Your Array of *Simultaneous* Responses

- **Intellectual**—awareness of the specific information; does it interested you?

- **Emotional**—feeling a particular way, responsive to sensory cues

- **Physical**—treating the card in a physical way, like touching or rubbing it. Do something with it, like folding it or writing on it; or best of all, acting upon it—like calling or visiting the business (an excellent way to verify initial impressions)

- **Common sense**—registering on your good business sensor

Some of these responses are at a conscious level. Others happen so fast that you are barely aware of them. The point of decoding is not criticism but to clarify what is puzzling or unfocused. Notice what appeals to you. Since most of the cards you encounter are mediocre, good examples stand out. They compel you to take notice!

The ideal card is without sour notes; it's pleasant. Any deviations from a good feeling are noticed—mental penalty or bonus points are awarded. Since most cards are mediocre, anything special stands out and demands extra attention. So-so cards barely register. You don't need a complicated scheme of analysis. The reaction may be as uncomplicated as **Good Job** or **Bad Job**, with an occasional **Really Good** or **Really Bad**. It could be as simple as WOW!

Ten Abilities Used to Decipher Business Cards

- **Making mental connections**, large and small, with your other facts on file

- **Gathering** information and impressions

- **Filing** information you notice away for future reference

- Sending appropriate **responses** (while giving or receiving cards)

- Showing respect and **interest** in the discussion during the time you're together
- **Registering contradictory** impressions
- Deciding whether to **trust** the person and what they say or do
- **Evaluating** the person's personality, status, style, values, etc.
- Deciding whether to **follow up** or get involved
- **Comparing** what you are observing with other similar types of businesses

Whenever you pay active attention, you gather information more efficiently and completely. As you collect clues from additional channels of awareness, some conclusions become obvious, others are seen to be irrelevant. In any case, you become better informed and more aware. Complex information is better integrated, so decisions require less effort (which means less stress). You also are more powerful, gaining an advantage over competitors who are just muddling along. Not a bad return for applying more focused attention.

OPEN THE MENTAL DRAWBRIDGE
Court the Fellow in Charge of Attention*

*trademark of Lynella Grant, The Problem D'Solver®

There is a little fellow (or gal) in everyone's head who is in charge of attention. He runs the mental drawbridge. You have one; every customer has one. Your drawbridge operator has the same gender, level of sophistication, and interests that you have. No matter what you may have decided to do, he's the one who **really determines where your attention goes**. He operates the mental drawbridge, which is opened when he's interested and closed as soon as he loses interest. He works long hours, but is very arbitrary about when he opens or closes the drawbridge. Since he stays in the background, most people are unaware that he's even there. This mental gatekeeper is very powerful because he's the one who decides what you notice and respond to—and for how long.

Fifteen Characteristics of the Fellow Who Runs the Drawbridge

- Can't concentrate and has a **poor memory**—doesn't recall what else he should be doing now
- Loves to **laugh**—forgets other priorities and leaves the bridge down
- Prefers **variety**, fun, excitement, and a good time
- Has **little tolerance** for sad, tedious, or yucky stuff
- Is vain—wants sincere flattery, **recognition** and praise; but will settle for any
- Reacts instantly and will shut the bridge without notice—often triggered by **fears** or old scars that push the *close* button
- **Lacks** a sense of **proportion**—can treat important things as distractions and trivial things as significant
- Is **motivated by wants** (impulses) rather than needs (basic requirements)
- Can be **bribed** by smooth words or lured by curiosity

- Responds to **passwords** and codes from those who touch him emotionally
- Is easily **impressed** by status or name dropping
- Becomes **bored** or frightened easily
- Can't keep track of **time**
- Doesn't like to think about business or **practical** things very long
- Will operate on the basis of **stereotypes**, if you let him

Enlist the Drawbridge Fellow

In spite of such contradictory attributes, the drawbridge operator is very powerful. He's the one who determines whether you get to first base or hit a home run. He will decide if you connect with the customer or make the sale. You cannot communicate unless the other person is available; for that you need to include her drawbridge gal. She's not business driven, but it's good business to know she's on the job. You should cater to her preferences whenever possible. Many of the card's messages should be for her benefit. Provide her some of the things she likes and she'll give you a better chance to connect.

The drawbridge fellow (or gal) is very adept at deciphering clues, though he seldom bothers to pass on the information in a rational way. Enlist his input on several things simultaneously. By being attentive at that subtle level of awareness, you will notice many tidbits of worthwhile information that are usually ignored.

Simultaneously notice:

- The **entire card**
- **Specific items** of information
- *Your own* **drawbridge fellow**, watching him go through his paces
- Your own **non-verbal reactions**

It's in the Brain

Humans are social animals with millions of years of instinctive responses built in. To survive in the past, the choice between fight and flight had to be made instantly. Distinguishing between friend (harmless) and foe (predator) was the difference between life and death—an error was fatal. The decision about what to trust was too vital to be left to reason, which is slow compared with instinctive reactions. The primitive non-verbal part of the brain determines whether or not to trust or flee, based on information that is so subtle and instantaneous that it is unnoticed by conscious thinking. Yet, it has determined your reaction: beware, get away, ignore, or relax.

The primitive brain (the part under the wrinkles) is the seat of our more basic emotions, among other things. It responds to pictures, images, symbols, and anything humorous. That's why you should create an emotional or sense-based connection if you want to gain another person's trust. All emotions are subjective personal responses. They touch us because they contact our common humanity. With forethought, you can establish such emotional connections by the way you develop your card.

All of the Senses Can Play

Perceptions just beneath the level of consciousness communicate directly with the fellow who runs the drawbridge. He then responds to them with interest or indifference. The more senses that are engaged, the more involved he becomes—he can't resist. The senses are tied to the instinctive centers, so respond instantly and without words. The more sensory messages being sent and received, the more ways you can connect with the other person. When an experience involves all the senses, it causes more intense impressions at that time as well as fuller recollections later.

Business cards depend on sight, of course, but don't stop there. Consider the sense of touch and how the textures of the paper and ink feel. For example, tactile feedback of the paper alone may be sensed as flimsy (cheap) or heavy (substantial and prosperous). If possible, form a visual and verbal connection between the senses and what your business provides. A wallpaper hanger who glued a piece of cheerful, textured wallpaper on the back of his card provides an excellent example of creating a sensory awareness about his business for the other person.

Sound is hard, but the suggestion of birdsong, or the trill of notes, or other obvious sounds can be indicated in such a way that you *feel* as though you've heard them. Slogans that have a rhyme, like jingles, can be printed in a manner that they almost "sound" like they are being chanted. Likewise, taste can be suggested by showing food or flavor-related images. Even smell or movement can be indicated. Subsequent associations bring all of the related sensations back again. That's why the experience of getting a card is vividly recalled whenever the card brings you to mind. Further, sensory triggers may occur at any time and remind the recipient of you and your product(s) and services.

Sky in gradu-ated blue screen; world, tongue and Frog Music in purple on white

Courtesy Business Card Archives

Full color still life of food against purple-gray background on heavy textured off-white stock

J·O·S·E·P·H·I·N·A

RESTAURANT · 1900 BROADWAY, 10023 · NYC
OPPOSITE LINCOLN CENTER · TEL 799-1000 · FAX 799-1082

Courtesy Business Card Archives

GARY WOHLMAN
PRESIDENT

INDIVIDUAL COACHING • TEAM BUILDING
PUBLIC SPEAKING • SEMINARS

PRESENTATION BREAKTHROUGH SERVICES

P.O. Box 638, Mill Valley, CA 94942 • (415) 381-6569 • FAX 383-7273
E-MAIL: gwohlman@well.com   WEBSITE: www.well.com/~gwohlman

Logo, name and title in dark red, other print in black on white glossy stock

Philip E. Orbanes
president

Winning MovesINC.

100 Conifer Hill Drive ★ Suite 102 ★ Danvers, MA 01923
phone: 508-777-7464 ★ fax: 508-739-4847
E-mail: WINNINGMOV@aol.com

Red swirling ball, black print on white stock, seems to move, and even "Moves" is leaning

HEALING DYNAMICS

Rita Bojórquez
Licensed Massage Therapist
Bi-Lingual. By Appointment
MEMBER
American Therapeutic
Massage Association

❖

Scottsdale Civic Center
7373 Scottsdale Mall. Suite 4
Scottsdale. AZ 85251
602-947-4614

Hands in purple screen, Name and diamond in purple, rest in turquoise on cream textured paper

Connect with Others through Symbols

During each social contact, attempt to connect with the fellow who runs the **other person's drawbridge**. Consider how to capture and maintain his attention long enough to establish a lasting connection. Too many attempts to communicate fail because they occur when the drawbridge is closed. Remember to court the drawbridge fellow long enough to effectively deliver your array of messages. Once you start noticing how your **own drawbridge fellow** participates, you'll communicate better with everyone else's.

Consider what emotion or reaction you are attempting to establish. Then everything about the card (from the choice of typestyles to color, images, and layout) should enhance that emotion. If you are handling someone's money, you need to convey reliability and level headedness. However, if you are selling dreams and adventure, there are more appropriate emotions that you want to arouse. When your card is not related to the type of business in some way, it sends a message that you don't care about it and that your interests are elsewhere.

Emotional signals engender emotional responses, and it is emotion that motivates people to buy everything beyond the bare essentials. They are buying the intangibles, the dream, the vision, the emotional connections. That is why emotional links are so hard to break once they have been established. Customers who have bought for emotional reasons have been shown to be the most loyal and least susceptible to lower-priced competitors. They are less concerned about price than about losing a positive emotional relationship.

What to Look for While Decoding

There is a saying that good editing is invisible; if it has been done well, you won't notice it. The same is true of good design and execution. If the card is done well and delivers its communication well, the editing or design (or lack of them) will not be the area of prime focus—your message will. Reading the card won't feel like a poke in the eye. Notice the importance of the emotional factor in describing an effective card. A laundry list of dos and don'ts will describe logical things to do, but the **feeling component is more important** than any such specific rules.

Although it is difficult to describe all the things that go into making a good card and a strong impression, when they all work together, the card conveys a good feeling. Cards that capture your attention have an "indefinable something" that just feels good to you. That "something" works best when it reflects an attribute of the business itself, and is not just a design feature of the card. When recipients resonate to the business personality, it isn't mysterious. The signs are there, and you should be aware of them.

On most cards you'll discover some positive and some negative messages, which may cancel each other out. It is easier to state **what not to do** than **what to do**. Much of the decoding effort involves spotting incongruities or sour notes. Some types of blunders can be eliminated as soon you become aware of them. Remember, an important purpose of decoding is to figure out what is puzzling or unfocused. The effort should sharpen your critical eye, not just find things to criticize. Decoding helps you give words to your powerful abilities to "see" beyond the obvious.

Delete Negative Messages Such as:

- ☐ I don't pay attention to details
- ☐ I don't know what is important
- ☐ I have bad taste (I'm tacky)
- ☐ I'm cheap, or my business isn't doing very well
- ☐ I'm clueless; I'm not aware of professional standards
- ☐ I'm just doing this until something better comes along
- ☐ I'm not successful
- ☐ I don't want to do what everybody expects
- ☐ I don't care what you think about me
- ☐ I'm doing the best I can, so bear with me or cut me some slack
- ☐ I don't have a coherent image of my business
- ☐ Don't bother to remember me
- ☐ I'll get around to dealing with such details one of these days
- ☐ I'm overwhelmed by all the demands on me
- ☐ I don't have time to plan
- ☐ This isn't what I really do; it's not my real job

You get the picture. Most of these are excuses that you are unaware you're making. They reveal inefficiency and lack of focus. Don't let your card say things about you that you didn't intend. Once you discover the messages being sent, you can replace them with others that serve you better.

It's a shame to provide a negative list without a positive one to match. However, most of these examples can be reversed to be positive statements—which is, after all, what you're trying to achieve. For example, "I do pay attention to details" or "I do know what is important" can be demonstrated by the many clever or competent details woven into your card and throughout your business.

Select the Hitchhiking Messages You Want to Send

- ☐ **Performance**—What actually is being done and for whom (particularly in a service business); the services provided; benefits enumerated or spelled out
- ☐ **Businesslike Methods**—Enhance credibility and trust; professional, informed, competent (See Chapter 4.)
- ☐ **Body Language between the Lines**—Written messages are always colored by emotional connotations and the manner in which they are delivered

An important aspect of any card is the *way* the receiver reacts to it. So far, the focus has been on refining your awareness of **your own reactions** to cards. Now shift your attention slightly, and notice **how other people react to your card as they receive it**. Notice **their body language**. It will tell you volumes about how well you are delivering your message. Pause, stop talking. Let them relate to your card—you'll be able to detect their reaction before any words are said.

Fulfill the Expectations You Establish

Back up your messages with policies and performance that **demonstrate** its reality. A card should reveal aspects of an enterprise that reflect what the customer can actually expect. A half-hearted card creates low expectations. It is always easier to exceed a low expectation, but this is a book about being consistent in image and performance. You need to back up your business image with a similar level of performance and service.

Further, don't confuse your messages. Strive to eliminate mixed messages and contradictory images. The messages that serve you best have a long shelf life. Where possible, they should be included in other business communications, like brochures, speeches, and newsletters. Never miss an opportunity to get the company message out!

JOHN HENRY'S
CONTINENTAL CUISINE

Neven Bajlo
Owner/Manager

Black on white glossy stock

(602) 730-9009
S.E. CORNER OF ELLIOT AND RURAL
909 EAST ELLIOT • TEMPE, AZ 85284

Avoid "Scratch and Dent" Cards

You've scratched out the old phone number or title or location and written in the new one as a temporary measure. (I once received a card with six things scratched out and changed—only the business name was not in pen.) So you're putting off the next printing because, after all, it's only temporary. Isn't it amazing how long a person can put things off—after the move, when the holidays are over, or the best one (and I hope this book doesn't make it a more likely excuse) "when I can really do it right." Good intentions do not compensate for the loss of credibility that results in the meantime.

Cards are inexpensive, a lot less expensive than what it is costing you to delay! Print new ones **now,** and incorporate some improvements. Call it market testing. Get feedback, invite suggestions, but start doing it! **You do not have to use up your whole box before you reprint.** That is a holdover from your mother's admonition about finishing your vegetables.

Everyone in the Organization Matters

Every employee should be:

- Sending the **same message**—providing a common business philosophy and image
- **Informed** about the company's priorities, philosophy, and products
- Aware of the **desired effect** of their cards
- Attempting to deliver value and **build trust**
- Sensitive about **customer service** and the impact of their job on it

Anyone involved in the business can shatter its good reputation. Remember, longevity in business requires building relationships and trust with your customers. Untrained or uncaring employees can undo years of good work. Every employee, from the owner to the "gofer," needs to be aware of his importance to the company's image and performance. Teamwork requires that all share the same priorities, and the success of the business depends on it.

Marketing is an on-going, company-wide activity. Marketing is part of everybody's job. All employees deserve to have a business card. Every one of them should be aware of being on a team with a shared common philosophy.

Big Fish in a Small Pond or Small Fish in a Large Pond

What "size image" do you want to convey? Are you a big fish in a little pond, or just the opposite? Subtle messages embodied in a business card can covey size, power, structure, status, or even access to power—whether truthful or not. Your card can enhance your image or trap you. It can mislead or truly inform. On this, you must be very careful!

When you work for a large company, your status is partly a reflection of the size and prestige of your employer. In a smaller business, status has to be indicated in other ways. (See Chapter 4 on ways to enhance credibility.)

THINGS TO DECODE
Your Tie to Technology

Several years ago an e-mail address was rare, but that has changed quickly. Already 40 percent of business cards are sporting an e-mail or electronic address. Sooner or later, each business must decide whether or not to have an electronic presence or a World Wide Web address. That decision also signifies that the business is committed to riding that wave into the future. It has stepped out of the "that's the way we've always done it" mentality and has joined the emerging trend.

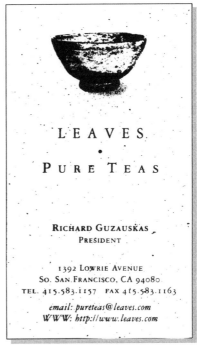

Shades of black and gray on speckled paper; back: muted dark green

Even a company whose card evokes the ancient Orient provides e-mail and Web addresses

For most businesses, the Internet is not yet a paying proposition, but many are choosing to establish a presence there. They are establishing contacts with others who do business that way. Some customers prefer to get information about products and services on-line, so you want to accommodate them. Eventually, most businesses will get involved, but for now your electronic identity indicates (in the decoding sense) an awareness of computer realities and a willingness to do business with others who are on-line.

Businesses vary greatly in the extent they are computer or technology oriented. Of course high-tech companies will have the skills and interest to use the latest "bells and whistles." However, even very low-tech businesses, like Bed and Breakfasts (a true mom and pop industry), market themselves on-line, and book a high percentage of their reservations electronically. Almost any business can benefit from being connected to computer networks.

Computers (and the software that they use) are being enhanced with glorious new features at a dizzying pace. Keeping on top of the steady upgrades is a challenge that must be constantly re-addressed. If your business can benefit from an Internet presence (or your competitors are already involved) get started on the requisite learning curve. Without some such indicators that you're aboard, you'll soon be treated as computer illiterate (and out of date).

Don't leave your low-tech customers behind. Some people won't have any interest or skill in changing the way they do business. They will leave you rather than alter their way of relating to you. Add options, but don't eliminate anything presently used for the convenience of your customers. You may even reap new customers from other businesses that leave them behind. One business got a lot of new customers because it was one of the few companies that didn't eliminate some dated methods for customers to order.

Provide Enough Information

Decoding also reveals ways you miss the mark. What is enough, but not too much information for a business card? It's a tough call how much you should put on your card, but there are some things that are so important that they are conspicuous by their absence.

Never assume "they will know" anything about your operation. **If the customer needs to know something in order to deal with you, make sure it's on your card!**

Your business card must have:

- ☐ Business **name**, your name, or both (See Chapter 3 on names.)
- ☐ What the **business does** and who it does it for, if it's not obvious from the name (See Chapters 1 and 3 on your identity.)
- ☐ **Address**—including city, state and zip code (See Chapter 5 on locations.)
- ☐ **Phone** numbers, including the area code (See Chapter 5 on your important numbers.)
- ☐ Depending on the type of business, there will be other "must haves;" for example, if you're a doctor, the card had better say MD

Think of the wasted opportunities of going to a national trade show and failing to provide your area code. It happens all the time. Take note of what you're always being asked. It might indicate something that needs to be added to your card. For example, if you're tricky to find, include a map or a comment like, "NE corner of Smith and Main" or "Next to the library."

Make sure your card is complete, so you're not a headache to those who are trying to track you down. You can't afford that. The customer you're trying to entice won't necessarily go out of his way to reach you, especially when you have competitors. Eliminate those things that could be barriers to doing business with you.

BUSINESS STAGES

Businesses Have Different Priorities at Different Stages of the Cycle

The card often indicates which issues have been resolved or are still "under construction." Spotting such priorities may signal where the business is in the cycle. Too new is often suspect, as is a business in severe decline.

Each Stage Confronts Different Issues

New Business

- Needs to get notice and established
- Inventing the wheel, with plenty of trial and error
- Attracting business and suppliers
- Lots of effort before sufficient financial returns or certainty about what works
- Under capitalization and delay in revenues

Growing and Expanding Business (Mature)

- More employees, along with the issues of training and managing them
- More services required
- Additional locations
- Changes in market conditions
- Competing trends and tastes emerging
- New lines of merchandise or services provided

Declining or Old Business

- Customer needs and priorities have changed
- Image out-of-date, seedy, or shopworn
- Dated marketing methods
- Loss of market share

- Key employees retiring
- Transfer of leadership or estate planning for continuity
- Demographic differences of customer base
- Old location, fixtures, and equipment require capital investment

Avoid Looking Like a Start-Up or a Has Been

Even with careful advance planning and a clear image of the business, it takes a while for a business to work out some bugs and get all the parts working together. It takes a while for its market to find it and become repeat customers. There are constant adjustments and new insights about what does and doesn't work as planned. A new business has many start-up issues and each of them feels like "inventing the wheel."

Among the messages that can be decoded is whether it is still a new business that is defining its identity. Or it could be a more mature business that hasn't upgraded and re-focused its image. In either case, the business hasn't provided a clearly defined image that is accurately positioned in the buyer's mind. It's not a one-time effort, but must be re-considered and adjusted throughout the life of the business.

Twelve Ways to Determine When Your Business Has Started

- Get your first **customer** or contract
- Sell a service or product and **get paid** for it
- **Name** the business; register your name or trademark
- Print your **cards** (or letterhead, flyer, menu, price list, etc.)
- Decide you're **open**; hang your signs or "shingle"
- Get your business **license**, tax ID numbers
- Set up the business **entity** (partnership, corporation, etc.)
- Sign the **lease** or when the lease starts

- Start **keeping records** or paying taxes
- Open your business **bank account**
- Order or receive your initial **inventory**
- Get into the **yellow pages**, or get a business phone or phone listing

It is usually not obvious exactly when a business gets started, since there are different "starts" that seldom occur at the same time. There are many ways to indicate when a business has begun, but sooner or later enough of them will occur that you'll be "in business."

Often the first step taken, once a decision has been reached to "go for it," is to have cards printed. Getting cards signals that you're inviting business. For a sole proprietor in a home-based business, printing the card may be all that is done. When that initial burst of enthusiasm cools, it is sometimes discovered that the "perfect name" isn't going to work or isn't available for your use. **Before** getting those cards made or taking any of the other above steps, check to see if your chosen name can be yours. Your librarian or attorney can help you determine whether your proposed name is trademarked or belongs to another business.

The Business Entity as a Clue to Business Maturity

The type of business entity (sole proprietorship, corporation, etc.) also can provide some indication about its place in the business cycle. Many businesses start as sole proprietorships (one person or couple). As the operation grows, legal and tax considerations encourage a more formal and less vulnerable business structure. Corporations can be anything from a one-person start-up to an international giant, but are the usual form for a larger or mature business. Incorporation blurs the size of the enterprise, whereas a sole proprietorship is seldom encountered beyond a certain size of operation.

Another clue to size and success can be found from the titles and job descriptions of employees. It takes a while for a business to grow large enough to have six vice-presidents or several subsidiaries.

As a business grows and finds its market it becomes a concrete presence. It will survive or perish on the strength of the identity it creates in the mind of those it seeks to serve. Businesses that can quickly create that recognition have a marked advantage. The messages on your card are to "hook" that illusive customer, and with it your future success.

DECODING IS DISCERNMENT
Use More than Your Eyes

As you gain practice, you will see that such abstract concepts as good design catch your eye. Before long, you'll see instantly that a business is customer-oriented, traditional, upscale, or trendy. You'll find yourself decoding the mood of the card without any apparent effort.

Many of the signals sent by a card are transmitted by touch. The *feel* of a card says much about the business. Flimsy often translates to cheap and insubstantial, while a heavyweight stock is more reassuring. A person is more inclined to trust the business that displays signs of quality. Such signals are sent independently of the printed words, which they will either reinforce or contradict. Here again, all the parts need to work together or a scrambled (unprofessional) message results.

Those businesses that select the deluxe options, for example, know that such details can pay off in increased respect. They have positioned themselves as valuable and discriminating. The following card screams quality in every detail—from the name, to the gold crown and crest, to the engraving, to the lush paper, to the design. Its European origin is signaled by its large size.

ROYAL ENGRAVING

MIGUEL SOLER-ROIG JUNCADELLA
DIRECTOR GENERAL

SERRANO, 41-3-3ª
28001 MADRID

TEL.(91) 308 40 08
(91) 577 05 33
FAX (91) 308 40 92

Gold engraved crown and logo with royal blue engraved text and large R; on heavy cream stock

But expense is only one way to stand out and communicate that you know what you're doing. Humor, uniqueness, interesting graphics, usefulness, and wit can all be equally effective to capture the receiver's attention and interest. Decoding skills will take you far beyond business cards and work just as well with a company's stationery and promotional materials.

To Recap

Your card is encrusted with many types of information. Not all receivers get the same messages. So take care that you send those you intend to send and eliminate those that can undermine your desired image.

Chapter 3

Tell *Who You Are* and What You Do

Figure Out Who You Are

Your card's primary job is to tell:

- Who you are
- What you do
- Who you do it for
- Why I should bother to remember you
- How to contact you

So, who are you, anyway? People need to know who you are before making decisions that involve you. Defining who you are is not simple and does not yield a single answer. This chapter primarily considers your business image, and ignores the psychological and philosophical issues.

Who you are exists in numerous simultaneous forms. Disengage from your customary way of identifying yourself to consider other equally relevant frames of reference.

Ten Relevant Business Whos

- Who as in **business name**—Jim James, Insurance; Homestead Relics (unique to you)
- Who as in **type of business**—pool cleaning service; retail office supplies (includes you and your competition)

- Who as in **business specialty**—not just a bakery, but a European bakery
- Who as in **person**—the one named on the card
- Who as in **title** or role—the title of the person named on the card; her job description
- Who as in type of business **entity**—partnership, sole proprietorship, corporation, agency, foundation, etc.
- Who as in **department** or division within a business—Regional Sales Office, Human Resources, Consumer Electronics
- Who as in the **public perception** of you—the low price leader; the place for ribs; your first choice for convenience (positioning)
- Who as in age and **stage** of the business—start-up, industry leader
- Who as in **affiliations**—exclusive distributor for Toshiba®; member, Denver Chamber of Commerce; Yale graduate
- Who as in **personality** and identity—the unique style that personifies the business; its ambiance or flair

Your card provides useful information about your relevant whos. It tells others what they need to know about you and defines the basis of your relationship. **It defines you.**

Show Who You Are and What You Do

Yellow moon and drop of honey; the rest is black ink on cream stock

ON-SITE
MASSAGE
(954) 878-6689
Home - Office
Chair • Traditional Table
Available
Co-Presidents
SEAN W. WARDEN   LIC# MA0012995
WILLIAM V. DADDIO   LIC# MA0019761

Full-color photo of an on-site massage; black print on glossy white stock

Let Your Card Be a Sample of Your Work

Pentkowski's Cartoons

THAT'S RIGHT! CALL (602) 264-5931...

...1735 W. MITCHELL PHOENIX, AZ, 85015!

IN CARE OF GREG PENTKOWSKI!

Black on white stock

Courtesy the Business Card Archives

A cartoon advertisement for a cartoonist displays his style

WILBER "Web" FRIEND, JR.
PRESIDENT

LITTLE'S EMPORIUM
ENGRAVING & PRINTING
INCORPORATED

833 ILANIWAI STREET · HONOLULU, HAWAII 96813
TEL (808) 591-8533 · FAX (808) 591-8530

Maroon on entire card with the fancy L and Little's Emporium garnished with gold; engraved lettering on heavy cream stock

Elaborately engraved card by an engraver

Also Consider Who You Aren't

Be aware of your limits. They are an important part of what defines you. Businesses thrive by being good within a limited area (geography, product lines, expertise). There will always be some things you cannot do as well or as cheaply as someone else can. Avoid them and build on your capabilities, because there are some areas where you shine.

Know Yourself

- ☐ What you are good at
- ☐ What you like or want to do
- ☐ What you like or want to do for money
- ☐ Who you have rapport with or who is attracted to you
- ☐ Who you have referral sources to reach

Don't try to be all things to all people. You'll fail, be disappointed, and worse yet, you won't be using your unique capabilities effectively. For example, learn from a well-documented trend that has been demonstrated in the catalog field. General merchandise catalogs are failing, even while overall catalog sales are greatly increasing. General catalogs are being replaced by much more specialized catalogs, which are targeted to specific groups or interests, like gardeners, gourmet food lovers, history buffs. Your business, too, will improve as you can more carefully target your messages to specific groups.

What Do You Do, Anyway?

The most frequently heard complaint about business cards is that you can't tell what the business does. A typical reaction: "If I can't tell what the business does, I dump the card." That's a sad end to what could have been a solid and enduring business relationship.

You know what you do, but don't assume the prospect knows. The card should leave no doubt about your line of business. If there are too many things you do, you look unfocused, and leave an impression that you're really not very good at anything. Be specific. Don't leave the receiver wondering. If you are too general, there is no clue about what you really offer. Is "Light Touch" a massage therapist, a lighting fixture store or a dry cleaner? If the name leaves any doubt about what the business does, state it with particularity. Use an illustration, tag line or slogan to make it obvious.

Jack of All Trades, Inc.
Joe Blow

Editor	Plumber
Chess Lessons	Home Repairs
Computer Sales	Vitamins

Aerobics Instructor

No Job Too Small.

(123) 222-3333   234 Main Street
Fair Skies, IA 12345

Too much information

Global Enterprises
We aim to please

Joe Blowhard

(123) 222-3333   234 Main Street
Fair Skies, IA 12345

Too little information

Too many identities or incompatible identities are considered a sign of mental illness in a person. In a business, you appear scattered, confused, inept, and unprofessional.

GET YOUR ACT TOGETHER
Unify the Perceptions of Your Business

The business card is a cost-effective method for aligning a customer's ideas about your company with what it really does. Clarifying the business identity improves customer awareness about you. Use your card as a portable billboard, a mini-brochure, a recurring reminder, a spur to action (call us; come in), which serves as a source of additional business.

Long before you see the first customer or client, you make many decisions necessary to launch the business. The business arises and grows from the vision of the founder. The resulting plan reflects many choices. How clear or realistic was the initial plan? How well was it thought through in the important conceptual stages? Then, starting from that blueprint, evaluate how well it has been brought into actuality. To simplify the complex factors involved, diagrams are helpful. Perfection is defined here as total overlap of the two impressions (circles).

A. Plan versus Reality

Compare how well the actual business matches the original plan. The purpose of this comparison is to discover what things don't correspond and then to find ways to bring them closer together.

Plan or *Blueprint for the Business*   *Actual* Business

Now these two images are placed over each other. The more they overlap the better. If there isn't a lot of overlap, it indicates problems.

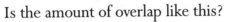

Is the amount of overlap like this?   Or like this?

B. Reality versus Perception

Now, compare what the business actually does or offers with the public perception of what the business does. Often there isn't a lot of overlap. One clue to a discrepancy is when your present customers or referral sources say, "I didn't know you did that."

*What your **Business Does** or Can Do*   *What the **Customer Thinks** It **Does** or Can Do*

Is the amount of overlap like this?   Or like this?

The closer that these two perceptions agree, the more you have eliminated disappointment and unrealistic customer expectations. However, if you are fuzzy about what your business does (or you're sending a mixed signal) or **do not communicate it clearly**, how is the potential customer ever going to figure it out?

C. Your Desired Customer versus Your Actual Customer

*Whom You **Want to** Attract*   *Whom You **Actually** Attract*

Is the amount of overlap like this?   Or like this?

D. What You Do versus What Your Card Says You Do

What the Business   *What the **Card Indicates***
Actually Does   *that the Business Does*

Is the amount of overlap like this?   Or like this?

Once you take the time to look carefully at the various kinds of perceptions and how they fail to agree, you will notice tangible ways to improve your communication.

E. Image versus Identity

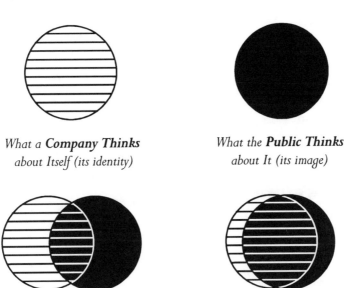

What a **Company Thinks** about Itself (its identity)

What the **Public Thinks** about It (its image)

How much do they overlap? How can you bring them closer together?

Clarifying the business identity expresses what is **already there** as an **integral aspect of the business**. It uncovers features of the company that already exist, but which have not been brought into focus. The qualities are inherent (internal, from the inside) rather than super-imposed (external, skin deep). Once you become aware of such unique features, capitalize on them. Stamp them as part of your "style." Such aspects of your identity emphasize and reinforce the image the public has about you. The connection is even stronger when **amplifying an existing feature** of the company, instead of making up one.

Your card should **reveal** the business identity, since that is what the public is going to be getting whenever they deal with you. If the image and identity don't agree (no matter how lovely the card), you're going to encounter an **expectations gap**.

YOUR BUSINESS NAME
Select the Right Name

There is a school of thought that a company's name should always embody the business identity, i.e., ABC Chocolate Company. A business, however, may change over time and have new products and services inconsistent with the prior name—which can lead to confusion and, ultimately, lost sales. ABC might eventually move into food distribution and away from candy production. A person looking for distribution services probably wouldn't contact a candy company to provide the needed services. Result—missed opportunities.

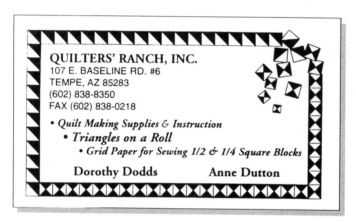

QUILTERS' RANCH, INC.
107 E. BASELINE RD. #6
TEMPE, AZ 85283
(602) 838-8350
FAX (602) 838-0218

• *Quilt Making Supplies & Instruction*
  • *Triangles on a Roll*
    • *Grid Paper for Sewing 1/2 & 1/4 Square Blocks*

Dorothy Dodds   **Anne Dutton**

Entire card is grayed turquoise on gray textured recycled paper

On the other hand, a descriptive company name might pull in customers on the basis of the name alone. A good example of this is "Teddy's Bear Company," a rapidly growing teddy bear manufacturing and sales firm whose name alone has garnered a lot of business. In choosing a name, you should include consideration of your long-range business plan (and you should have one) and the possibility of expansion and diversification. Would your company name be appropriate, for instance, if you moved to a different state, or changed your product line? For an established business, a name change can be costly—not only in direct expenses (advertising, letterhead, logos, etc.) but also in lost sales continuity.

If growth is one of your business goals, try to avoid "local" sounding names such as "Third Street Market," or "South Wabash Deli." Don't tie your business name to a particular location unless that location provides tangible benefits. An example of this would be the *Wall Street Journal*, a name universally associated with the financial capital of the world.

If, however, your "success plan" depends on a small-town image, adopt a company name that you could apply to any locale or growth situation, such as "Your Neighborhood Grocer." If size is considered important in your particular field of endeavor, strive to find a company name that does not reek of "small potatoes" or indicate that your are too small to perform at the expected level. By the same token, if you are not a multi-national conglomerate, don't pretend that you are.

Some Business Names From the Archives

It's For the Birds (Bird Farm)
The World's Wurst Restaurant (Sausage)
Hat's in the Belfry (Hat Shop)
Stay Tuned (Piano Tuner)
Rag Time Cleaning (Janitorial)
It's a Crewel World (Needlepoint, Yarn)
Shady Deals Realty (Real Estate Sales)

Courtesy the Business Card Archives

Ten Criteria for Your Business Name

- ☐ **Distinct** and unique
- ☐ **Memorable**
- ☐ Able to communicate an image or **emotional connection**
- ☐ **Appealing** to the customer
- ☐ **Protectable** (See trademark information in Chapter 8.)

- ☐ Can be easily **pronounced** or spelled
- ☐ Free of **unintended** or negative **messages**
- ☐ Unlikely to be **confused** with other businesses
- ☐ Can be **translated** without meaning anything offensive or inappropriate
- ☐ **Compatible** with the business image

Representative

300 West Lowe Ave., Suite 108
Fairfield, Iowa 52556
Tel: 515-472-0906
Fax: 515-469-6310

Jim Moore
owner

4103 E. Mission Ave., Spokane, WA 99202
Bus. (509) 534-7255   Fax (509) 534-5564
"http://www.ohbrines.com"

Blue-green logo with screened drop;
black letters on glossy white stock

Forest green on white stock

It is entirely possible for a small operation to go head-to-head with larger competitors. Now that technology is so reasonably priced, a few talented people can deliver work that was once the exclusive province of big corporations. Your products and services can scream "quality" without being associated with the big guns in your field. Unfortunately, some of your potential customers will equate quality with size. This is where your choice of a company name can either pay large dividends or kick you in the teeth. Quite often, you and your company won't even be considered if the image you portray is that of a small-scale wannabe—no matter what your capabilities actually are. Should you find yourself in this situation, consider adopting a name with little or no connotation of size.

Within an industry, business names often sound very much alike. A limited number of words are linked up in all sorts of combinations that result in a certain sameness. An example is illustrated with high-tech words like: tech, soft, link, micro, and serve. The various combinations may be different enough to meet the requirements to secure a trademark, but they tend to get lumped into one global category and are not distinguishable (except to insiders). Such names are inclined to be very jargon laden. The companies are all trying to sound like insiders. That presents a challenge: sound like they're part of an industry while using a name and image that stands out.

Avoid Business Names that Cause Problems

- **Empty words** or symbols that convey nothing: J&J, Sunset Sales
- Names that make customers think of **someone else**, especially your competition
- Words that do **not translate** well, especially if you are involved in international trade (See Chapter 14.)
- Names that could **infringe on existing trademarks**
- Words that are not **politically correct** like Squaw Peak Cafe or Hooters®
- **Limiting** names that won't let you grow; Polk Country Enterprise
- **Misleading** names that are not what customers expected; for example, XXX Restaurant was not sex oriented

- **Tip-off words** like *"Enterprises"* or *"and Associates"* or *"Unlimited,"* or *"Consultant,"* which usually suggest you are small or confused about what the business does

- Dated or **quaint names** unless related to that kind of business, like a tavern or antique store; The Olde Time Shoppe

- Names that people don't get; **too clever**, cryptic or jargon laden

Names that are hard to spell or pronounce are easy to forget. This may be especially true of foreign terms that lack tangible associations. Be careful of initials, jargon, slang or acronyms, either because they **have** associations or because they **lack** them. For example, TLC does stand for "tender loving care," so if you mean something else with those letters no one is going to remember your variation. (See section on alphabet soup and acronyms in Chapter 4.)

Beware of Distinctive Names that Can Create Confusion

Some names are unusual because they **intentionally change** well-known words into new forms, or use letters creatively.

- Unusual **spacing**: adding spaces where not expected or running two words together

- Altering **capitalization**, either not using it at all, or using capitals when not expected, like in the miDDle of the word, as in BonBons© or TexAZ®

- Altering the **spelling**, although the word still **sounds** recognizable; Kwik Kopy® or Problem D'Solver®

- Adding or eliminating **punctuation**

- Overlapping or arranging **acronyms** (letters) so it is impossible to tell the word or letter order; is it ABC or BCA or CBA, etc.

- Vernacular or unusual **pronunciation**: example Po Folks® Restaurant

LYNELLA GRANT, J.D. is

The Problem D'Solver®

Using Problems to Open Doors

Periwinkle
blue ink
on apricot-
colored stock;
the business
name is in
copper foil

Phone: (602) 970-4672   Author • Speaker   ®
P.O. Box 1269, Scottsdale, Arizona 85251
Fax: (602) 970-3925 • E-mail: frivel@aol.com

My own card is tricky to spell because of the "D'S," which looks puzzling

Darshan Singh Khalsa
MIS Project Director
MicroAge, Inc.

Direct (602) 804-2265

Internet: dkhalsa@microage.com
Mobile (602) 919-1445
Fax (602) 929-2477

Post Office Box 1920
Tempe, AZ 85280-1920
2400 South MicroAge Way
Tempe, AZ 85282-1896

Mountain and
logo in red
foil; the rest
is in black
on white

These forms of a business name may be distinctive and are often clever, but should be used carefully to avoid confusion. Is the unusual variation clever or perplexing? Do people "get it" or does the name usually have to be explained? While the symbol may make a good graphic element, the nuances behind it may easily be lost. When the name tends to confuse, write it both ways (with the simple form in small parentheses).

Apply this test. Could you address an envelope using only the information on the card? What would this name look like typed, rather than in a glorified logo, where it may not be apparent which is the first letter?

Next, pronounce the name aloud; is the spacing clear or lost? Recently, I was evaluating yellow page listings for Cardservice® (one word) International in various phone directories. Some branch offices were listed as one word, others as two words (Card Service). The placement in the yellow pages had a considerable impact as to which office got the bulk of the inquiries. Although company employees knew there was an official spelling, the public didn't. Those who deviated from the proper spelling (one word) were getting most of the business, because they were listed first in the directory.

If you have a name that depends on such devices, list yourself under **both** forms or spellings so that the customer is not confused by a distinction that goes against convention. There may be a protectable trademark in the odd form, but if it costs you customers, reconsider. At least make sure you can be found in the standard as well as unique form.

Consider Coining a New Word

Some of the strongest business names owe their recognition to the fact their name was created just for them—Kodak®, Xerox® and Exxon®. Words such as these are free of associations, except for those created by the company. The decision to use a made-up word is tricky because of the risk that the name will not make sense or be memorable. Persistent promotion is required to make such coined words familiar.

Creating a new word means it is yours alone. You can trademark it and prevent its use by others. The lack of prior associations serves as both its primary advantage and disadvantage. Though you may not be confused with another word, you could get mentally thrown into a catchall category that "doesn't mean anything" or "one of those names I can't remember." Try combining familiar concepts or words in a new way, like "Uncola" for 7 UP® or choose a name that sounds like something else that is well known. For example, Altima® doesn't mean anything, but sounds like "Ultimate," which is very nice indeed.

Finding new words isn't easy. The safest letters to use are the least used ones like X, K and Z—but using such letters results in words that often seem contrived and awkward. Try not to get KUTZY (too cute). Unfamiliar letter combinations could be offensive or have established meanings in another language. Even if you know the literal meanings of a foreign word, always ask a native if there are any connotations that would destroy the image the name is designed to establish. (See Chapter 14 on using your card abroad.) Double entendres and sexual innuendoes lurk everywhere, even in our own language.

Red band and black text and figure on white stock

Variable gray screen on grayed-yellow stock

The Professions Restrict Business Name Options

Traditionally, the professions have been law, medicine, banking, accounting, architecture, and similar fields involving personal services. Individuals in the professions are initiated members, often characterized as being "in practice," (which leads to the old saying: when are they going to stop practicing and do it right?). The cards for professionals are very conservative in design, with little room for variation. The way to stand out is through very subtle refinements. Anything dramatic, like use of bright colors, could be seen as bad taste and a sign of unprofessional behavior (which sheds doubt on the rest of your skill). Professional standards define such things as what business names may (and may not) be used by the members. The content of the card must reflect the standards of that professional organization.

The operative word is "tradition," since these fields have historic roots that determine not only what members do, but define what practices are considered to be appropriate (hence professional and ethical). Professions connote more than jobs. They require obligatory training, ethics, standards, and methods that prevent anyone except members of the profession from performing those services. That is why the business name is usually the names of the person(s) performing the services. The business is started by "hanging out the shingle," and the quality of performance should affect the degree of success.

Distinguish yourself by using very high quality options like engraved printing, watermarks, embossing, and deluxe stock. (See Chapter 9, when you want to be impeccable.) Strive for **understated elegance** rather than dramatic effect. Stay within the stringent limitations, while making a positive impression with exquisite layout, visually interesting professional symbols, a tag line and your credentials. Consult your professional organization for its guidelines and prohibitions. It may also have special logos or designations that you can display on your card as "badges of achievement," like the National Speakers Association microphone logo for professional speakers.

The New York State Society of Physician Assistants
322 8th Avenue, 14th Floor, New York, NY 10001-8001

ROBERT BLUMM, RPA-C
President - Elect

69 Robbins Avenue
Amityville, NY 11701
Home (516) 598-1081
Work (516) 484-8886

NYSSPA Phone
(212) 206-8300
NYSSPA Fax
(212) 645-1147

Name of the organization is blue foil; the rest of the print is black on gray stock

Standard symbols have evolved for the professions. Common examples are the caduceus (twisted snakes) used by doctors or the scale (to weigh justice) used by lawyers. These symbols differ from a logo created for an individual business, since anyone in the profession can use them. There are also many variations of such symbols, so develop a more creative version to set you apart. It is inappropriate for anyone to use the symbols unless they are members of, or connected to, the profession itself.

If Your Business Name is Your Name

In some service businesses or professions, the card does not show a business name, only the name of the person who runs it.

Dale V. Cavan

CAVAN

Real Estate Investments

15880 N. Greenway-Hayden Loop, Suite 700   Scottsdale, Arizona   85260
PH. 602-627-7000, Ext. 108   FX. 602-627-7010   MB. 390-4560

Fine engraved card with black ink on heavy white stock and name in gold

Your Host:
Angelo

1000 W. Bristol
Elkhart, IN 46514

(219) 262-9815
Fax (219) 262-0534

Turquoise on gray patterned and textured paper

Your name alone is unlikely to tell much about the business and what it does, so additional information or a tag line is recommended. Using your name often implies small—unless it has become a household word like Walt Disney and Calvin Klein, and they didn't get well known overnight. The business is perceived as local, small and a probably a sole proprietorship. Often, a small business begins using the owner's name, and then grows to become an entity apart from the originator. If people know you, like you, and trust you, they know they want to do business with you. If you are in a service business, your name operates as the prime association of the intangible services you provide. Also, you bring your reputation and identity to the business. Trust is higher because they sense a "real person" who cares about them.

Take into account the drawbacks in using your own name. The distinctions between you and your business get blurred. If there is a business problem, such as litigation or bankruptcy, it reflects back on your personally. It also works in reverse. Your personal problems or reputation could lead to negative publicity for the business. So think twice before deciding whether it is a good idea to use your name as the business name.

If you sell your business that is named after you, the business name is treated as one of the assets of the business. It is no longer useable by you as your business identity. You also run the risk that the new owner may tarnish your name, and with it your reputation.

Even though they have a right to use it, you will be affected by **how they use it**. The professions have guidelines that govern the sale or transfer of a practice, as well.

If you are going to use your name as a trade name, treat it the same as any other business name. Trademark it; make it obvious it is the business name. Just to stay safe legally, also abide by any corporate or reporting formalities. If you wear more than one "hat," make it clear which one you're wearing.

Signatures as Designs

An actual signature can become a visual image on the card. The owner's signature personalizes the business name. Like a font style, it should be compatible with the rest of the card design. Some large companies have attempted to avoid the impersonality of a standard company card by adding the employee's signature to the card, along with his name and title. If a card doesn't show your signature, you may want to add it, along with a brief note when you give it.

Screened photograph of hair stylist, signature and print in black on white

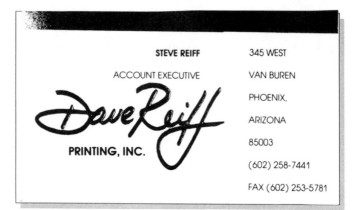

STEVE REIFF

ACCOUNT EXECUTIVE

Dave Reiff

PRINTING, INC.

345 WEST

VAN BUREN

PHOENIX,

ARIZONA

85003

(602) 258-7441

FAX (602) 253-5781

Graduated blue-green and purple bleed along top edge; black print and copper-embossed signature on textured cream stock

---

THE PERSON WHO IS NAMED ON THE CARD
What's in a Name?—The Individual Named

A person's name is **very important**—especially to him or her. For the customers, that individual personifies the business in their minds. The person's name on the card can be whatever they want to be called. The name used need not be a legal name or their married name. It needn't be their full name. If the name is difficult to pronounce or is a foreign name, it helps to say: "sounds like _____ "or "rhymes with _____" under the name. Such a comment could even be turned into a memorable slogan. Nicknames are O.K., or you may say Joseph "Tiger" Brown. If a visual connection exists, that is even better, like Red Baker—because of his prominent red hair.

When it is unclear whether the name belongs to a man or a woman (Pat, Lynn, Marion, J.J.) consider adding Mr. or Miss, Mrs. or Ms. Otherwise, these terms are not appropriate. (See Chapter 4 for other titles.)

Caveat: If the company cards are all the same, tailored only to reflect the name and title, make sure the design can accommodate a v-e-r-y l-o-n-g n-a-m-e.

Green marbled bleed on left; black print on off-white stock

Cards without Names or Titles

Some businesses use a card identifying the business, but no particular person is named. In a restaurant or beauty shop, the individual service provider is part of the staff, so if an employee want to identify herself in particular, she writes her own name on the common card. An attractive variation of such a card is to rubber stamp a person's name or appropriate symbol.

Some cards will have more than one name. For example a husband and wife, as the owners of a business, may say Herb and Hilda Reynolds. A card may also name all the owners or employees. A family-owned business might list all the members of the family. In that case, everyone gives out the same card.

Red Party Music and a graduated screen of the city; the rest is black on white stock

One of the secondary reasons for a card is to personalize the business, to make a person-to-person contact with the receiver. Having individuals named on the card furthers that goal. Some people prefer dealing with personalities instead of impersonal and remote (as in emotional accessibility) businesses.

Who Is on Your Team?

The person whose name is on the card (as well as his or her title) will differ, but in most cases, everyone in a business should use the same card to maintain and reinforce a unified business image. Full-time employees should have their own cards. The morale-building power of an employee's card can not be exaggerated. The value of being included as a team member transcends the minuscule cost. For example, teachers now often use a business card, even though they are not in a business in the customary sense.

Team players:

- Leased employees
- Telecommuters
- Temporary employees
- Independent contractors or subcontractors on special projects (including former employees) and others who perform services on an ongoing basis

It may not be readily apparent who should be using a company card. In this day of virtual businesses and joint ventures, people may be working for a company, even though their role isn't permanent. The business needs to decide whether all the team members will use the same card and appear to be part of the same organization. Consider also the pros and cons when a person instead uses his or her own business card (when acting as consultant or trainer) while serving on a project.

The Common Card and the Executive Card

All the employees of a company may use the same card, but some companies embellish the card used by executives. The changes are often subtle, but those enhancements exude status and power. Enhancements appropriate for an executive card:

- ▢ Heavier weight of stock
- ▢ Beveled edge
- ▢ Beveled edge with gilt or color or gold
- ▢ Embossed images, metallic foil or other special effects
- ▢ Engraved printing

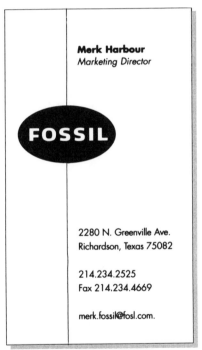

Both show the rust, black and yellow logo and black type on a cream background. The employee card has a vertical screen in light yellow; the executive has a heavy textured blue back and an embossed centered logo.

Although these cards use the same colors and type style, the feel is very different for the executive and employee cards.

This executive card is engraved in black on a heavy cream stock with a gold crest.

A Prop Can Embody an Image or Name

When you have a distinct image that is both on your card and a tangible object, you create a powerful connection. For example, George Hedley's business soared after he added a hardhat symbol to his card and called his programs Hardhat Seminars. He also used a related sticker on everything and started wearing a hardhat during presentations. The clients from those industries had no difficulty in picking him out from his competition because he was signaling them that he understood their needs. Employing a 3-D symbol assures that you are noticed and remembered.

Photo and printing in black on white glossy stock; the hardhat and the band on the bottom are orange

Props are also used to reinforce the images you want the customer to have about your product or service. I've made a vest festooned with business cards for events related to this book. A restaurant feels more like "home cooking" when every server is dressed in a wig, spectacles and long apron—like granny. (Even if your granny never looked like that, the association is still clear.) Whatever you choose will help to make a physical statement that sets you apart from your "duller" competitors. (See Chapter 4 to credentialize yourself.)

YOUR TITLE
Tell Your Title or Position

Most business cards show the person's position or job title. Sometimes it is sufficient to state what department he works for. Consider whether a job title indicates the real job function. Some titles are so nebulous it is impossible to tell what the person's function is. It will be assumed that the person is qualified to do whatever the job says. It's OK to have fun with your title and create a title that's just for you, like call youself "Queen."

If you're the owner or CEO, you're obviously a big fish, even if the pond is small. If you're one of 400 account representatives, it's not the status of the position but the status of the company that matters. Be careful not to look pretentious or misinformed by using an unsuitable title. For example, too often, a sole proprietor or partner inappropriately uses "President" on his card, undermining the credibility he seeks (which is a title related to a corporation).

When selecting your title:

- Give some thought to whether or not you need or want a title
- Your title should give a clue about what your function is; use a term that isn't cryptic or jargon
- Your title gives some indication about the size of the company
- Avoid "owner"—it sounds small
- It needn't be the same as your job description
- If your organization is large, show your title relative to the department or team

Navy blue on white stock

Purple on gray with a light screened pattern

Navy blue
with gold rules
(bars) and
around the
gold on gray
stock

Ten Reasons to Have More than One Card

☐ You are engaged in **more than one business**

☐ You wear **different "hats"**

☐ To promote **different aspects** of the business

☐ To **test** various card designs

- To reach **more than one market** or language; to provide a translation of your data
- To match the unique **expectations of a customer**
- To provide **offers**, coupons and specific marketing devices
- To **highlight special** events, products or affiliations
- To show different offices, **locations** and hours
- To appeal to different **demographics**, ages, or occupations

Each business you actively pursue deserves its own card. If you wear different hats, create a card for each hat. You'll leave fewer fuzzy impressions and sharpen your own awareness of what you do in each of them. Your focused clarity enhances your credibility. Using more than one card allows you to tailor your identity and skills to the needs of the person who gets your card.

Skeleton in turquoise, along with the rules; text is in black on turquoise and cream paper

Turquoise print on white stock

d🦆kmint

MARIA ORT

THE DUCKMINT
PARTNERSHIP

PERFORMANCE ENHANCEMENT
FOR BUSINESS PARTNERS &
MANAGEMENT TEAMS

POST OFFICE
BOX 30390
PHOENIX, ARIZONA
85046-0390
602.266.4433

Maria Ort
Principal

Representing Fine
Building Products

THE

**FIRST
TEAM**

1110 East Missouri
Suite 700
Phoenix, AZ 85014
602/266-2900
800/866-2900

Duckmint is blue-green along with the Duckmint Partnership; the little duck feet in the logo are embossed; the rest is black on white stock

Die-cut card is brick red with reversed print on white stock

To Recap

Customers need to be aware of who you are and what you do. Develop a consistent image to avoid an expectations gap. Make sure your business name communicates what you do. If not, indicate on the card specifically what it is that you do or are involved with. If you wear more than one "hat" have more than one card.

Chapter 4

Build Customer Confidence with Expertise and Slogans

Develop Customer Confidence

An image of credibility and success inspires confidence. Customers need to trust a business in order to want to buy what it offers. Even if they buy once, unless customers think you're trustworthy, they won't come back. Dispel any doubts by showing that you are well established, competent, and professional.

Many businesses have little face-to-face contact with their own customers or suppliers due to telecommunications, the Internet and mail order. Often, the perception of the business rests solely on its printed materials. Thus, the quality of such correspondence and promotional materials permits a small business to compete head-to-head with much larger organizations. If you **appear to be competent**, the actual size of a business often matters little. You are more likely to be judged on your ability to deliver and the perceived quality of your work.

If you want to be successful, you need to **appear** successful. Avoid any signs of poor or borderline taste. Ironically, good design or expensive embellishments are most evident when understated. If overdone, the result can become crass. You may have a very expensive card, but it may still seem tacky.

Business is not conducted in isolation. People whom you meet socially or through various activities are potential customers (or clients). Your personal life is related to your business; therefore, your successful image should not be confined to business hours.

What Makes People Buy?

The American Retailers Association researched why customers buy from a business. They found that confidence was the most important criteria. Any or all of these reasons should be an integral part of your card.

The reasons people buy (in this order):

1. **Confidence**
2. Quality
3. Service
4. Selection
5. Price

It pays for a business to build a reputation based on customer confidence and loyalty. As you establish and reinforce the message that you are trustworthy, customers will stick with you (customer retention). It's much less expensive, and easier, to keep a good customer than to find another one. Never forget: **Your customers are your competitor's prospects.**

Inspire Confidence by Appearing to Be:

- ☐ **Well established** and stable
- ☐ **Risk free**
- ☐ **Reliable** and respectable
- ☐ **Businesslike** and professional
- ☐ **Competent**—with all the ability expected
- ☐ **Successful**—others are attracted to you
- ☐ **Easy to do business with**—convenient, available, cooperative
- ☐ **Customer service** oriented
- ☐ Able to offer **support services**
- ☐ **Trustworthy**

Notice that these traits are all intangibles, rooted in early impressions made long before any purchases are made. (See Chapter 1 on making impressions.) Your card plays an active role in establishing your personal and business credentials. It has the power to produce both a high level of expectation along with a feeling of confidence in you. As you quietly reassure your targeted customer, deliver what your promise (and it helps when performance even exceeds expectations).

Your card should strengthen confidence-building perceptions by its good taste and attractiveness. Indicate that you are capable and hassle free by explicitly stating your credentials and any business policies that reassure those the company serves. This chapter shows various ways to bolster your perceived credibility—without stretching the truth.

Strive to be Credible

- Don't **over-promise**
- Don't be **unbelievable** or absurd; be careful when using superlatives like: only, biggest, best, most, fastest, cheapest
- Don't be **"too good to be true"** or you arouse suspicions
- Don't **insult the intelligence** of your audience
- Don't be too **abstract**
- Don't be too **flowery**
- Don't be **brash**, aggressive, or pushy
- Don't be **inconsistent** in your claims

Customers who have confidence in your business will continue to buy from you and will remain resistant to offers from competing businesses. Your card should remind them in every way possible that they were correct to rely on you. Demonstrate intangibles like good value, reliability, and consistency. Make them glad they chose you! **Cards build confidence.** Beware of that word "build"; it doesn't just mean "to put together once." Confidence must be **consistently re-built and reinforced at every opportunity**.

Establish Your Credentials

- **Yourself** and your own capabilities
- The **business itself**—its products and services
- The **business location**
- **Convenience** and all the ways you make it easy to do business
- **Payment options**—credit cards and other appropriate terms
- The many ways you **make the buyer's life easier**

What They See Is What They Expect

Everyone prefers to deal with businesses that are reliable, that don't leave a sour note. And once you find those gems, you want to continue doing business with them. In a world that so often provokes uncertainty and disappointment, everyone longs for those products and services that can be counted on to provide what was expected in the first place.

Perception is important, but you need to do more. Provide **concrete verification** of your skill and ability. Part of what the buyer expects is expertise beyond his own or outside his scope. Buyers come to you for specialized knowledge in a particular field and need reassurance that they are getting what they're paying for.

Products and services with high-perceived value are not very price sensitive. A higher price tag can, in fact, increase perceived value of a product or service. Just purchasing something considered valuable enhances the buyer's prestige (and if you doubt it, notice how people react to a friend's new BMW). Intangibles such as professional services are also less price sensitive when supported by expertise and specialized training. In such cases, performance is expected to exceed the norm.

A business card is a tool with many uses, not the least of which is inducing people to buy your product(s) or service(s). Make sure they are compatible with what the prospect **thinks** he is getting.

Be careful; **expectations must be met**! Don't indicate that you can deliver more than you or your company can capably provide. If your promise is a Cadillac®, don't deliver a Chevy®.

What Kind of a Job Is Consulting?

Those who call themselves consultants are often perceived as being out of work. They're treated as self-employed by default and waiting to get hired to do a "real" job. (Cartoon of businessman with sign: Will consult for food.) While that perception is often inaccurate, you should take care when putting "consultant" on your card. Be clear as to your areas of expertise and provide ample credibility-building cues.

Eliminate Sour Notes

Be sensitive to any cues you could be sending that could raise doubts about your reliability, stability or competence. You're asking for the customers' trust along with *their* dollars. A stable and reliable appearance is saying you'll be around if anything goes wrong. For example, if you provide only a post office box, but no location, you risk looking like a fly-by-night operation. Strive to be so professional that no one has any reason to question either your ability to perform or the quality of the products you sell. You can't afford to make people nervous. The reassurance that you can provide exactly what they want, on time, leads to more sales. Professionalism is the standard, so strive to personify those businesslike-standards.

Don't be so clever, cute or strange in your promotions or image that you lose the customer's respect. It may be a fine line, but it is apparent to the prospect when it is crossed. If something on your card could be considered borderline, use it as a second card reserved for special situations or for those who will "get it." Here again, you're flirting with the fine line between memorable and adolescent, between attractive and amateur, between being businesslike and being weird.

Credibility Strengthens Referrals

Referrals are the lifeblood of many businesses. They are more important than all the promotions you can lay end to end. The person who refers business is often endorsing the quality of your goods and services, so if you don't satisfy expectations, referrals dwindle. Often, it works as a two-way street, when both businesses serve the same clients in related but non-competing ways.

Sixteen Reasons Why People Refer Business to You

- They know you will **treat customers well**
- They **don't sell** or produce what you offer
- You provide **specialized products** or knowledge beyond others in your field
- They are **too busy** to produce what you offer, or have run out of the product
- They are engaged in **higher priority** projects
- They **like you** and want you to do well
- You have developed a **joint promotional** relationship (it goes both ways—you refer to each other)
- You're **less expensive**, faster, more convenient, etc.
- You have **specialized** staff, resources or equipment
- You are the only **authorized provider**, distributor, licensed source
- The know you have **satisfied customers**
- They owe you a **favor**
- They are your **contacts**
- You **share advertising**, publicity and marketing efforts
- You **pay for referrals**, or provide some other reward
- It enhances **their own credibility**

Your card needs to inform the world of your capabilities. All these referral sources are candidates for your business card. They are also candidates for handing out your cards and vice versa. (See Chapter 12 on ways businesses can distribute each other's cards.)

USE SLOGANS
Tag Lines State Your Message

Tell people in a short phrase or sentence what you want them to know or remember about the business. It should conjure up a strong mental image that will be forever linked with you in their memories. Choose one that people will relate to and remember. For example, the tag line of the publisher of this book is "Turn Notions into Motions"—which is exactly what this book strives to achieve. A printer's card showing camels in a row and stating "We take the humps out of problems," emphasized its service orientation.

A tagline can be as important as your logo; it delivers your most direct message. It should provide a reassuring message to attract the customers you can best serve. Credibility-enhancing statements, like the ones throughout this chapter, can augment your tag line. Once you have adopted one, use the slogan often. Have everyone in the organization employ it in every business contact, telephone greeting or transaction.

Kinds of Tag Lines

- **Statement of purpose**, philosophy, or mission statement
- **Motto** or slogan
- **Pledge**
- **Policy**
- **Guarantee**
- **Jingle**
- **Pun**, joke, or play on words
- **Relevant quote** or aphorism—or a takeoff on one

(504) 738-7700
FAX (504) 738-5255

Wanda Perret
Sales Representative

P. O. Box 10482
New Orleans, LA 70181

"Our business stinks but it's picking up!"

*Black on
white stock*

**PHOTO TOURS
(602) 282-4320**

*"Imagine yourself on a
Photographic Safari...
Traveling into Ancient
Red Rock Country..."*

 TROY WILLIAMS
Manager

252 N. Hwy. 89A
Sedona, AZ 86336

WHERE IMAGINATION AND
EDUCATION GO HAND IN HAND

Peggie J. Pelosi
President
(416) 738-8877

*Rock structures, Photo Tours and
phone number in red, the rest in
black on mustard yellow stock*

*Folded card in red, green, blue and
yellow*

"One look at the production plan and I said, 'I can see you're new at this, aren't you?' (he nods timidly as I continue) 'Let's start gathering the team together. There is enough talent here to make your wildest dreams come true.' A few synergistic lightbulbs explode—whamo! We begin by

Back side of card for Shinetop Productions (4067 Santa Nella Place, San Diego CA 92130 (619) 481-6561) It is one of four cards that grabs your interest and then...

The Castle Keepers

"We'll mind your manors"

Pets · Plants · Property

P.O. Box 220
Charlottesville, VA 22902

804.977.1681
References Upon Request

Black print on gray stock

Courtesy the Business Card Archives

Arthur Maranjian
Vice President

Tel 970-493-3793
Fax 970-493-8781

The Intrepid Group, Inc.
Book, Line & Thinker ❑ the Bookmailer

Corporate Offices
6280 East County Road 60
Fort Collins, CO 80524

Distribution Center
1331 Red Cedar Circle
Fort Collins, CO 80524

Square logo and name of business in dark blue; the other print is black on beige stock

The Qualities of a Good Tag Line are Also the Qualities of Good Copy or a Good Business Card

- ☐ Every word **carefully chosen**
- ☐ Makes an **impact**
- ☐ **Catchy**
- ☐ **Clear** and memorable
- ☐ **Unique** or distinctive
- ☐ Doesn't violate **trademarked** slogans—although a paraphrase or parody can be effective, witty, or humorous
- ☐ **Concise**—with good cadence and rhythm
- ☐ **Relevant** to the business and the customer
- ☐ **Attractive** to the eye and ear, when said aloud

Avoid using slang in the tag line or the business name unless it is integral to the image.

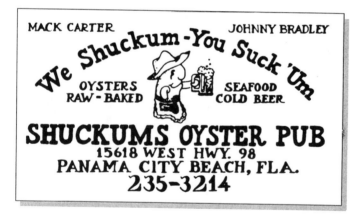

Dark brown on light blue stock

Courtesy the Business Card Archives

Images chosen should not be superficial, but should reflect the true nature of a business. Make sure there is connection between a symbol or slogan used and what is offered. Make it catchy. Whenever possible, tie the slogan to a memorable experience. For example, a car dealer offered free hot air balloon rides that people recalled fondly when they were ready to buy their next vehicle. Sales improved over the following months, even though the balloon rides were not otherwise related to automobile purchases. The purchasers felt positively toward the dealer because of the enjoyable free rides, so returned when they were ready for a new vehicle.

Bullet the Copy on a Card

Since space is severely limited, complete sentences are not necessary on a card. Use sentence fragments or phrases, as long as their meaning is clear. Punctuation isn't critical, either. In fact, an argument can be supported that you should **not use a period** at the end of a slogan because it inhibits comprehension. Bulleted lists convey abundant information, using just a few carefully selected words. Bullets can be vertical, like the lists throughout this book, or random, simply to separate horizontal items, like this listing of branch outlets: ◆ Crossroads ◆ Bayshore ◆ Civic Plaza

EXOTIC • HANDMADE • ACID-FREE
DECORATIVE • ART PAPER • TOOLS
BOOKBINDING • CASTING SUPPLIES
PAPER MAKING • MADE TO ORDER PULP
PAPER MILL • WORKSHOPS • BOOKS
INVITATIONS • STATIONERY • GIFTS
CUSTOM CUT CHOPS • WAX & SEALS
RETAIL • SHIPPING • CATALOG

PAPER ARTS
MILL & STUDIO, INC.

930 WEST 23RD ST. • SUITE 16 • TEMPE, AZ 85282 • (602) 966-1998

Black on textured paper

Lake Shore
Joan N. Hupp, Owner/Chef

• Cooking Classes
• Recipe Development
• Menu Development
• Food Consultant
• Demonstrations

Chic
Le Cordon Bleu
Member: IACP, AIWF

Chefs

Phone and Fax
312-280-1143

111 E. Chestnut,
Chicago, IL 60611

Green trees and name line; the rest in black on white laid stock

Such bulleted lists help to organize the information so that it becomes easier to read. Bullets create a block of information, which uses white space to advantage. Lists need to include similar items. For example, use all verbs or locations, or products carried, etc.

When using bullets, you can make them part of the overall design by picking a symbol that relates to the business or the card design. Such bulleted items can be used to unify and connect the images on the card. Use small dots (·) or larger ones (●), or choose a shape related to your business, like the little card shapes used as bullets on these pages. A business that featured gifts from the heart reinforced that image with tiny heart-shaped bullets (♥). Or, if there are lines or bars (rules) on the card, the bullets can be little squares the same thickness, to echo the design feature. Just be careful that what you choose isn't so busy that it clutters the card. Also, choose one simple shape that is easily recognized, since bullets are quite small. Don't mix bullets in the same list or on the same printed piece.

SAGEBRUSH

Publications

Gwen A. Henson
- ◆ Book Editing & Indexing
- ◆ Book & Publication Design
- ◆ Book Publishing Consultation
- ◆ Computer Typesetting
- ◆ Graphic Design

(602) 777-9250
Fax: (602) 777-9270
Email: sagebrsh@netzone.com
957 East Guadalupe Road, #17
Tempe, Arizona 85283

Your own editorial & production departments

Black on textured sage green stock

VEGETABLE SOUP—ALL THOSE LETTERS DON'T SPELL ANYTHING: DEGREES, ABBREVIATIONS AND ACRONYMS

Take Care With Acronyms (letters like AMA or IABC)

An acronym is made up of the first letters of a series of words. In themselves, the letters mean nothing, so you need to link them to other mental associations. Some acronyms are designed to spell something specifically related to an organizational slogan or purpose. Such combinations of letters are more easily remembered (MADD for Mothers Against Drunk Driving).

Acronyms and jargon come and go. They can date the card or your business image as they are superseded by new and better jargon. Also, people forget what they mean, even if they once knew. One wit put DMN after his name. When pressed, he said it meant "**D**on't **M**ean **N**othing." Some acronyms succeed at becoming indelible, so that over time everyone remembers the initials and the original words they stood for may be lost. For example, IBM is better known than International Business Machines.

Be kind to the poor card recipients. They neither care about nor want to know all of the complexities of your company. If too much is encoded into some of these symbols, it can easily turn prospects off. Avoid terms that cannot be deciphered by anyone outside of your field. Consider spelling out acronyms in some way that indicates what the letters actually stand for. Spell out words completely somewhere on the card so they can help to deliver your message.

Some people have so many initials after their name that instead of being impressive, the effect is intimidating and perplexing— rather like "vegetable soup." Not all designations are equally important. Although MD or Ph.D. are easily recognized, with the proliferation of letter combinations, it's often hard to tell what the person is actually saying. For example, those within the profession (insurance) may know that being a CLU is a good thing, but others may not be well enough informed to be impressed.

You don't need to load every achievement on your card. Be selective. In most cases, state only the highest or most important designation or degree. If you have both a masters and doctorate in the same field, only show the doctorate (unless it is important to the customers you're courting or in a different field than the Ph.D.).

Peter Homer, Jr.

NATIONAL INDIAN
BUSINESS ASSOCIATION
8280 GREENSBORO DRIVE, SUITE 550
McLEAN, VA 22102

Office (703) 486-7933
Fax (703) 486-7944

Phone (703) 893-3749   Fax (703) 893-3540

Brick gray on mottled textured gray stock

ATTITUDES
INSIGHT
MOTIVATION

SEMINARS   (602) 730-0164

Folded card with bright turquoise on glossy white stock

Since there are only 26 letters, you run the risk of sounding like "someone else" or becoming another company with "all those letters" (without being too clear about your specific letters). Initials often fail to conjure up a tangible image or mental association. Companies with initials as their name need to be especially clear about what they stand for or at least what the company does. In the case of mergers and consolidations, hyphenated names are often used in an attempt to preserve the previous identity of each company. The danger is that the resulting name will be such a muddle no one can sort it out.

Even if an acronym is well known, like ABA (American Bar Association), there are only so many letter combinations. On a national level, such a combination stands for 16 different organizations, from Bandmasters to Booksellers to Bakers. Make it clear to which one you are referring. If you are forming your own logo or acronym, check to see if the combination of letters you intend to use could be confused with a well-established or common acronym.

Michael R. Hill
Vice President, Controller

Motor Coach Industries International, Inc.
10 East Golf Road, Des Plaines, IL. 60016-2291

Ph. (847) 375-1236   (800) 428-7626   Fax: (847) 299-7843
1-800-SKY-PAGE   Pin: 3194625   Cell: (312) 590-3438

Engraved royal blue type on gray stock; silver foiled embossed bars on logo

Avoid Abbreviations

Abbreviations are used to save space and aid comprehension. Unfamiliar abbreviations defeat that purpose. Avoid using abbreviations on your card, even if the meaning is clear. It is better to write out "Road" than "Rd."

Rules regarding periods: Capital letter abbreviations (CBS) do not require periods. If it is an abbreviation with upper and lower case letters or all lower case letters (Inc. or c.o.d.), use a period. However, all capital abbreviations of **places** take periods (U.K.).

It is best to completely spell out the state where you do business on your card. However, if you do abbreviate the states, use only the standardized two-letter form of abbreviations shown here. No periods are required. Discontinue using the prior state abbreviations like Mich. or Ala. They date your image.

Standard Abbreviations for States

AL—Alabama

AK—Alaska

AZ—Arizona

AR—Arkansas

CA—California

CO—Colorado

CT—Connecticut

DE—Delaware

DC—District of Columbia

FL—Florida

GA—Georgia

HI—Hawaii

ID—Idaho

IL—Illinois

IN—Indiana

IA—Iowa

KS—Kansas

KY—Kentucky

LA—Louisiana

ME—Maine

MD—Maryland

MA—Massachusetts

MI—Michigan

MN—Minnesota

MT—Montana

NE—Nebraska

NV—Nevada

NH—New Hampshire

NJ—New Jersey

NM—New Mexico

NY—New York

NC—North Carolina

ND—North Dakota

OH—Ohio

OK—Oklahoma

OR—Oregon

PA—Pennsylvania

PR—Puerto Rico

RI—Rhode Island

SC—South Carolina

SD—South Dakota

TN—Tennessee

TX—Texas

UT—Utah

VT—Vermont

VA—Virginia

WA—Washington (state)

DC—Washington, DC

WV—West Virginia

WI—Wisconsin

WY—Wyoming

List courtesy of the US Post Office

BUILD YOUR OWN CREDIBILITY
Tangible Things to Say about Yourself *Personally*

Provide the *bona fides* (Latin for "in good faith") which show that you are worthy of trust, like these:

- ☐ Education, degrees, titles
- ☐ Awards and honors
- ☐ Inventor of _____; could even be silly like *"the half-pound hot dog"*
- ☐ Founder of _____; could be unrelated to the business, but helps if it is connected
- ☐ Author of _____; contributor to _____
- ☐ Brag lines (if they're true): first, biggest, last living, hometown, former, winner of, only
- ☐ Years in business
- ☐ Philosophy, motto, statement of purpose
- ☐ Years of experience—your own, staff, combined total
- ☐ Emblems, military ranks, retired
- ☐ Member of _____
- ☐ Sports, teams, prizes, sponsor of
- ☐ Hobbies, especially if related to expertise, or if you're known for them
- ☐ Elected or appointed to boards or committees, especially if related to your expertise
- ☐ Special interests, especially if related to your business, logo, or image
- ☐ As seen on, at, with _____
- ☐ Former _____ or *emeritus*, or retired

Member
23 Years

Gordon Taylor
GENERAL MANAGER

SUPERIOR PONTIAC-CADILLAC
1717 S. Dort Highway
Flint, MI 48503

Bus: (810) 744-1000
FAX: (810) 744-1077

*Black on
white glossy
stock with
gold emblems*

Show Your Credentials and Expertise

If you have degrees, special designations or awards, proudly display them after your name (Ph.D., CLU, Winner: Contractor of the Year—1995). They will also provide cues to your status. But be careful, if your awards were received long ago or if you have newer things to brag about it could make you look dated. If you're doing business with foreign countries, (See Chapter 14 on international business.) showing your credentials is essential. Since you want to make your business credible and trustworthy, please only tell the truth. Don't make things up to enhance your status. Don't make claims to competence that you haven't earned.

T<small>RAUMATIC</small>
S<small>TRESS</small>
I<small>NSTITUTE</small>

Daniel J. Abrahamson, Ph.D.
Clinical Psychologist
Administrative Director

C<small>ENTER FOR</small>
A<small>DULT</small> &
A<small>DOLESCENT</small>
P<small>SYCHOTHERAPY</small>
<small>LLC</small>

22 Morgan Farms Drive
South Windsor, CT 06074-1369
Tel (860) 644-2541
Fax (860) 644-6891

*Gray print on
gray recycled
stock*

Disclose Required Credentials

The trend is toward increasing regulations of occupations to protect the public and assure acceptable levels of proficiency. Hairdressers, building contractors, surveyors, morticians, detectives, etc. must all establish their right to conduct business in their chosen field. Many schools not only grant degrees but also offer specialized certificates of accomplishment. Magic words: certified, licensed, authorized, registered. Use them. In addition, the professions themselves often have specific designations, which are required for membership. (See Chapter 3 on the professions and business names.) Such careers have degree requirements plus ways to demonstrate specialization or unique achievement.

BLACK,
POLCYN &
BROWN

GLEN E. POLCYN, CFP
ADMITTED TO THE REGISTRY
OF FINANCIAL PLANNING
PRACTITIONERS

4133 E. PASADENA AVENUE
PHOENIX, ARIZONA 85018-1618
602•840•6122
FAX 602•952•1695

A PROFESSIONAL FINANCIAL
PLANNING ASSOCIATION

Dark forest green vertical band bleeds off the page with silver foiled diagonal edge; bottom line also in green; text in black on cream textured stock

★

Black Star
RESEARCH & INVESTIGATION

Barry A. Kintner - AIA
5714 North Eighth Place No.2   Phoenix, Arizona 85014-2203
Ph & Fax: 602.266.1646 - E-mail: a2z@inficad.com

Arizona P.I. Lic.# 9508011

*Black print on
white stock*

Be aware that some states require that a person's license number or other type of notice be shown on their business literature. For example, a private investigator (detective) needs to show a license number, or an attorney must state a Bar registration number. Anyone who is licensed should determine whether disclosures are required, then make sure they're dutifully shown on your card. Ironically, the more status a person has, the less information is needed on the card. In the upper ranks, others are expected to know of your status (so less needs to be said).

JOHN M. SAUER
PRESIDENTIAL COMMUNICATIONS

WHITE HOUSE COMMUNICATIONS AGENCY
(202) 395-2000

*Blue picture
of the White
House; text in
black on off-
white textured
stock*

Courtesy the Business Card Archives

Membership is Smart Business

You're known by the company you keep. Membership both enhances your professional education and is an ongoing source of business and referrals. Belonging to organizations provides abundant tangible benefits:

- □ **Networking** and referrals
- □ **Affiliation**
- □ The opportunity to be an **insider** and with other insiders
- □ **Contacts** with those who are not otherwise in your sphere of contacts
- □ Enhanced **community spirit** and opportunity to "give back"
- □ **Enjoyable** experiences
- □ **Perspectives** outside of your business frame of reference
- □ An environment for **developing skills** not used in your business and expanding on those you use
- □ All the benefits which come from **volunteering**, like being on committees with powerful contacts
- □ On the pulse of **industry trends**
- □ **Reflected glory**

Master Ahn Sung Chung

1382 Industrial Drive Suite #1
Saline, MI 48176

Tel: (313) 944-8023
Home: (313) 429-4839
Fax: (313) 944-3922

U.S. Taekwondo
JiDoKwan Saline

Logo and seal in old gold; text in black on beige stock

```
4234 N. Winfield Scott Plaza        Phones: 602 970 0101        Dark blue ink
Suite 101                                  602 970 6272         on light blue
Scottsdale, AZ 85251                 Fax: 602 423 0526          stock

        Edward E. Scannell, C.S.P., C.M.P.
             • Keynotes • Workshops • Seminars

PAST NAT'L. PRESIDENT              PAST INT'L. PRESIDENT

ASTD                                    MPI
                                 MEETING PLANNERS INTERNATIONAL
AMERICAN SOCIETY
FOR TRAINING AND
DEVELOPMENT
        1991-92 President         ® National Speakers Assn.
```

Professional Organizations and Unions Have Their Own Rules

Members of a specific profession usually belong to affiliated professional organizations. These organizations have standards of admission for membership or stages before a person becomes fully qualified, like apprenticeship or internship. Often, special training is required, with performance or ethical standards imposed on members. Some such organizations have optional membership, like the American Psychological Association. But others have mandatory membership in order to function within that profession, such as the State Bar Association to practice law. Members are permitted or required to display the organization's logo. Check the policy of organizations related to your business.

Membership also serves to show that you are part of a profession and thus leads to referrals from your peers. In some fields, more business comes from referrals by other practitioners than in any other way. In that case, you are really marketing yourself to them and showing your advanced qualifications and specialization. Some cues speak to peers and may not be as relevant to customers. Get feedback from both groups (peers and customers) when you develop a card, since you may have different things to communicate to each.

Personalize the Impersonal—Stand Out in a Large Firm

Within a big organization, it is especially important to stand out as an individual. There may be hundreds of other employees with similar jobs and identical business cards. Even in such circumstances, however, there are ways to personalize your company card. Show that you're doing something special for the company. You're displaying leadership traits. Add a tag line or symbol that shows activities beyond the norm. Even if you have to cover the printing costs yourself, it's worth it! President, Smallville Chamber of Commerce; Member: Million Dollar Club; Coach, _____ Company Softball Team; Chairman, Scholarship Committee; #1 Salesman, 1996 are a few examples.

Have stickers made to embellish your company-supplied card. The one-time charges for dies or set-up seem cheap when you realize that it costs no more to make 3,000 than a thousand, and you only pay for them once. Stickers come in any shape you could imagine and beautiful colors, metallics, and special effects.

Adapt a characteristic symbol or graphic that applies to you alone that you use in a variety of ways, like on your fax sheet or bid proposals. Or you could use a rubber stamp, colored pens, or markers to add a distinctive color or cartoon-type flourish.

One salesperson used a small graphic so consistently that it moved with her from one employer to the next. The customers who followed her valued the consistency in her materials, as well as in her services.

Reveal Other Kinds of Expertise

Don't stop there. Be aware of what interests, motivates, and reassures your ideal customer. There are many things that can be said about you that do not involve academic or professional accomplishments. Even when you offer identical merchandise to others, the customer is often buying your unique technical advice or judgment. For example, as an owner of a camera shop, you understand the advantages of various cameras, so you can point out which features will best serve the *particular* customer—who comes to trust you and rely upon you when making such buying decisions.

That kind of reliance is the best hope for the survival of small retail businesses. The impersonal superstores and on-line shopping networks do not compete well at the level of personalized service. Customers will pay extra for that kind of input. Become known and sought out for your expertise. Then indicate your expertise and product knowledge on your card or promotions (e.g., we have over 30 years experience in repairing music boxes).

Black ink on white

Bragging about the best BBQ (and it is!)

BUILD THE CREDIBILITY OF THE BUSINESS
Show Reasons the Business is Memorable

- ☐ Established or founded in _____(year); in business since _____; open more than _____ years; _____ years at the same location
- ☐ Founder of _____
- ☐ Awards earned from organizations or for special services
- ☐ Winner of _____
- ☐ Sponsor of _____
- ☐ Memberships in various organizations; include their logo or symbol
- ☐ Group(s) you represent or participate in
- ☐ Authorized dealer, distributor, agent; exclusive source for
- ☐ All major name brands in stock, or name brands offered
- ☐ Formerly known as _____; formerly located at
- ☐ State unusual services; visit our _____
- ☐ Who you serve: "for the fisherman," "supplier to the meetings industry"
- ☐ Years of experience: your own, staff, combined total
- ☐ All sales, services are done in-house
- ☐ Personnel are _____ certified, or have at least _____ years of experience
- ☐ No beginners
- ☐ Come in and see the _____; something interesting, beautiful, noteworthy, or humorous
- ☐ Ongoing contests (how many pennies in the jar?) drawings, surveys, monthly winners

Profit From Being Local

A simple statement, such as "local" may be a big factor in attracting business. Tourists are looking for authentic local products or experiences and people like to buy locally. Use your knowledge of conditions in your community to determine if a local emphasis would enhance your appeal.

- ☐ Locally owned
- ☐ All products made in _____ (your town or region) or "on site"
- ☐ Made from locally grown/mined/produced ingredients
- ☐ "Authentic"; made by members of the _____ Tribe; provided or produced by our graduates

Capitalizing on Religious, Ethnic or National Affiliations

Showing your religious or ethnic affiliation is a two-edged sword. It attracts some, offends others, and is a matter of total indifference to yet others. For example, some businesses display the cross or fish symbol to show that they are Christian and to attract others who are also Christian. If your ties relate to what you're selling, like a kosher deli or a religious bookstore that depends on you "knowing," that background is very important. It comes down to understanding who your market is and what your customers expect from you.

When you want to capitalize on national or ethnic connections, identify the origin of the products: Danish designs, Oriental Market, Indian Bazaar. As an example, your ethnic products can serve as a meeting place by providing foods, newspapers, music, etc. from wherever "home" is. Such a targeted market could be sufficient reason for two different cards: one for the affiliated group and another for the general market.

BE EASY TO DO BUSINESS WITH
State Clearly *How* You're Easy to Do Business With

- ☐ Easy to **find**
- ☐ Easy to **buy**
- ☐ Easy to **park**
- ☐ Easy to find **open**; state hours, extended hours, after-hours options
- ☐ Easy to **pay**
- ☐ Easy to get **repairs**, updates, modifications
- ☐ Easy to get **delivery** or installation
- ☐ Easy to get **parts**, supplies, or related items and answers
- ☐ Easy to **find products** or select what you want
- ☐ Easy to get **expert advice** or assistance
- ☐ Easy to get **training**, workshops, or classes

Tell What You Provide

- ☐ Free, covered, or valet parking
- ☐ Free pick up or delivery, or within a certain area, radius or time frame
- ☐ Secured location; guards on duty
- ☐ All competitor's coupons accepted
- ☐ Open 24-hours a day or 365 days a year; we never close; open weekends
- ☐ Pharmacist on duty round the clock; mechanic on premises; alterations in house
- ☐ Express check-in or check-out
- ☐ Join our Frequent Flyer, Parker, Eater Bonus Program
- ☐ Unlimited refills, batteries, adjustments, repairs
- ☐ Walk-ins welcome
- ☐ Free demonstrations

- Technical support available; on-site assistance
- Same-day delivery; one-hour or one-day processing; same-day order processing; orders ready or shipped within 24 hours
- Convenient locations
- Free _____: gift wrap, dinner, pass, carwash, lesson, visit, shampoo, color
- Any special service offered, like trip or menu planning
- Checkout times, free continental breakfast, newspaper, local calls
- Ask for discount for _____ or coupon good for _____
- No minimum order
- Free installation or delivery
- Trial period, introductory offer, or options available
- Free or discounted classes, related products and supplies
- Free newsletter, book, or information related to products or services
- Incentives for repeat business or referrals
- All staff are board certified, licensed, graduates of _____

Features such as these lend themselves to bulleted lists on your card. Whatever you choose to highlight should reflect the desires and preferences of your targeted customers.

IDENTIFY YOURSELF TO THOSE WHO REQUIRE EXTRA ATTENTION
Serve the Special Needs of the Customer

Send a signal to those who have special requirements that you can provide what they need. Often, such features relate more to customer service than to the actual products or services sold. In some cases, you are supporting a philosophical stance, such as a smoke-free environment. Someone out there is looking for all sorts of specific assistance, so if you provide it, help them to find you.

Be caring enough to provide special services, when appropriate; not only does it help those you serve, but it encourages other businesses to do so also. When I was a small town attorney, I was proud to be able to say "I make house calls." It may not make sense for others in larger cities, but it was an unexpected bonus that increased my value to my clients.

Handicapped

- ☐ Wheelchair accessible
- ☐ Special accommodations provided
- ☐ Elevator access
- ☐ Braille—cards, signs, information
- ☐ Sign language available

JILL SCHRAMM
Office Manager

Center for the Blind, Inc.

3100 East Roosevelt, Phoenix, Arizona 85008
(602) 273-7411 • West Valley (602) 972-9382

Member
United Way

Dark blue on white stock with Braille letters at the bottom

Card is both printed and in Braille

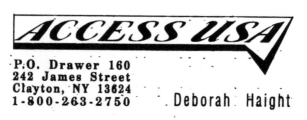

Braille sample—black ink on white stock

Make your card easy to read. Avoid dark backgrounds or low contrast between ink and card stock. Make addresses and phone numbers larger. Don't crowd the information. Also arrange text to correspond with the flow of the eye. (See Chapter 6.)

Travelers, Immigrants and Foreigners

- ☐ Use and post standardized language-free international symbols
- ☐ State languages spoken
- ☐ Offer instructions or information in several languages
- ☐ Bilingual classes available
- ☐ State the products country of origin; Korean grocery; products from Israel
- ☐ Advertise in their ethnic publications; as served in _____ (name of country)

Those Who Are Young or Old

- ☐ Make signs and printing larger
- ☐ Childcare available on premises
- ☐ Rides available upon request
- ☐ No charge for children under 6
- ☐ Ask about the Senior Discount; Saturday is Seniors Day

- □ Seniors, 25 percent off on Tuesdays
- □ Children eat, stay, ride free; ask about our youth rate

Pets

- □ Pets welcome
- □ Personalized pet care
- □ Corral on premises
- □ Kennel facilities

Food and Dietary Concerns

- □ Vegetarian or vegan
- □ No pesticides
- □ Kosher meals available
- □ All organic materials or products
- □ Special diets: low or no fat, salt free, wheat free, egg substitutes
- □ No MSG
- □ No preservatives
- □ Authentic _____ cuisine
- □ No sugar added; sugar free
- □ Low calorie; _____ calories per serving or entree
- □ Percentage of entree, product, meal that is fat
- □ Fresh; first of the season; _____ crop
- □ Authentic (state origin); imported cheese, wine, seafood

ISBN 0-9680631-1-X

Distributed by Prima Publishing
(916) 632-4400

Mahmmud Jaafari

4426 N. 19th Avenue
Phoenix, AZ 85015

*A Vegetarian
Main Attraction*

Phone (602) 265-5992

Janet Podleski
Author

Granet Publishing Inc.
51 1/2 West Adams
Fairfield, IA 52556
toll free (800)470-0738
fax (613) 247-9162
e-mail spoons@magi.com

Black on beige card

*Red and yellow Looneyspoons; red
pants, green shirt; rest is in black on
white stock*

Support Causes You Care About

- Products made in America
- Made by union members
- Made from local products
- Made by native craftsmen, students, residents, members
- Smoke free environment
- Allergy free
- All natural ingredients; 100 percent natural
- Percentage of every sale to _____ organization; support the local band
- Collecting for a charity; all proceeds to _____; collections for flood victims
- Made from recycled materials

- No foreign parts or ingredients
- Biodegradable

REDUCE THE RISKS OF DOING BUSINESS WITH YOU

Use Reassuring Language

Give any assurance you can to minimize the customer's feeling of risk. If the buyer is on the verge, such reassuring claims can often tip the scale in your favor. When you increase confidence, you increase sales. At some point before a purchase is made or a contract is signed, the customer has to feel that he is making a wise and safe decision. Reassure your customers with third-party endorsements, testimonials and quotes from satisfied customers. Be constantly on the alert for such spontaneous reactions. Capture the quotes then trumpet them.

- Full money-back guarantee
- We stand behind our work
- No reasonable offer refused
- Licensed; certified; bonded; insured
- Satisfaction guaranteed; lifetime warranty
- Guaranteed for the life of the product; one-year guarantee, or 30 days or 90 days
- Guaranteed as long as you own your car
- No repair over $_____
- Installation free or $_____ with purchase
- Ask about our _____ policy or guarantee
- Return policy; we have a "no hassle" return policy
- Flat rate per hour or job
- Maintenance contract included or available

- ☐ Extended warranty at no charge or for $_____
- ☐ If not completely satisfied, your money will be cheerfully refunded

NANCY COXE
Vice - President

124 W. Orion, Ste F-4
Tempe, Arizona 85283
(Lic. No. 075554)

Pager (602) 498-7694
Mobile (602) 710-8801
Office (602) 752-7807
Fax (602) 752-3086

- Installation
- Maintenance
- Design-Build

Gray mountains medium blue sky; the rest in black on grayed textured stock

Full Service Has Become the Name of the Game

- ☐ Describe the kinds of services or products; list services
- ☐ Provide and spell out a complete range of services
- ☐ Even if you are not in a service business, always realize and perform as though customer service matters; treat the customers as though they are trusted
- ☐ State who you are affiliated with for service or repairs, or outlet for _____ clinic
- ☐ All services provide by _____; state specific qualification or certification

STATE THE PAYMENT OPTIONS
Provide Various Ways to Pay

- ☐ In-store financing, or checks accepted with two IDs
- ☐ Barter system, will trade
- ☐ Member trade or barter organization
- ☐ Apply for our credit program (or card) today

- ☐ Credit card same as cash
- ☐ Ask about our Christmas Club
- ☐ Layaway available
- ☐ No interest until _____
- ☐ Discount for cash
- ☐ No payments until _____
- ☐ 90 days same as cash
- ☐ We finance on site
- ☐ Bankruptcy O.K.

Accept Credit Cards and Debit Cards

One of the ways to show the financial stability of the business is to indicate that you accept credit cards. If the company is large enough to have its own credit card, that's even better. The ability to take credit cards has been controlled by banks, which are reluctant to provide merchant status to small businesses or those that lack a storefront. Therefore, having a merchant account indicates that you are established and recognized by creditable financial institutions.

Use some of the most recognizable logos around: Mastercard, Visa, American Express, etc. If you accept them, you have a right to display their logos, and that includes putting them on your card. It is an additional method to accommodate your customers and distinguish yourself from your competitors, especially if they don't accept credit cards.

Display Credit Card Logos

As you provide more payment options, the customer has more control and you will have fewer collection problems. Customers also feel less risk since they know it is easier to return goods or handle disputes if the purchase was initially made on a credit card. Take advantage of the increased impulse sales. Accepting credit cards increases business since customers are inclined to spend more with less hesitation. Stores routinely increase ticket size or sales volume about 20 percent when they start to accept credit cards.

Even if you don't take credit cards, eliminate negative statements like "No Credit Cards Accepted" or "No Checks." It sets a negative, who-cares-what-you-want tone. It is better to **state what you do accept and inform by omission.**

Stores now accept debit cards, and that trend will expand. It is good for the merchant since the procedure eliminates bad or bounced checks and purchases are instantly credited to the business account. Every bank now issues such cards to its customers so they can use the 24-hour automated teller services.

To Recap

Confidence is vital to business survival. Use tag lines and credentials to build credibility for the business. Spell out your features and benefits for those who are looking to buy what you offer.

Chapter 5

Display Your Addresses and Phone Numbers—If You Tell Them How, They *Will* Call

"Give Me a Call"

A major function of the card is to provide the business name, address, and phone number, and rests on the assumption that, "If they know how to reach me, they will call." But these days few businesses have only a single telephone number and address. There are multiple ways to communicate with each other. Displaying your numbers communicates much more. They also reveal the business's priorities, price range, positioning, and sophistication.

Kinds of Telephone Numbers Frequently Used on Cards

- Business telephone numbers
- Emergency or after hours contact number
- Home telephone number
- Fax number and fax-on-demand number
- Voice messaging number
- E-mail address
- Web site or web page
- Pager, digital or voice
- Cellular phone number

- 800 or 888 number
- 900 number
- Extension number or voice mailbox, within a large organization

Where Do You Put All Those Numbers?

Businesses are assaulted by the proliferation of telephone lines, equipment, services, and options that accompany the rise of electronic communications—and we're nowhere near the end of it. Technology will continue to make us more easily accessible and efficient, although this point is often debated. You undoubtedly already have a variety of addresses and phone numbers, (with the likelihood of additional ones down the road). The unavoidable question is, **how do you fit them on the card?** With space at a premium, how much do you provide? You may need to make a judgment call, since you need not disclose all of them to everyone.

The large assortment of numbers does, indeed, create design and layout difficulties. An easy solution is to print them on the back or on a folded card. However, as will be shown in Chapter 6 on card shapes, some very real problems come with that remedy. If it is at all possible, decide which numbers are most important, and print only those on the front of the card. Another solution is to print only the important numbers and write any others at the time the card is given. That personalizing touch can reap other rewards (See Chapter 12 on distributing cards.), since it then becomes something you have "given" in a special way: "Here's my home phone number, if you need me over the weekend."

Most cards print the phone numbers too small or really too small. Now that the population is aging, those tiny numbers simply cannot be read. If a number can't be read, it won't be called. (See Chapter 7 on font sizes.) Also, the more numbers stacked up on the card, the harder they become to read or find the one you're looking for. If you have a primary business number, make it apparent in some way, so that it will be the one called first.

Set Your Principal Phone Number Apart

- ☐ Make it **first**; avoid placing it last in a string
- ☐ Make it **larger**
- ☐ Make it **bold**, italic, underlined, etc.
- ☐ Make it a **different font** or color
- ☐ Put a **box** around it
- ☐ Add something special, like a **star** or check mark
- ☐ Place it **apart** from the other numbers
- ☐ Add a special **design feature** to emphasize it

Rainbow colors in box; rest in black on white

Keith Moore
ACCOUNT REPRESENTATIVE

IMAGE
GRAPHICS, INC.

Printers
& Manufacturers of Books

Specializing in short /medium run 4/C and black

P.O. Box 996
2701 Wayne Sullivan Drive
Paducah, KY 42002-0996
800.445.6163 · Fax 502.442.5810
502.442.6163

The Positive and Negative Considerations of Phone Numbers That Spell Words

- ☐ Easier to remember; the word is often related to the business identity
- ☐ Can be too cryptic or clever, like vanity license plates

- Not every phone has letters on the keys; letters often are not readable or well-lighted
- Letters are slower to dial and awkward to translate into numbers
- Can't keep the word combination if you move (unless it is an 800 number)
- Can choose a word related to your slogan or identity
- Limits word length; restricted to words that match the available prefixes (all 7 letters) or four-letter words (last 4 digits)
- Phone company reserves the right to change numbers or prefixes
- Provide the numbers after the word (SOLD - 7653)

Loan By Phone™
221 LEND
1 800 352 5363
(Outside Metro Phoenix)

Red circle and the rest of logo and text is medium blue on white stock

Hours:
Monday – Friday, 8 am – 8 pm
Saturday, 9 am – 6 pm

BANK≡ONE

Whatever it takes.

Bank One, Arizona, NA
Member FDIC

* Loans subject to credit approval.

Paul Baker
Sales Associate

ORTUNE

Fortune Properties, Inc.
2525 C Street, Suite 100
Anchorage, Alaska 99503
(907) 562-SOLD (7653) HM. 337-5062
Mobile 244-5474

Orange triangle around the "F"; type in dark blue on white stock

Be careful about O and 0—when printed they look very much the same. One is a letter (O; oh); the other is a number (zero), but people are often careless and intermix them ("My number is 666-oh 724 (0724)"). Computers distinguish between oh and zero, even if you don't; if they aren't entered correctly in your contact lists, the person's data can't be found or retrieved later. Being clear about which one you mean is even more important when words and letters are intermixed because you're spelling a word.

Fax Numbers Are Fax of Life

Think of the power of a fax machine:

- Direct transmission to the receiver—almost anywhere
- No delay—transmits in seconds
- No postage costs
- No middleman (except phone lines)
- Connection through computers or fax machines
- Inexpensive
- Simple to own or operate
- Lacking a fax (and fax number) today rates as a business card blunder—you look like an amateur; having the same phone and fax number marks you as very new or small

Avoid the Problem with Fax Numbers

How often have you dialed a phone number, and then felt chagrined to be greeted by the piercing shriek of the fax mating call? It happens much too often and is annoying because, in every case, you didn't expect it. You hadn't intended to dial the fax number. The problem is even more annoying when you have just paid for a long distance call without reaching anyone. Such an annoyance can be avoided if the fax number is not found in the place where you expect to find the phone number.

Distinguish fax numbers from main phone numbers. Make the principal number prominent. The fax is only sought by those wanting to fax to you. Some people print fax numbers upside down, so that they are not accidentally dialed. Such originality may solve the problem, but lacks elegance and can undermine the card's design. I invite anyone who has figured out a remedy to enter the contest (#3) in the back of the book. so that a consistent method of displaying fax numbers can be developed. Let us all strive to stamp out the screaming menace.

ADDRESSES
Ten Kinds of Business Addresses

- Store or retail outlet(s)
- Office or home office
- Warehouse
- Billing address
- Sales office
- Mailing address: post office box or commercial mailing address
- Corporate or company headquarters
- Virtual office location
- Wholesale facility
- Shipping address

Assess the Business Address

The old real estate maxims, "Location, location, location," and "Location is everything," may seem shop-worn and hackneyed, but they're just as true and appropriate today as when some genius first identified the concept as a major precept of property sales. Location, however, is important to **any** business. It's fairly obvious that the mere location of a business can send either positive or negative messages. An upscale location, for example, can indicate success, class, and good taste, while a slum location on the "wrong side of the tracks" sends an entirely different message.

Unfortunately, available funding often dictates a less-than-desirable business location. This need not be a strike against you, if handled properly. Your "lousy," inconvenient, or run-down area doesn't have to be trumpeted on your card through your address. Remember, your business card should be a positive statement about you and your company. Negative messages should be eliminated if possible, minimized if not.

If a business is service oriented or can be conducted by phone or other electronic means, why not overcome a negative address with the simple expedient of a post office box in a better location? In some cases the company address may be eliminated altogether—with positive results.

Consider the situation of a friend of mine. He was, and is, an excellent appliance repairman. As an employee, he was the darling of his large company's appliance repair division, its star repairman. He had always wanted to have his own little business, and, after a particularly trying day "at the office," he made the leap from employee to owner of his own little company. Unfortunately, he was over-eager and under capitalized. Because of zoning restrictions he wasn't able to operate out of his residence, and the only building he could afford was in a run-down neighborhood. Walk-in business was almost nonexistent and he was too late for that year's Yellow Page listing. His only advertising tools were his business cards, flyers, and newspaper ads. In each case, his address was killing him. After a brainstorming session one night, we decided to eliminate his "negative" address entirely. In place of an address, his business cards (and other advertising) simply stated: "Area-Wide, Four-Star Service at Your Door." He upgraded his basic phone service, acquired a quality mobile phone, and passed out his business cards at every opportunity. In less than two months, he was forced to add another service truck and two employees. By **omitting** his address, he turned a negative into a positive and substituted one mental image for another.

Royal blue on white stock

Red type on dark yellow diagonal box with white reverse for Hotline; on white stock

Choose Location With Customers in Mind

The most important word in selecting an address to put on your business card is "appropriate." If your targeted market consists of people in lower economic levels, a high-end address is more of a hindrance than an attraction. By the same token, an upscale beauty salon will benefit from a trendy address. Numerous studies have indicated that people tend to stick with the familiar. In most cases, your location should fit the type of customer you seek.

You can bask in the reflected glow of success due solely to your address (Wall Street, Paris, London, "Biltmore Plaza," etc.) or share the image of other businesses associated with a particular area. However, "location status" can be an extravagant amenity if it fails to enhance your business. It may add unnecessary operating costs and distract from activities that could use improvement, such as upgraded equipment.

If you depend on walk-in traffic and your address might be difficult to locate, try putting a miniature map on the back of your card, or a phrase such as "conveniently located next to _____" (a well-known landmark, store, public building, etc.). Or provide street coordinates. Disclose something that makes you easier to find.

15th Street Studio

a frame shop & gallery

1725 15th Street
Boulder, Colorado 80302
(between Arapahoe & Canyon)

Robert Colachico   303-447-2841   **Stephen Grant**

Tuesday-Friday 10-6 · Saturday 10-4 · or by appointment

Red box around 15; black print on white stock

Rethinking her accessibility gave a friend of mine a much more desirable business card address and increased her gross profits several times over. Her one-woman sign and banner company was located in an area that generated little walk-in traffic. As a result, she was spending a disproportionate amount of her income for advertising. Determined to find a more favorable address and cut her advertising expense at the same time, she negotiated a lease for some unused space in a compatible business—a quick print shop located in a large mall. The equipment she used for making her signs and banners was moved to her garage. The small space she leased provided enough space for a desk, some display area and a few chairs—exactly what she needed in the first place. Once she realized that her office didn't have to be located in her production area, she was able to upgrade her address—and increase her business in the process.

Many companies have several specific addresses. Whether these locations are appropriate for business cards or not depends on the purpose of the card. For instance, the sales office address would probably serve a company salesman better than a warehouse or shipping location. On the other hand, those addresses might be perfect for those who sell to you. Any or all of these addresses could apply to your operation and may need to be specified on the card.

Brick red and black printing on gray stock

Post Office Boxes Have a Negative Reputation

When you provide only a post office box, you run the risk of looking transient. Also, shipments by Federal Ex, UPS, or others cannot be delivered to a postal address. There are valid reasons for omitting an address altogether: security, not serve customers directly, virtual location, zoning, home based business, etc., but consider the message you are sending if only your post office box is provided.

There are inexpensive alternatives, like a shared location with another business, an office suite, or a business service center with mail-receiving capabilities. You can rent a mailbox from a location that sounds like a street address. Most of the proprietors of such businesses will also accept your not-postal packages. Be careful, though, to specify that customers must call for an appointment. When they do, you can provide your street address, so they won't be frustrated by seeking you at your mailing address.

Maps Help Them Find You

Two-sided card; Prussian blue crab and business name...

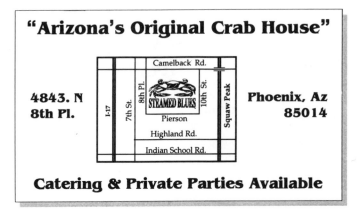

...rest of the text and map in black on glossy white stock

PLANNING DEPARTMENT
TELECOPY (907) 262-1892
BUSINESS (907) 262-4441
262-4255

ROBBIE HARRIS
PLATTING OFFICER

KENAI PENINSULA BOROUGH
144 N. BINKLEY ST. • SOLDOTNA, ALASKA 99669-9988

Gold spot on map; the rest in black on white stock

Or show the location itself.

THE CITY OF
PASADENA

Department of
Information Services

GENI SOWELL
Librarian III
Outreach/Programming Coordinator

Pasadena Public Library
285 East Walnut Street
Pasadena, California 91101-1556

(818) 405-4037
(818) 585-8396 Fax
gsowell@ci.pasadena.ca.us

Red City of Pasadena and dome; remainder of logo in dark green; the text is in black on white stock

The College Inn Guest House

A European-Style Bed & Breakfast
4000 University Way N.E., Seattle, WA 98105
(206) 633-4441   Thomas Wall, Manager

Black print on gray textured and mottled stock

Locations All Over the Place

In addition to the **kinds** of business addresses a company my have, it may also have **multiple locations**, each occupying a different address. For example, a multi-national corporation may have locations in different countries with numerous branches in each. Some companies have multiple functions at widely different locations. For some of these companies, deciding which address to put on a card is not so much a question of informing the public, but rather, deciding how much to reveal!

In some cases, large, multi-national corporations may simply state something like: "with offices in London, Rome, Athens." No specific addresses are given except the main corporate office. Individual locations will have their own version of the corporate business card with appropriate local or regional addresses and numbers.

Jennifer Morris
Publicity Coordinator

the world's best travel guides

lonely planet

155 Filbert Street, Suite 251
Oakland, CA 94607

t: 510/893-8555 f: 510/893-8563 e: jennifer@lonelyplanet.com

Two-sided card; full-color sketch on the front...

Lonely Planet Publications

Australia	PO Box 617, Hawthorn, Victoria 3122 Tel: (03) 9819-1877, Fax: (03) 9819-6459
UK	10 Barley Mow Passage, Chiswick, London W4 4PH Tel: (0181) 742-3161, Fax: (0181) 742-2772
France	71 bis, rue du Cardinal Lemoine, 75005 Paris Tel: 1 44 32 06 20, Fax: 1 46 34 72 55
USA	155 Filbert St, Suite 251, Oakland, CA 94607 Tel: (510) 893-8555, Fax: (510) 893-8563

www.lonelyplanet.com

...with black print on the back

Should You Print Your Home Phone Number?
Pros

- ◻ Friendly gesture; customer service oriented
- ◻ Available and can be easily reached
- ◻ Treats customers like friends, not just business contacts
- ◻ Type of business that has emergencies (like plumbing or towing) or after-hour services
- ◻ Saves time and frustration in getting reached
- ◻ Accepted convention in your town or business

Cons

- ◻ You're never off duty
- ◻ Blurs the distinction between home and work; lack of privacy or boundaries
- ◻ Security is imperiled
- ◻ Can be abused by the intrusive
- ◻ Not everyone needs it (be selective about giving it out)
- ◻ Can make you seem new or small
- ◻ Connotes that it's not the "day job," or that it is a part-time business

Home-Based Business—Is It Necessary to Obscure Your Size?

Home-based businesses are growing both in number and respectability. They represent a $450 billion revolution that will only accelerate. If we consider the telecommuters who work from home, the numbers are already in the millions. It's a trend that will continue to grow as technological innovations make "being there" less important. Much of the "stigma" once associated with a home business no longer exists. However, when living and working at the same location, it is important to create some distinctions. You may find that working in your robe and slippers is rather nice, but some of your customers may not find it quite so charming. Therefore, your living and working conditions should not be allowed to "blend" until any distinction between the two is obscured (unless you are an artist, in which case, you are **expected** to blend).

Don't compromise your business image by cutting corners where it would be obvious. Avoid any hint of being a hobbyist, amateur, or part-timer with its "here today and gone tomorrow" aura. Anything that makes your potential customers feel that you're not a "real" business can compromise your credibility and the rates you'll be able to charge. Avoid being "penny wise and pound foolish." This is especially true when it comes to telecommunications. Never use your home phone number as your business number. You may think your three-year old sounds cute on the phone, but the account executive you've been courting for months might have a different image in mind. Separate lines cost very little and are considered essential by most successful home-based business people. (A fax machine that is hooked up to the family phone is a dead giveaway that you are small potatoes!) **Use a business number on your business card!**

For years, I've dealt with a company that was very professional and the service was outstanding. I had the impression that I was dealing with a large, well-run firm. Certainly, they gave me no reason to think otherwise. While in California on an unrelated business trip, I decided to visit their office and say "hello." Was I ever surprised to find out that this "large firm" was run out of a small, two-bedroom house, and the "office" was not much larger than a big closet—proof that "professional" doesn't necessarily mean big.

Occasionally there are benefits to a home-based business that acts and sound like a home office. If part of your success rests on an image of memories of grandma's kitchen and the smell of fresh-baked bread, then by all means, don't attempt to replace it with a sterile facade of marble, chrome, and glass. Stick with what works for you. Many large companies spend zillions of advertising dollars to cultivate a home-spun image. Be clear on what image you want

to project from your home office. Conduct yourself accordingly—
and let your business card reflect that image.

Include Zip Codes and Area Codes

Don't forget to use your zip code and area code. Omitting either rates as a business card blunder. Better yet, use your zip plus four.

TELEPHONES MAKE CONNECTIONS
Display Numbers of All Kinds

The **kinds** of numbers you provide show that you are a legitimate, established, and well-connected business (pun intended). It also indicates whether or not you're part of the global electronic community, with instant research and communication links readily available. You may have a communications setup that was state-of-the-art several years ago, but is outdated now due to advances in technology. A relationship with your local phone company will help keep you abreast of changes that might benefit your business or enhance your capabilities.

Select Either Dots or Dashes

In the U.S., the customary way to show a phone number is with the area code in parentheses (or followed by a dash), with a dash between the first three digits and the final four digits, thus:

(123) 222-3333 or alternately, 123-222-3333

In Europe the convention is to use periods instead of the parentheses or dash, thus:

123.222.3333 or alternately, 123 222 3333

The periods are being used on more and more American business cards. The dot may be small (•) or large (●). However, being less familiar, they are harder for Americans to read and relate to. The arguments for periods or dots are artistic or simply "a change." Since they are harder to decipher, the author recommends you stick with dashes unless you're conducting business in Europe.

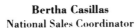

Bertha Casillas
National Sales Coordinator

WILLIAM BOUNDS, LTD.

P.O. Box 1547
3737 West 240th Street
Torrance CA 90505-6003

310.375-0505
Fax 310.375.0756

*Brick red
diamond;
black text on
white stock*

TERRI LONIER
President

914.255.7165 voice
914.255.2116 fax
terri@workingsolo.com
http://www.workingsolo.com

**Reaching
independent
entrepreneurs**

WORKING SOLO, INC.
111 Plains Road
New Paltz, NY 12561

*"Working
Solo" in
bright yellow
box; text in
blue on white
stock*

Phones and Your Business Image—Don't Risk It!

Telecommunication is the lifeblood of business. At the very least, it is considered essential by anyone other than a cave-dwelling recluse. Troglodytes may not need a telephone, but **you do!** Few businesses can survive in seclusion. Sure, your favorite hot dog stand may not be dependent on telecommunications for the bulk of its business, but if you'll look closely, you'll probably find a cell phone in the proprietor's back pocket. Our modern world simply couldn't exist without communications, be it plain-Jane telephones or the Internet. People **need** to contact each other—and the ubiquitous business card is one way to tell them how to get in touch. If you and your business are accessible by phone, fax, or Internet, put that information on your card, and let the prospects decide how they want to get in touch with you.

Once you get them to call, make it a positive experience—right from the start. A busy signal or being put on hold, either by a person or a machine, breaks the vital momentum that made them pick up the phone in the first place. Constantly evaluate your system or procedures to eliminate such turn-off signals. You will never know the amount of business lost because you couldn't be reached. Remember; if they can't get through to you, they will eagerly go to someone else.

The first few seconds on the telephone are a vital link to the public, with a dramatic impact on the bottom line. I have never forgotten hearing Joseph Charbonneau (a professional speaker) say that the most important person in his company is the person who answers his phones. She determines where his kids go to college or where he gets to take his vacations.

Who among us hasn't felt the frustration of telephone hell where we select from mechanical menu after menu, unable to reach a living soul or get the information we need? The first impression that you give about your company is usually the voice that answers. Harvey Mackay says "How your telephone is answered says more about your company than all your slick advertising and marketing plans can ever hope to accomplish. Your telephone receptionist is the most important salesperson in your company."[1]

Nowadays, a personable human link stands out. One day recently, I made about thirty business calls and only reached two humans—and they made me feel very appreciative. Consider the importance of the person who answers your phone. Don't just put your trainees there. Think carefully before eliminating the vital human contact. Sure, the technology makes it easy to replace a warm body. But people do notice! A colleague told of receiving a special promotion from American Express about an exclusive new service he had qualified to receive. "Just call the provided number." When he called and was greeted by a machine, he didn't feel so special after all. The value of that expensive promotion was vaporized for him, and who will ever know how many others? He hung up, having lost all interest—but it did bother him enough to puzzle over the incongruent messages he had received.

The Ideal Telephone Receptionist

☐ Has a warm and resonant voice

☐ Can be understood; speaks plainly and without a thick accent

☐ Sounds professional and businesslike

☐ Knows the company's products and services; directs you to the best person to help you

☐ Has longevity and remembers callers over time

☐ Cares about people and sincerely wants to be of service

☐ Is paid enough to be considered the professional that he or she is

☐ Makes callers feel "reasonable," valued, and glad they called

☐ Answers promptly, and if you're put on hold, remembers to come back to you; also gives you a chance to respond yes or no when asking if you will "please hold"

☐ Treats customers like they are special

When You're Not by the Phone, You Needn't Be Out of Touch

☐ Emergency numbers; after hours numbers

☐ Live answering service (not in your office)

☐ Live switchboard or receptionist (in your own office); messages referred or "patched" to you

- Voice mail and answering machines
- Ordering lines, answered 24-hours a day or at specified times to handle orders or queries; also fax-on-demand systems
- Beepers and pagers
- Cellular phones, PCS phones, and mobile phones
- Home telephone number provided
- E-mail addresses and bulletin boards

With such a variety of contact numbers, it's difficult for the caller to know which to try first. Or the receiver may check the wrong system and miss a timely message. Organizer systems use a central link to track you down and inform you that there is a message. For example, a pager might alert you when messages are received by your voice mail. Such capabilities are bound to become more complete and efficient over time.

Take care with the message you leave on your message devices. Often, it is impossible for the caller to determine if he's gotten the intended person. You want to set a tone that is both personable and businesslike. Make it interesting. Like your card, it should convey a flavor of "you."

Put Your Number Where People Can Find You

- Yellow page listings and ads; business phone number required
- Yellow page listings and ads in other communities, even around the country
- White page listings
- 800 and 888 number directory
- Information—411 calls and 800 information
- On-line (electronic) directories
- Business cards, promotional literature, and ads
- Other listings and directories, such as membership directories

Reduce Telephone Tag

- If someone leaves a message, respond promptly
- Leave a complete message so a call back is not required or expected
- Be available for calls at a certain time of day, and let everyone know that you can be reached then—schedule other activities around it
- State in your messages when they should call you back
- Make telephone appointments and then honor them

Examine Local and Long Distance Options

Local phone companies vary considerably regarding the quality and sophistication of their offerings or equipment. We have little choice about how quickly some of these systems are being upgraded. The major long distance phone companies are stumbling over each other in an effort to acquire your business. Any one of these carriers can provide excellent service and offers plans to reduce the cost of long distance communications. All have packages that include numerous options, which are constantly being improved.

Since the competition is ferocious and promotional programs are frequent, you probably can negotiate a deal that provides more service for less money. It's worth listening to the sales people who call soliciting you to change carriers. Then evaluate how well your own carrier compares (or is willing to match). The quality of long distance service is usually good, since most carriers share the same lines or satellite links. The distinctions among carriers are revealed in their customer and support services, as well as their pricing structure.

Try Phone Features That Come in Handy

- **Call Forwarding** or Selective Call Forwarding—Phone can be programmed to forward your calls to another number; with selective call forwarding, only the calls you designate are forwarded

- **Call Waiting**—Provides a distinctive sound to let you know when another call is coming in when you are already on the line; does not ring as busy to the caller; you can go back and forth between the two calls (beware that some business lines don't provide this feature)

- **Distinctive Ringing**—Allows you to distinguish business calls from personal calls by assigning two different numbers with two distinctive rings to a single phone line

- **Call Transfer**—Allows you to transfer a call on one number to another number in your home or elsewhere; frees business line for more incoming calls

- **Market Expansion Lines (MEL)**—Provides you with local numbers and directory listings in other communities; calls are toll-free for customers, and automatically forwarded to ring at your office; creates phantom office in other locale

- **Dedicated Lines**—Phone lines used for a single purpose, like a fax machine, so they don't compete with other uses

- **Roll-Over Lines**—All calls come in on main number and roll to other unused business lines; only one number listed on card

- **Back Lines**—Line not listed on the card or given out, except to "insiders;" also used for roll-over lines

- **Teleconferencing** and 3-Way Calling—Permits more than two locations to talk together at the same time

- **Caller ID**—Permits receiver to know who is calling before answering the ring; unfortunately, too many calls come from "anonymous" and "unavailable"

Cellular Phones, PCS Phones, and Car Phones

The various versions of portable phones have gone from being expensive and rare to everywhere. Just be aware that a driver using a car phone is likely to cause as many accidents as a drunk driver. Although the cellular phone number on your card doesn't carry the cachet it once did, cellular phones still can't be beat for keeping you accessible. Decide if that number is to be provided on your card, given out selectively, or be used only for your office to relay messages to you. The costs of using such phones do not arise from buying the equipment as much as the monthly fees and the per-call charges.

The issue of privacy on cordless and cellular phones should not be ignored. People can and do listen in on your "broadcast" calls. It is critical that professionals, like doctors and lawyers, never use cordless phones when talking to their clients. The legal concept of **confidentiality** of any communication a person has with his doctor, lawyer, and minister (they cannot be required to testify or disclose what they know about a client) is destroyed. That means the simple use of the cellular phone **waives confidentiality** and will **imperil all communication** with the client (not just the calls made on cordless phones). New technology may deliver better protection for calls over the airwaves in the future, but for now it's not worth the risk.

Provide Toll-Free 800 Numbers or 888 Numbers

- Receiver pays for long-distance calls, flat time charge; free call for the caller
- Portable—can move with you anywhere in the country or to other long distance carriers
- Permanent—the number is yours as long as you care to use it; it belongs to you, not your long distance carrier
- Not apparent where in country it rings (problem about time zones)

- Creates positive public perception—customer friendly
- Customers are about seven times as likely to respond when an 800 number is provided—even if it is not a long distance call for them
- Often used for information services or messages, and may not be manned

Full color photo card on glossy stock

900 Numbers Can Sell Services

900 numbers are the numbers that the caller pays at a per-minute rate. However, the charges are paid to the 900 number operator through your phone bill. The amount of per-minute charge is determined by the 900 number provider. No longer are these being used mainly for pornography. It has become an effective a way to sell all kinds of services: legal advice, computer coaching, medical information, etc. The caller gets the information needed and pays for the time of the person providing the assistance. Even govern-

ment agencies have installed 900 numbers to let those requesting some kinds of information pay for it.

To Recap

You need to be easy to find and easy to reach. Your address and "how to contact" information will be one of the main reasons people keep your card. Make certain they get all the information they need.

Section II

Build a Better Business Card— Create a Silent Ambassador

An effective design develops through the investment of time and attention. It doesn't just happen, any more than a great structure just happens. The whole design results from the coherent assembly of details. With an effective design, all the parts in your business package **work together** to make a pleasing and memorable impression. That identity should strengthen the concept of the business, while connecting with the customers' needs. When you consider its impact on your bottom line, it is not sufficient just to have a pretty image. It must also be positive and powerful.

"A letterhead and business card tell more about the way a business or individual wants to be publicly recognized than any other form of graphic communications. These are at once brands, like those burned into cattle hides; banners, like those carried into battle; and signs, like those that provide directions. The design of these materials may often appear simple, but in fact, they are among the most charged, and therefore among the most difficult, problems a graphic designer must solve."[1] A coherent image saves money and time. A standardized look and procedures can be replicated on all documents.

All your business documents should show that you are professional and competent. That visual identity is a valuable business asset, as important and as tangible as your location. It should not raise any questions about whether you are "as good as the next guy." Be prepared to invest the time and money necessary to develop the most potent and professional image that you can. You are going to live with it a long, long time. Whether or not it is a good one, it will become the image that people will associate with you (even if you change it later).

Up to this point, the emphasis has been on deciding **what messages** go onto your card. Section II considers all the things necessary to arrange the words and images to create your visual identity. Precise language and unambiguous symbols are necessary. Since a card is so small, each part needs to be in scale, in harmony, and support the desired image. The experience of creating your card also helps you to "invent yourself."

The chapters in this section appear in no particular order. Each focuses on the development of your card from different angles. Some aspects, like visual images, fit into any of the chapters. An attempt has been made at continuity; however, read the entire section, rather than relying on any single chapter to develop your card.

Section Table of Contents

Chapter 6

Consider the Card as a Whole

Searching for the Perfect Card

Attempting to describe the ideal business card is like trying to describe the ideal dress, dream vacation or perfect automobile. No answer makes any sense unless you consider what you want to accomplish and what is best for you. You are faced with infinite variables, with your choices constrained only by your budget, imagination, and the incredibly small area in which you get to work.

Finding your ideal card is not an epic quest, like seeking the Holy Grail of marketing and design. There is no perfect card just waiting to be discovered. Since the card is a reflection of you and your company, the objective is to develop one that **accurately reveals your unique style in a way that attracts the kind of business you desire**. Your identity acts as the consistent factor in any card you develop.

Just as you did not decorate your home overnight, it takes time to create a card that fits you. Some parts work better than others, so you keep them and embellish those features. Other parts don't work as well, so out they go. You experiment. You make the best card you can, then tinker with it from time to time. Like your home, you move furniture around, change the color scheme, add pictures and accents, replace things that don't quite fit. Your card needs to have the basic parts like name, title, and address, just as your home needs chairs, beds, and shelves. You try out various arrangements and decorative details. What's too much? Too little? Or a pleasing arrangement? After enough tinkering, it melds into something that suits you, works for you and, indeed, is a reflection of you—just like a comfortable room.

The chapter ahead considers attributes of the whole card: graphic images, the impact of colors, and card size. There are a zillion ways to go about expressing your own business identity. The process of discovering yours can help your business evolve and prosper. Creativity, ingenuity, and resourcefulness will serve you better than arbitrary card design standards. Such qualities are highly prized in creating an enterprise. Display them with a flourish.

Effective cards are noteworthy because they are all too rare. **They do get noticed!** And once someone notices the card, they notice the person behind the card, the person behind the business. They grant both the card and its bearer a second look.

Guide the Eye to What is Important

Since, your card is the handshake that you leave behind, knowing how the human eye perceives that "handshake" can determine whether yours will be remembered as firm or weak, outstanding or faint-hearted. Realize that your card's effectiveness ultimately depends on the way the receiver responds to it. But first she must see it, and that viewing is largely physiological. Make a design that **guides the eye** through the card. Use type, placement and images that "capture the eye" and lead it to those parts that are most important.

In the Western hemisphere, we tend to read from left to right, top to bottom. Studies have shown, most of us unconsciously view any printed material in the same way. This trait is considered by psychologists to be a "learned habit," because learning to read overcomes any natural tendency that had previously existed to view printed material any differently. As our reading skills progress, we reinforce that reading pattern until it becomes a distinguishing feature of our culture.

Since the eye sweeps across the card from upper left to lower right, the eye resists going to the two other corners, unless carefully guided. The eye habitually goes to the focal point (just above the center) and then trails off down to the right, unless captured by something the brain finds interesting. Without a lure to pull the eye down to the left or up to the right corner, your eye simply won't notice those areas. Eye movement applies to your business card because **whatever you want to be noticed should appear in that band**. Assuming that many people only glance at a card, knowing where that glance will focus lets you arrange the message so that even a casual scan delivers.

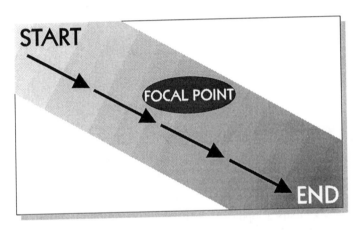

The **primary message** you intend to send on your business card should be the overriding focal point of its design. The rest of the information on the card supports its total message and adds to the overall impression the little piece of paper imparts to its viewer. A picture or visual image is likely to be the first thing noticed; color is noticed next. Type size also disrupts the left to right habit. If you decided that your name, for example, should be the principal message, both size and location can be used to call attention to it.

Although we know that eyes naturally move from left to right and top to bottom, studies also indicate that if a person is **asked** where his eyes first focus on printed material, he will inevitably answer "the center." Perhaps this is why so many people design their business cards with their name precisely in the middle. In itself, this is not an undesirable location, provided the rest of the card is subservient in size and color, and the card is relatively uncluttered.

This characteristic eye movement can be, and has been, exploited commercially—usually in a subtle manner. The knowledge that our eyes function in a predictable pattern has been helping advertisers shape commercial messages for years. Technically, it is a function of the brain, but it is manifested in eye movement. Likewise, shapes and colors that our brain finds pleasing can be measured by eye response. In fact, the use of shape and color can momentarily divert the eye from its left-to-right habit. The **way** you arrange elements on the card can be a powerful, if subtle, method of controlling the viewer's attention.

Bright purple and turquoise card with each of the four corners colored, on recycled cream stock

A centered card

Establish a Hierarchy of Attention

Steer the attention to what you want to be noticed first, second, and third. Manipulate several qualities to create a hierarchy of attention.

- Size—the first thing a reader sees is the largest item on a page and what will usually be considered the most important. "As size decreases, so does perceived importance."[1] Consider size first, and design the other elements around it

□ **Contrast**—Whatever has greater contrast gets more notice. Make sure what you want to stand out does, indeed, stand out. Use contrast sparingly and **only** for things that are of consequence

□ **Position**— Place the more important information in the area between the top left of the card and the bottom right. Another position cue occurs when a person's name is above the logo, which signals that they are significant

□ **Form**—Visuals and pictures are easier to grasp than words. The reader looks at the written items second. Visuals have more impact than their size would suggest

□ **Content**—Select words and concepts that are attractive and interest sustaining

Ten Ways to Make a Card Easy to Read

□ Arrange elements to follow the natural **flow of the eye**

□ Convey a **theme**, unifying concept, or coherent image

□ Select elements that fit and **work together**

□ Shun too many typestyles or capital letters

□ Use type that is **large enough** to be read easily

□ Create a clear and interesting **graphic image**

□ Avoid being too **crowded** or too busy; it's confusing

□ Provide plenty of **white space**

□ **Cluster** the parts into blocks of information; then frame them with that white space

□ Make **important things larger**

Piece of Mind Books

230 S. Buchanan
Edwardsville, IL 62025
(618) 656-7277

Andi Romick-Allen
Owner

*Turquoise on
white stock*

Be Stingy with Words and Space

Never forget, a card is very small. Since there are a number of things that have to be on it, economy of words is important. Make every word be clear, concise, and tightly expressed. Every word or image should be essential. Be ruthless! Carefully select every single word, making sure it is precisely what you mean. Too much crowded on the card becomes a jumble. Tighten up your language, and eliminate anything that distracts. Sometimes just changing a word or two yields an entirely different impact.

When I was younger we played a game called Scottish Telegrams. [Note: The phrase refers to frugality, and is not meant as a social slur; there is no intention to offend anyone who is Scottish.] Since you had to pay for each word in a telegram, the goal was to use the fewest number of words to send a message for the least amount of money—just like a Scottish telegram. For example, send an eight-word message for the price of one word:

Havtagotatonasat (1 word) *means*

I have to go to town on Saturday (8 words)

This may be an absurd example, but it serves the point.

The Whole is Greater...The Card is Bigger than Its Size

A card's message is achieved, in part, from the **interaction** of its many parts and the **way they are combined**. The whole impression conveyed is greater than the sum of the individual parts (ala Gestalt).

And part of that augmentation is a result of the hitchhiking messages (See Chapter 2 on decoding hidden messages.) that accompany the printed images. Additional elements arise because of the assembly and operate together to deliver a complete picture. Discussing the many separate components of the card ignores the *way they work together*, their inter-relationship. Further, the harmonious combination of the parts sends an overall impression of competence and reassurance.

THE INFLUENCE OF COLOR
Colors have Emotional Connotations and Impact

The addition of color(s) adds many more options and much more interest to your card. (Look for additional information on colors and PANTONE MATCHING SYSTEM®* colors in Chapter 11, on printing.) As Jan V. White says, "Color can help by highlighting the utility—to the individual recipient—of bits of information and thus adds benefit. It must be used to reinforce signals. Used cannily, in the context of a clearly-designed document that takes advantage of color's potential, it creates greater reader attention, leading to clearer comprehension, which causes longer retention."[2]

Colors provide many ways to touch the receiver and are greatly favored by the Drawbridge Fellow described in Chapter 2. It helps you to capture and hold his attention, and it makes mere printing become more interesting and attractive. "Color is not something to be added to the surface like cosmetic makeup. It is not just "prettified," but a language. It must be used as an integral part of a coordinated effort to make printed information faster and easier to understand."[3]

Colors are not just nice to look at. They affect us physically as well, giving rise to a scientific specialty, which studies the physiological effects caused by color, called chromadynamics. "Scientists have proven that certain colors effect vision, hearing, respiration and circulation."[4]

---

*   PANTONE® and PANTONE MATCHING SYSTEM® are registered trademarks of Pantone, Inc.

Color Adds Impact

- **Grabs attention**—stands out
- **Spotlights material**—gives it importance
- Looks (and is) more **expensive**
- Adds more **beauty** and is visually interesting
- **Organizes** information
- Adds **emotional impact**, more recognizable
- Reveals **mood** and personality
- Assists **comprehension**
- Sends **subliminal communication**; emotion-laden messages

Colors have personalities, so choose those colors and tones compatible with the business personality. Make sure you select an appropriate color for the type of business, not just one you like. The nature of the business often dictates the appropriate color range. Use those shades as unifying elements in borders, frames, and rules around the words. Adopt a signature color as part of your image, like IBM® blue or Kodak® yellow. Many businesses adopt a PANTONE MATCHING SYSTEM® shade (with a designated number, like PANTONE® 182) as part of their business uniform.

Masterpiece

CATERING

LUCKIE BOSSELMAN
(602) 996-6934

gourmet artistry for every occasion

Picture accented with yellow, blue and red spots; text in black on glossy white stock

Full color vertical bleed on textured stock; burgundy text on cream stock

CHILDREN'S WISH
FOUNDATION
INTERNATIONAL™

Arthur J. Stein
President

8615 Roswell Rd.
Atlanta, Georgia
30350-4867
(770) 393-WISH
1 (800) 323-WISH
Fax (770) 393-0683

Be Sensitive to Ways Words, Images, and Colors are Linked

Some colors have such a strong association in a special use (such as orange and black together mean Halloween); it is hard to use those colors without triggering that idea. Other images are so strong you won't get the desired effect without the appropriate color. For example, a black banana is not appetizing; neither is a purple one. Don't choose colors that run counter to their familiar associations. One year I put green food color in the mashed potatoes (St. Patrick's Day). The taste wasn't affected, but they were unanimously declared "inedible."

Notice Color Associations

The symbolism of color is greatly influenced by culture. Then there are the factors like age, gender, and economic class that "color" those influences. Nevertheless, colors have recurring associations arising through our training and culture.

- Avoid using red and green together since many people have red/green color blindness and cannot differentiate between the colors
- Red-yellow-green have meanings regarding traffic signals
- Color words have their own associations: "yellow" means coward; "green" means inexperienced; "blue" means sad
- Don't risk pastels because they are perceived as weak and frilly, unless your business is about summer, flowers, babies, or caters to feminine interests
- Strong colors should be incorporated in small amounts, like a banker's tie
- The eye sees bright colors first, so use brighter shades for emphasis

Common Color Associations

Red	Danger, hot and heat, intense, alive, sexy, impulsive, stop signs and red lights (stop), bloody, passion, Communists (reds)
Blue	Calm, military, first place, peaceful, conservative, water, skies, spiritual
Green	Lush plants, conservation and environmental issues, fertility, nature, spring, money, green light (go), envy, healthy, lushness and prosperity, safety and security
Yellow	Sunlight and sunny, warm, spring, fresh, lemony, caution, yellow light (caution), coward, cheerful, idealistic, imaginative, intellectual
White	Purity, snow, virginal, cold, clean, honest and trust-worthy, unsullied, refinement
Black	Powerful, authoritative, dark or evil, somber, trendy and sophisticated, death, unknown, frightening, witches
Orange	Citrus, ripe, autumn, fire, cheap, warm, informal, cheerful

Purple	Royal, expensive and valuable, ceremonial, powerful, traditional, luxurious, fruity (like grapes or plums)
Brown	Earthy, basic and simple, agriculture, autumn, reliable, grounded, plain and not luxurious
Gray	Elegant, established, classic, secure, mature, neutral, old, well-established

Since the use of color is so linked to emotional responses, carefully consider your card color(s) for its non-verbal messages. Bold colors with high contrast come across as garish and tacky for an accountant, but just right for a toy store. Whereas, pale colors may suit a flower shop, they would be seen as weak and wimpy for a sporting goods store. Various professions have their own characteristic colors, from the red and white barber pole to the white of a nurse's uniform, to the gray of a banker's suit (although such connections are mutating). The intensity of the color also communicates. Bright or loud colors are seen as vibrant and often reflect youth or ethnic preferences. Dulled tones indicate mature, established, or upper-class tastes.

Color is determined by:

- **Hue**—the name of the color
- **Value**—the darkness or lightness of a hue
- **Chroma**—intensity of a color; brightness; the amount of saturation; strong chroma is colorful, and weak chroma is gray

Any comment about color needs to consider the hue, intensity, shade, brilliance, as well as the surroundings. The appearance of an ink's color is partly determined by what it is printed on and whether it is a PANTONE MATCHING SYSTEM® color or results from 4-color process (as discussed in Chapter 11 concerning printing with color).

Choose Colors for Their Heat or Coolness

Consider whether colors are warm or cool.

- ☐ Warm colors: yellow, orange, red, yellow-green, peach, salmon, brown
- ☐ Cool colors: green, blue, violet, lavender, indigo, mauve, maroon

Warm colors are perceived as active and encourage mental activity. Such emotional colors get attention. They are more upbeat, fun and happy, so are associated with getting things done. As far as design goes, they are best used in small areas on a card.

By contrast, the cool colors represent authority, respect, and reliability. They are perceived as cool and clean, or associated with nature. These colors can be used in larger areas on a page or card.

Consider Color Early in the Planning Process

When you intend to use color, it figures prominently in the tasks of your design person. Bring color decisions into the planning from the outset. Your printer will also have valuable input on how your color choices will impact on your printing job or costs.

The information in this chapter is primarily related to the impressions that colors create. Their impact on the receiver can be so strong that it adds immeasurably to your card's appeal and should be considered for your next design. In some situations, the cost differences are not great, and they become minuscule when you divide the price of the cards by 500 (or 1,000) that come in the standard box.

PAY ATTENTION TO LEGIBILITY
Colors Influence Legibility

The way colors are placed next to each other influences their legibility. Nothing is clearer to read than black ink on white paper. No color combination establishes as good a contrast as black print on light stock. Much of this is determined by the science of light-waves and the physiology of the eyeball. Still, on a little card go for impact, since there really isn't a lot to read. Jan V. White (a guru on using color effectively in printing) provides some generally accepted concepts about legibility, but warns that they may not be accurate:

"Best legibility   Black text on white (but not white text on black)
Dark green text on white background
Dark blue text on white background
Brown text on white background
Warm color text on cool colored background
Worst legibility   Red text on green
Green text on red
Blue text on yellow
Green text on blue
Red text on blue
Black text on color that is darker than 20% black
(See Chapter 9 on screens.)
White text on black"[5]

Colored ink has less contrast than black does. Make colored letters larger, so they are more legible. Be careful that the background or paper stock is not too dark to create a strong contrast. Also, don't overlook the effect of printing on cream or colored stock—it will change the color of the ink.

Another factor that influences legibility of type is the x height, which shows how high most lower-case letters are relative to the capital letters. High x height fonts are easier to read because they appear larger than other type styles the same size.

The man has a dog—High x height

The man has a dog—Low x height

Colored Type Reduces Comprehension of Type

Studies conducted by Colin Wheildon demonstrated that reading comprehension is greatest for black and is reduced significantly with type of any other color. They found a paradox; while 61 per cent of the respondents found that colors were attractive and pleasant, "64 per cent said they found the color intruded while they were trying to read the text."[6] Comprehension fell from 67 percent for black (the highest score) to 17 per cent for bright colors, and even more for low-intensity colors. The darker the type, the "greater the comprehension level. This poses the question, why not black? Ink doesn't come any darker."[7]

CHANGING THE SIZE OR SHAPE OF A CARD
Increasing the Size of the Canvas (fold patterns)

The standard business card is a fixed size and shape in a horizontal or vertical format; however, ingenuity has expanded the size of the canvas used to display your message. Variations take several forms. In each case they result in more room to convey more information. Sometimes, even the shape can be changed, which opens further symbolic possibilities.

Black print on white stock

Horizontal card (called landscape orientation)

Brick red on glossy white stock

Vertical cards (called portrait orientation) permit interesting design variations.

Dark blue print and screen (two different shades) on textured lavender stock

Sometimes you encounter a horizontal and vertical card at the same time.

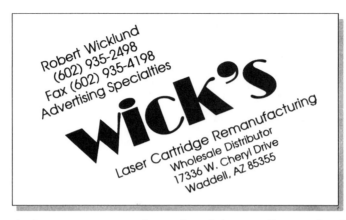

Black print on glossy white stock

A design variation is a diagonal card, but usually is confined to the standard size and shape.

Two-Sided Cards Double the Print Area

Printing on the back doubles the amount of space to deliver the impact of the message. The back has become a ready answer to the question "Where do you put all those numbers?" However, as pointed out in Chapter 5, there are some disadvantages to putting such information on the back.

Two sided card: dark purple circle and print with amber wheat sheaf...

...back purple print on orange shape

Two sided card; dark green and blue on white; bleed on top and bottom; back blue with green accents

Disadvantages of Large, Folded, Two-Sided or Odd-Shaped Cards

□ They **don't fit** card carriers (including yours); get dog-eared easier

- They **don't fit** into most card storage systems (theirs), which only show the information on the front
- They get put in a **separate** or "special" place—and then buried and forgotten
- It is **inconvenient** to see the information on the inside or back
- Folded or odd shaped cards are **bulky**
- They are **more expensive** to design and print

Advantages of Large, Folded, Two-Sided or Odd-Shaped Cards

- They permit **more room** for information
- Provide **more complete** information; usually less crowded, so easier to read
- More likely to be **noticed** and commented on when received
- Can serve as a **mini-brochure** or mini-catalog
- Often **ingenious** or clever; likely to be remembered and kept (but does that translate to sales?)
- Usually **well planned;** permit more design options
- **Novelty value**—they are kept; makes your card stand out from other cards

How About a Postcard as a Business Card?

Why not go directly to using a postcard? Make no pretense of it being a business card. It's one way to stand out; they are inexpensive and available in full color. Larger means there is plenty of space on two sides. They can go through the mail cheaper than a letter. They're perfect for a quick personal note that gets past the gatekeeper—so they get read. They do, however, share all the disadvantages of any non-standard-sized business card.

Remake the Shape of the Card

Beyond these standard shapes, anything goes! Size and shape can be bent into unlimited variations. Such cards are likely to create a strong impression. What you gain in cleverness, you may lose in other respects, so changing the conventional shape is a calculated risk. People cannot easily put an odd-shaped card in their wallets or card cases. Any non-conforming card doesn't fit with the others and ends up being put "somewhere else." If you have an unusual size or shape of card, offer a standard-sized one as well, so they can keep you in both places.

Unusual shapes can simply be larger (like the cards in Europe, see Chapter 14 on international business) or smaller, or have a corner trimmed off. Or consider rounded corners.

Two sided card; pastel turquoise border on all sides, front and back; with dark blue and light blue printing on gray textured stock

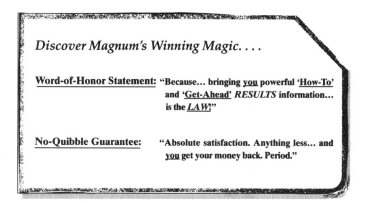

Two sided card; lavender on glossy white; back: Purveyors of enlightening books, audio & video tapes

PURVEYORS
OF ENLIGHTENING
BOOKS,
AUDIO & VIDEO TAPES

JEFF VOLK
603-659-2929
FAX 659-2939

219 GRANT ROAD
NEWMARKET, NH
0 3 8 5 7

THOMAS J. LINNEMEIER   **(219) 426-0555**
Senior Vice President

PAY
TO THE
ORDER OF _____ $ _____

100% Attention to Your Needs ___DOLLARS

FORT WAYNE NATIONAL BANK
FORT WAYNE, INDIANA

Black print on green check stock; they tear off little pads, like checks

A suitable card for a banker; he's used this one for over 30 years

Die-Cut Cards Are a Standout

Die-cut cards permit you to make a card in any shape you desire. Although they require the expense of having dies made, and take longer, the effects can be stunning! It is even possible to have a stand-up or three-dimensional card. Such cards will not work on all materials, so consider stock choices early.

JOHN GRIFFIN WOOD, D.D.S.
GENERAL DENTISTRY

—

SATURDAY APPOINTMENTS AVAILABLE

1717 W. NORTHERN AVE.
SUITE 109
PHOENIX, AZ 85021

OFFICE HOURS
BY APPOINTMENT
602/870-7707

Navy print on white textured stock, with bite out of corner

OKLAHOMA GROCERS ASSOCIATION

ELDEN G. ROSCHER
President & CEO

25 N.E. 52ND STREET
P.O. BOX 18716
OKLAHOMA CITY, OK 73154-0716
405/525-9419
IN OKLA. 1-800-OGA-4229
FAX: 405/525-0962

Brown recycled paper like a grocery bag; black print; gold embossed "G" with state of Oklahoma on it; with bag-like shape

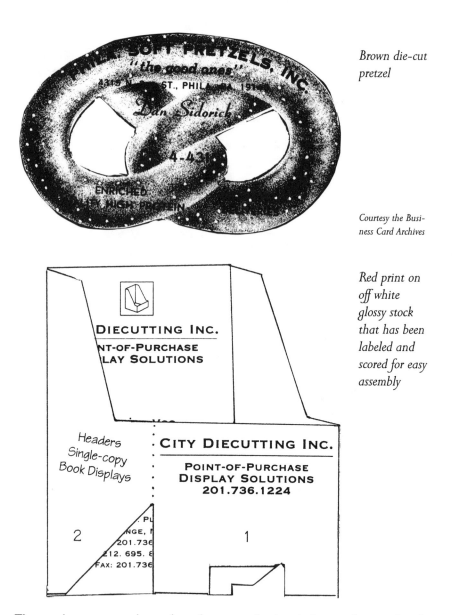

*Brown die-cut
pretzel*

*Red print on
off white
glossy stock
that has been
labeled and
scored for easy
assembly*

This card is too complicated to show in a flat book, but is designed to be a business card and a tiny 3-D display—a business card dispenser; it's a product sample the scale of a card

Slide charts can be standard or custom designs and can be rectangular or circular styles.

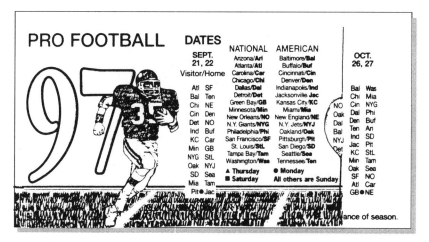

Slide chart: two-sided with card on one side; sliding information (shown) on back; green and black on white stock

3-D telephone is reduced in size; cream with greeen trim and print

Standard Odd-Shaped Cards

One kind of odd-shaped card has two parallel cutout holes on the bottom edge, in order to slide on a track. These cards are filed in tracked boxes or in rotating storage systems. Trademark issues prevent identifying the brand name, but you will recognize the familiar cuts. Now that the trademark has expired, there are several suppliers of products for these systems. (See Chapter 13.)

Victor Graphics, Inc.

"Printers and Book Manufacturers"

1211 Bernard Drive
Baltimore, Maryland 21223
Email: pineapple@victorgraphics.com

Maryland/DC		410-233-8300
Customer Service		410-233-8301
	Fax	410-233-8304
New York		212-929-5424
	Fax	212-691-6452
New England		
	Boston	508-541-6900
	Fax	508-541-6393
New Hampshire		603-772-7176
	Fax	603-772-7176

Dark green print on cream stock

Another special shape that can be employed to make your card stand out has a tab. The card will be easily found in a card filing system. The tab may show the business name (The Mane Event) or the business category (Beauty Shops). Here again, a tab is handy for those who file their cards with such a system, but, due to its irregular shape, it is a hindrance for those who don't. Offer a choice of card, with or without a tab.

Dark-brown and light brown animal on beige stock; text in black

Or you could simply round the corners.

*Royal blue
and silver on
heavy white
stock*

DAVID C. MCCLINTOCK
PRODUCT MANAGER

126 WEST FIGUEROA STREET
SANTA BARBARA, CALIFORNIA 93101
E | DCM@CONNECTEDSYSTEMS.COM
T | 805 962 5066 F | 805 962 5044

FOLDED CARDS TAKE MANY SHAPES
Folded Cards Permit Many Variations

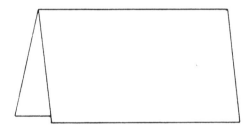

Top Fold (tent fold); front and back the same size

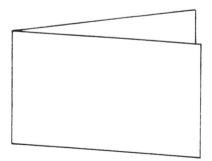

Side Fold (book fold); front and back the same size

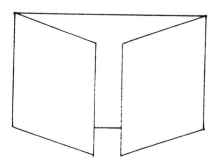

Gate Fold

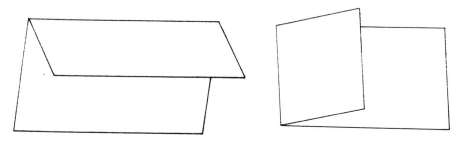

Short Fold; either top or side

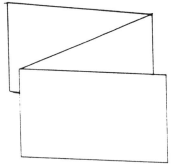

Z Fold or Accordion Folds

To Recap

In planning a business card, start by considering the entire card. Make it easy to read. Think about the way colors can alter its impact. Changing the shape creates unlimited possibilities. Use the back or a folded card to greatly expand the printing surface. Any such global effects can add points of interest to make your card, and you, more appealing.

Chapter 7

Display Graphics and Type That Make You Stand Out

Symbols and Images Connect with the Emotions

Visual images are filed in the brain as pictures, which make them much easier to recall than words. Every business has a visual identity; consider it part of the "business uniform" (pun intended). The image is conveyed on its letterhead, signs, vehicles, packages, ads, and, yes, its business card. That impression is "absorbed at a glance [and] has so much force. The graphic image is fast (sometimes instantaneous), powerful, and often subliminal."[1] Part of that visual identity is the **totality of the appearance**, so a single flaw may throw the image off. When there is harmony, it transmits a subliminal message that the business is integrated and organized. Much of the "heavy lifting" of a business image is done by the logo.

"Remember that people's initial response is usually subconscious and emotional. Details and 'atmosphere' count for more than is generally acknowledged, especially for products and services such as insurance and transportation, that are often purchased sight unseen. As a result, prospective clients make 'buy/don't buy' decisions based on"[2] those signs of competence and attention to detail.

Ten Goals for Business Images and Symbols

They should be:

- **Easy to remember**, recognize and relate to
- **Triggers for the senses** or affect emotions in a positive way
- **Representative of related things**—as a rattle symbolizes a baby
- **Unique** and distinctive
- **Balanced,** with the right size and proportion
- **Good looking** and feel good
- Recognizable after being **photocopied** or faxed
- **Compatible** with the rest of the card and the primary business message
- **Consistently** used on all communications
- **Timeless, not dated** or over-done

Abstract concepts are often easier to show as pictures than through words. For example, a flag stands for our country and all it represents; but it is hard to find a word that brings the same emotional connections as the flag. An abstraction like luck can be represented by a four-leaf clover or rabbit's foot. A birthday cake symbolizes making wishes, getting older, or receiving gifts.

Reading's Fun LTD.
QUALITY BOOKS • DISCOUNT PRICES
School Discount Book Program Nationwide
Fund Raising Sales • Book Fair USA
NESRA Member

Tim McCormick
Regional Bookfair Representative

2740 South Hardy Drive, Suite #4, Tempe, AZ 85282
Phone: **602-968-1999**   Fax: 602-968-6888

Red and green apple; red, blue and green books; text is black on white stock

Books with an apple symbolize school and learning, even though the "apple for the teacher" days are long gone.

Communicate with Functional Illiterates

In this day of inconsistent education and an influx of immigrants, don't assume that someone can read very well. Depending on which sources of information you consult, functional illiterates make up 20 percent of the U.S. work force, about 44 million Americans—and that figure is not going down! Poor readers may be able to make out your phone numbers, but they rely more on images or symbols than on words. Using symbols and maps on your promotional materials helps to compensate for poor reading skills. Besides, as the population has grown older, making out the fine print gets harder to do—even when there's ample reading skill. So establish strong visual images to help deliver and reinforce your messages.

Logos Reveal Your Identity

A logo is a particular graphic image that is identified with a business. It symbolizes the business and provides additional cues about its personality. The mood and feel of the logo should be compatible with the business personality. It can be created from letters (acronyms) and/or words, letters combined with graphic images, or images alone. Its design can be formal or informal, complicated or simple, familiar or novel.

Many logos result from emphasizing something with which you already have a connection, like a family crest, monogram, or sketch of the product. It usually is combined with a distinctive font style arranged in a special way, frequently with a color accent. A logo is often the initials of the company rendered in a dramatic type style or arrangement. Letters may be intertwined, re-sized, overlapped, and contorted into visually interesting shapes. A logo may appear to be very simple, but when it is combined with other factors like size and color, it becomes something all your own.

david smallwood

7915 Silverton Avenue
Suite 317
San Diego, CA
92126
619/695-2702

Logo is silver foil; black text on gray textured stock

SOUND
LISTENING
& LEARNING
CENTER™

BILLIE M. THOMPSON, PH.D.
Director

2701 E. Camelback Road.

Suite 205

Phoenix, AZ 85015

602/381-0086

FAX 602/957-6741

Black on recycled off-white stock

Dark red on white stock

A logo shares the same qualities as a corporate image. (See Chapter 1 on defining your business identity.) It is flexible, memorable, pleasant to look at, and unique. It reproduces well, has staying power, and creates a positive impact. If there is no logo or visual image, what is the focal point of the card? Where does the eye go? Is that the most important thing to be noticed or remembered?

Design of a logo can cost thousands of dollars. Larger companies realize it is a good investment. They then spend much more promoting that symbol until it is easily recognized. But small businesses also need one, and it can be achieved economically. Designing a logo only needs to be done once, yet it will be used constantly on everything related to the business for a long time. Although good logos may look simple, there is a lot compressed into them, and getting one to capture the company spirit takes skill.

James R. Spencer
President

15838 N. 62nd Street
Scottsdale, AZ 85254-1988
(602) 596-9970
FAX: (602) 596-9973

FAX ON DEMAND: (602) 596-6628
COMPUSERVE: 75460,563
INTERNET: http://www.videolearning.com

Video Learning Library in red; rest of the card in black on white stock

Black print on dark yellow stock

**Quality Videos
for Young Children**

**Gina Lamb
(310) 672-2357**

BO PEEP PRODUCTIONS, Inc
P.O. Box 982 Eureka, MT 59917
phone/fax (406) 889-3225

Categories of Images Often Used for Logos

- ☐ Geometric shapes and abstract forms
- ☐ Natural objects like birds, flowers, and mountains
- ☐ Things that have been built or imagined
- ☐ Objects related to historic, ethnic, or geographic places or events
- ☐ People and human body parts: a baby, a hand pointing, Elvis
- ☐ Sports and activities; doing things, or using tools and equipment
- ☐ Decorative motifs that symbolize other things; i.e., red checks to suggest casual dining
- ☐ Letters, numbers, and calligraphic symbols
- ☐ Monogram, family crest, picture, or sketch of product(s)
- ☐ Pictures that personify a slogan, emblems
- ☐ Locations, either specific or indefinite: a mountain, Mount Rushmore, the business headquarters

Just look around; pick up a magazine, walk through a retail store. Logos are everywhere, so take the time to notice them, and you'll get some good ideas for your own.

Black on white textured stock

Riordans Sporting Goods in dark blue; remainder in black on dark gray stock

Alice Blackmer
National Sales Manager

205 Gates-Briggs Building
Post Office Box 428
White River Junction, VT 05001
(802) 295-6300
FAX: (802) 295-6444
email: blackmer@sover.net

Olive green on light green stock

Your Logo Should Not Be:

- **Faddish**; needs to have long-term imagery
- **Hard to read,** understand, or decipher
- **Incompatible** with the company goals, image, style, and clientele
- "Cutsie" or done in **bad taste**
- **Diminish credibility**
- A reminder of your **competition**
- **Dated** or leave a shopworn impression
- Printed with **inappropriate colors**, or those that will not create enough contrast

Clip-Art for Logos

Advantages

- Copyright-free images, which can be used without permission
- Available from books or computer software
- Widely available; many sources; many categories of images
- Abundant choices; wide variety
- Easy to use; can be clipped (scissors), copied, or scanned (computer) into your designed piece

- □ Inexpensive
- □ Can be manipulated to have different size, orientation, etc.
- □ Can be reused

Disadvantages

- □ Not unique; used by many other users
- □ Familiar, people have seen it already
- □ Known to be the "low cost" option, so may make your seem amateur or "on the fly"
- □ Hard to find exactly what you want
- □ Time consuming looking through so many sources
- □ Can be used with taste or without, so often perceived as tacky

If you intend to use clip art, do something to it that gives it a custom look. Flip it over; cut it into parts; change the direction or orientation; add another element or image; juxtapose it with another image or with lettering; use it in an unusual way. The section in Chapter 8 on using templates shows ways to use clip art effectively.

Make Common Images Uniquely Yours

Be careful whenever you have more than one logo or visual element on the card, so they don't compete with each other. When there is more than one image, it should be apparent which is the center of attention (by size, placement, color, etc.). A cactus can be used by many companies and isn't unique to any business (even if it is in the name, like Cactus Burgers). Do something different with even a common symbol to make it seem uniquely yours. Join several objects; juxtapose two things that don't normally go together. Change the angle, size, and scale. Your imagination is your only limitation.

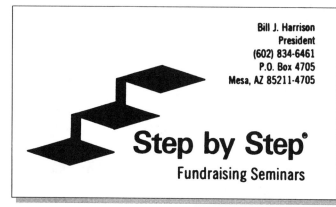

déminie designs

Deborah Deminie
(602) 296-4890 Tucson, Az. 85715

Copper foil for
Déminie
Designs, box
and cactus
in copper; text
in blue on
apricot stock

Bill J. Harrison
President
(602) 834-6461
P.O. Box 4705
Mesa, AZ 85211-4705

Step by Step°
Fundraising Seminars

Black print on
white stock

The logo must be able to survive being faxed, laser printed, and photocopied. Check by sending it through the grubbiest fax and copier you can find several times (get 5th and 8th generation impressions). If the image can't survive that treatment, you're going to have problems—because it will happen. When it is reduced to shades of gray, will the image still come through?

Be careful that there are enough differences in the color hues that the image doesn't fade away or look like a blob. One remedy is the stained-glass effect with a band around each color so the colors still look distinct, even when the color is reduced to gray. Avoid complicated graphics or dark blocks if the image will be faxed. What arrives will not look very good and you may offend the receiver for tying up his fax machine longer. Consider using a very small logo or one that is an outline form of the logo.

Brown, turquoise and yellow logo; black print on white stock

DESERT FOOTHILLS
R E A L ◆ E S T A T E ◆ C O M P A N Y

Office: 759-4300   **SLAVICA KANISKI**   Fax: 706-0000
Pager: 209-6578

REALTOR   3636 E. Ray Rd., #14 • Phoenix, AZ 85044   EQUAL HOUSING OPPORTUNITY

Factors in Logo Design

- ☐ Image must work well when reduced or expanded—on a pen or on a billboard
- ☐ Appears on everything the company has printed—as well as buildings, vehicles, and products
- ☐ Colors chosen for high contrast; can be reproduced as black and white, reverse printed, or done in an outlined form
- ☐ Makes you stand out from your competition
- ☐ Produces strong, clear, and consistent impact that "says something"
- ☐ Includes a ® or a ™ symbol on the logo (if trademarked); make it very small

RAYMOND A. KELLER, JR.
Catering Director

(602) 273-7088

BILL POTWORA
Service Captain

Pager 201-0063

Apropo Catering

FULL SERVICE PROFESSIONAL CATERING
1602 N. 46th Street • Phoenix, Arizona 85008

Red business name phone number and flames; the rest is black on white stock

*Lavender and
lavender
screen on
white stock*

FINDHORN
Press

Thierry Bogliolo
Partner

Findhorn Press, The Park, Findhorn,
Forres IV36 0TZ Scotland
Tel (01309)690582   FAX 690036
e-mail address thierry@findhorn.org

CATERING
by *LauRen*

LAURETTA E. WILLIAMS
RENNIE-RENEÉ WARREN
(313) 864-2956

*Silver tray, red
tie and but-
tons; the rest
is black on
white stock*

Logos Age

Every so often, you need to consider whether your logo has
become dated. Styles change over time. Fashionable font styles
come and go, or the nature of the business may change. (See Chapter
3 on the reasons a business name may need updating.) Sometimes,
the method of printing or the color combinations can make a design
seem out of date and out of touch.

Prudential Insurance

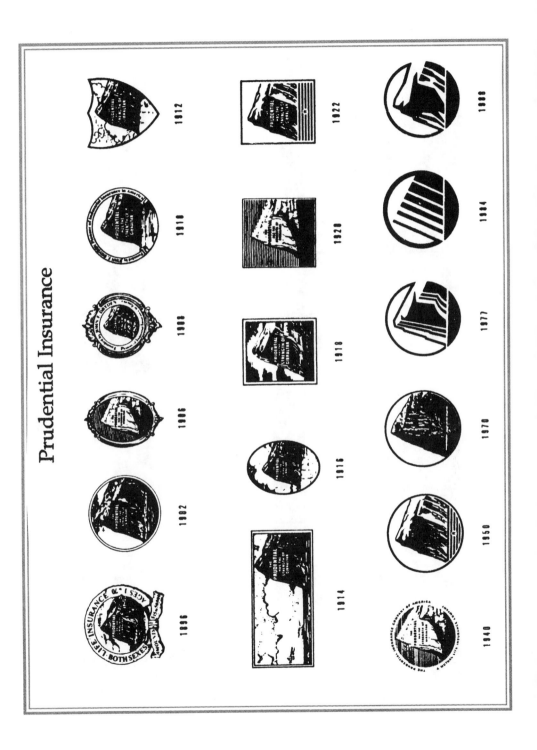

The Betty Crocker Portraits

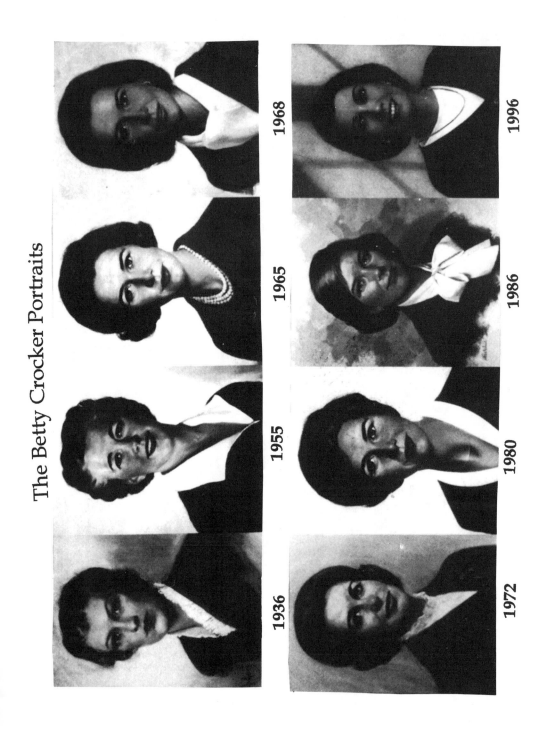

1968

1996

1965

1986

1955

1980

1936

1972

Even something as unchanging as a rock changes, when included in a graphic image. Prudential Insurance has invested considerable effort and money in keeping its logo, the Rock of Gibraltar, current. Revisions of an image can also result in other dilemmas, like how to make certain that everyone and every department is using the same, most recent version.

The human appearance can, likewise, date a logo because hair styles, priorities, and fashions change.

LETTERS HAVE PERSONALITIES, TOO
Select Your Type Style(s) with Care

Letters are every bit as unique and laden with associations as graphics can be.

- Stay in the same font family; use a different font for emphasis

- Never use more than three different type styles on a card; it confuses the eye

- Some typefaces go together harmoniously, but others do not. One of the giveaways of an amateur is mismatching typestyles

- Be careful about punctuation or fonts with small serifs that may not be readable, especially with raised type (thermography)

MarketAbility and ribbon in red; the text in black on white stock

TAMI DEPALMA
Book Publicity & Promotion

(303) 279-4349
Fax (303) 279-7950

813A 14th Street
Golden, Colorado 80401

E-Mail: twist@marketability.com
http://www.marketability.com

MarketAbility
Marketing & Public Relations   *with a Twist*

Using two font styles to make a point regarding what the business offers

Brief Font Table

Characteristic	Example	Name of Example
Serif (with "little feet")	Little Feet	Times Roman
San serif (without "little feet")	No Little Feet	Helvetica
Weight of letters	**HEAVY**	Informal Black
Shapes or strokes	**Fat or Circle**	Poster Bodoni
Expanded type	Extended	Eurostile Extended
Contracted type	Condensed	Arial Narrow

The variety of fonts is infinite, and, beyond that there are many variations within each type family. Then consider the ways type can be altered such as shadows, orientation and distortions.

Two Type Families

Serif Family—Goudy	San Serif Family—Helvetica
Goudy	Helvetica
Goudy Italic	*Helvetica Italic*
Goudy Bold	**Helvetica Bold**
Goudy Bold Italic	***Helvetica Bold Italic***
Goudy Oldstyle	Helvetica Narrow
Goudy Oldstyle Italic	*Helvetica Narrow Italic*
Goudy Oldstyle Bold	**Helvetica Narrow Bold**
Goudy Oldstyle Bold Italic	***Helvetica Narrow Bold Italic***
Goudy Oldstyle Extra Bold	**Helvetica Black**
Goudy Handtooled	Helvetica Light

Experiment With Upper- and Lower-Case Letters

- ❑ Combination of upper and lower case
- ❑ All upper case
- ❑ All lower case
- ❑ Inappropriate case, like capitals in the miDDle of a word, or with customary spacing altered (See Chapter 3 on Names.)

9680 east sutton drive   scottsdale, az 85260   (602) 451-1357

jennifer scott
personal growth counselor

self help systems

Circles and self help systems in lime green; trunk and text in black on white stock

All lower-case letters

DAVID MCDONALD

WORKS IN CLAY

LIMBERLOST POTTERY
721 FIRST STREET
PRESCOTT, AZ 86301
(520) 778-7854

STUDIO VISITS BY APPOINTMENT

Dark green on white recycled paper

All upper-case letters

Sample Decorative Type Faces

Sample (All are 24 point type)	Typeface Name
ABC 123*	Algerian
*ABC 123**	Balloon
AaBbCc 123	Colonna
ABC 123*	Desdemona
ABC 123*	Goldmine
AaBbCc 123	President
AaBbCc 123	Vineta

*Only uppercase letters are available in this font

Select a font style that suits the mood of business.

gryphon house, inc.

Kathy Charner
Editor-in-Chief

P.O. Box 207 - 10726 Tucker Street
Beltsville, MD 20704

(301) 595-9500 x304
1-800-638-0928
FAX (301) 595-0051

E-mail: kathyc@ghbooks.com
http://www.ghbooks.com

Royal blue on textured white stock; book is read (as well as read)

CANYONLANDS

PUBLICATIONS & INDIAN ARTS

Leah L. Paletz
Regional Sales Manager

4999 East Empire, Unit A
Flagstaff, Arizona 86004

(602) 527-0730
1-800-283-1983

FAX (602) 527-1873

Black print on caramel-colored textured stock

ADD HAND LETTERING AND FLOURISHES

Calligraphy can be hand lettered or computer generated versions of hand lettering.

Advant-Edge Technologies, Inc.
A Division of Consulting Alliance, Inc.

Don Imler

Business Coaching
Management Consulting

602 968 8780
602 895 2348

9340 Parkside Dr. • Sun Lakes. AZ 85248

Green print on gray stock with green flecks

DAVID CONVERY

BOBBY MORROW

Artworx

CREATORS OF FINE JEWELRY,
COSTUME JEWELRY, AND UNIQUE GIFT ITEMS

SCOTTSDALE, ARIZONA

(602) 945-8260

Maroon ink on glossy white stock

GAMING ENTERPRISES, INC.

Harlan Bohnee
Treasurer

1-800-WIN GILA
1201 South 56th Street ◆ Box 5074 ◆ Chandler, AZ 85226
520-796-7777 ◆ FAX 520-796-7712
Owned and operated by the Gila River Indian Community

Gold foil business name; balance of type in blue, red and black on glossy white stock

Some script styles are **not** hand lettered

Sample Script Type Faces

Sample	Typeface Name
Abcdefg 123	Brody
Abcdefg 123	Brush Script
Abcdefg 123	Brush 455
Abcdefg 123	Freehand
Abcdefg 123	Kauflinn
Abcdefg 123	Lydian Cursive
Abcdefg 123	Mariage
Abcdefg 123	Mural Script
Abcdefg 1 2 3	Vivante

CHOOSE THE RIGHT TYPE FOR YOUR PURPOSE

Select the Right Size of Type

Every business card represents a conundrum, how to fit enough information in a very small area. Often, the type is made smaller so more can be packed on. Since larger connotes importance, by inference, everything small is treated as less important. Yet, what you choose to say on your card *is* important. It is better to say less, so that it won't be too tiny or so jammed together that it becomes a hardship for the reader. Also, since smaller does use less room, it leads to crowding and poor use of white space. (See Chapter 8 on white space in design.) Font styles also influence the type size, so not all printing in eight point is equally difficult to read.

At some point (and point size) type is so small that it becomes hard to read. The problem is more pronounced when the cards are printed with raised letters (thermography). Also, letters like "a" or "e" or "8" get clogged as the little spaces get filled in with ink.

I've passed the time in my life when I can read find print unassisted, yet I refuse to use a magnifying glass to read a business card. If the print is too small to be read, it goes directly into the trash. When a number is not readable, I don't bother to call.

Sample Point Sizes

Point Size	Serif Font	San Serif Font
6 pt.	Times Roman 1234	Helvetica 1234
8 pt.	Times Roman 1234	Helvetica 1234
10 pt.	Times Roman 1234	Helvetica 1234
12 pt.	Times Roman 1234	Helvetica 1234
14 pt.	Times Roman 1234	Helvetica 1234
16 pt.	Times Roman 1234	Helvetica 1234

Make Type Readable and Understandable

Colin Wheildon's book, *Type & Layout*, studies the ways that type and design influence the communication of a message. In a series of studies, the author demonstrates that type choice or placement *alone* can either assist or interfere with the reader's ability to comprehend. He contends that "typography fails if it allows the reader's interest to decline. It fails absolutely if it contributes to the destruction of the reader's interest."[5]

"Devices that lead a reader on a wild goose chase, disturb an efficient pattern, or cause the slightest measure of distress should be eliminated."[6] If you want people to read and remember what you write, there are some things you should diligently avoid. Much of the research is on longer pieces than a business card, but if you're striving for consistency throughout your communications, this research should influence your style and design choices, and hence be reflected in your card. Two factors studied, however, do apply to card design.

Comprehension suffers when material is printed in san serif type. This is serif and this is san serif.

Comprehension also declines when material is printed in reverse type.

This is reverse type.

Therefore, save san serif fonts and reverse type for accents.

PHOTOGRAPHY ON BUSINESS CARDS
Photographs Add Personality

Photographs are very popular on business cards. One problem with photocards is that they don't change—and you do. People age, alter hair styles, and suddenly need glasses. Vanity being what it is, this could lead to some embarrassing moments! If people squint at the picture, look hard at you, and then ask, "Is that you?!" you need a new picture—or none at all.

Don't just think about using photographs of yourself. That is one of the least effective uses for them on a card. Showcase a product, building, or even a "before/after" situation, such as an auto body repair shop might use. When applied thoughtfully, a photograph can certainly enhance a business card.

The photograph should be an integral part of the card, and that begins in the design process. A photograph shouldn't be just stuck on simply because it's what you've got around. The picture should be taken or selected because it adds the right personality note you want your card to convey. It should be compatible with the style, layout and mood of the rest of the card (and the business). It would seem that a disproportionate share of photo cards belong to real estate agents and insurance salesmen. Presumably, this provides a recognition factor so that if you see one of them on a street corner, you can run up to them and buy another insurance policy or a lot in the Shady Acres Retirement Community. A real estate agent may be better served by a picture taken in front of a home with a "sold" sign. Another strategy could be to replace the photograph with a drawing or caricature instead. If your competitors have a similar card or treat photographic cards as the standard, find a way to avoid appearing like their clone.

A photograph can be black and white, full color, or a duotone (two color, as is often seen in period photographs). These alternatives are integral to the design process as well as what needs to occur at the printer. (See Chapter 11 on working with your printer.) Color choice will also effect the costs of producing your card.

Guidelines For Using Photographs

- Use photos that are clear and in focus; not fuzzy
- Crop or set off important parts
- Reprint from the negative, not too many generations (reproductions of reproductions)
- Don't print photographs in weird or unnatural colors

- Choosing black and white, two-color (duotone), or full color influences the mood of the card
- Use a photo that shows personality—that makes you (or the object) interesting
- Cut around the head or object for added emphasis and to eliminate clutter
- Use photographs with pleasant lighting: not too harsh, no shadows on the face, no squinting, etc.

Photo Enhancement Improves the Image

- Sharpens features and details
- Corrects shadows or blemishes
- Improves or changes contrast between lights and darks
- Compensates for lighting or other minor flaws
- Permits cropping of images (cutting away parts)
- Improves old or faded images
- Can be achieved by computer software or at the photolab
- Can overlap images or turn several objects (or people) into a single image
- Permits colors to be changed
- Allows special effects, like morphing (changing an image into something else)

Try Different Ways to Use Photographs on Cards

Use photographs to make you or your business more interesting. Start with a good picture.

A. Photo of a person's head (mug shot)

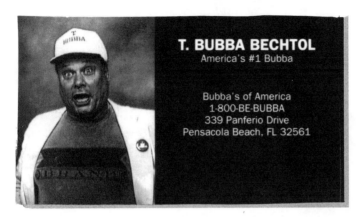

Full color photograph; black square with reverse type

B. Photograph of person named on the card covers the entire card

The photograph covers the entire card (bleeds to the edge). Text information is reverse printed on the photograph or printed on the back side. The person pictured is often involved in an activity.

Full color photograph with information reverse printed on front

Full-color photograph with information on back: Dan Poynter (805) 968-7277 at the North Pole

C. Photograph related to the business, but not of the bearer

Put the product or service in the spotlight, and show an example of your work, i.e., food prepared by a caterer, flowers arranged by a florist, new puppies delivered by a veterinarian.

Black and white photograph of cat with printing and eyes in yellow

Full color photograph with information on the back

D. Montage of small photos or slivers of pictures arranged as part of the layout

Show a variety of shots, arranged in an interesting way. For example, a travel agent could show great destinations; a photographer some special shots from his portfolio; a contractor could show before and after shots on a remodeled kitchen.

Full-color photograph with black printing and red rules on glossy white stock

E. Photoprocess Business Cards Offer Infinite Color Options

Photoprocess cards are the marriage of photographic methods and computers to achieve a unique graphic design. All the colors portrayed on the computer screen are usable. Any graphics or photographs are scanned into the computer and combined with all the design techniques available with computers. Special effects are no trick at all.

The result is a truly customized card, with full, vibrant color. Such cards are priced competitively, and certainly do attract attention. The card is produced as a photograph, rather than being printed. (See the discussing of printing colors or photographs in Chapter 11.) A card produced in this way has the feel of a photograph, with either a gloss (shiny) or matte (dull, non-reflective) finish. Depending on the equipment used, a message may also be printed on the backside. See ordering information in the Resource section to get attention-grabbing photoprocess business cards.

Full color card with black printing on photographic stock

Full color card with information reversed, on photographic stock

Use a Drawing Instead of a Photograph

Why not use a drawing or caricature instead of a photograph to convey the image you want to present.

EINSTEIN ALIVE!™

Speeches ▼ Workshops

™1991 **Arden Bercovitz, Ph.D.**
Speaker

10565 Caminito Banyon
San Diego, CA 92131-1710
619-695-9506 ▼ 800-748-6967

*Royal purple
and black on
recycled gray
stock*

ELLIS IN WONDERLAND
MANAGEMENT • ENTERTAINMENT

ELLIS PAILET
PRESIDENT

518 S. RAMPART ST.
NEW ORLEANS, LA 70113
(504) 525-0000
FAX (504) 581-1112

*Red Ellis and
tie; rest is
black on white
stock*

Courtesy the Business Card Archives

Get Permission to Use the Photographs

Every photograph is a customized form of illustration. It is a creative expression and unique (just as every one of the millions of pictures of the Statue of Liberty is unique). It was taken by someone, so you have copyright issues to consider. When you want to put a photograph on your card, make sure you have the right to do so. Printing an unauthorized photograph can be very expensive.

Even if you hire someone professional to "take your picture," you need to get a release from them at that time, if you intend to reproduce the photograph. When you decide to include a photograph in any printed piece, it either already exists or it must be specifically made (or commissioned). Deciding which to use may hinge on how difficult it will be to deal with the copyright question. Rights to use a photograph should be established from the beginning (while in design phase).

Consider Copyright When Selecting Photographs

- No copyright issue if bearer took the photograph; has all the rights to its use
- Photographs taken by family or friends; get a written release to eliminate any potential issue
- Photograph from picture libraries and rights to reproduce is licensed for a one-time particular use; you have no further rights to use the image without paying an additional fee
- Photographer hired (commissioned) for a photographic session, and client buys all the rights; photography must provide an assignment of copyright to the client, or the original work, along with the copyright, belongs to the photographer

These same cautions apply to any illustrator hired to create a customized drawing, caricature, or cartoon for illustrating your card.

To Recap

Symbols and images communicate more effectively than words. But symbols and words together create a distinctive business identity. Adopt a font style and logo that are compatible with the business personality. Another strategy could be to replace the photograph with a drawing or caricature.

Chapter 8

Work with Design and Designers

Make a Design that Works for You

Design is the servant of the infinite and varied commercial images that we encounter wherever we look. "Everyone is a spectator of graphic design, eagerly sometimes, involuntarily at others. During the last decade and a half or so, changes in both technology and society have allowed many more people to participate. Today the business card, tomorrow a home page on the World Wide Web."[1]

Design is like good taste—it's hard to say what it is, but you sure can tell when it's missing! Taste and style do not suddenly materialize full blown. They reflect a combination of decisions and the ways those choices fit together. Demonstrating how well all these elements work **is itself** part of your message, a reflection of the quality of your skill in every area of business performance. Design always considers **how** information is presented not just whether it is appropriate.

An effective card need not be designed by a professional, but it should be apparent that someone paid attention to what she was doing. The design should reflect an identity, personality and taste compatible with the business. While the cards of a lawyer and a toy store convey very different images and court different customers, each should create positive impressions that correspond with the image. Design and message should also be consistent with the customer's expectations of what the business actually provides.

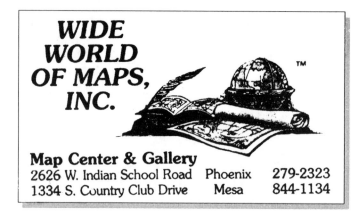

WIDE WORLD OF MAPS, INC. ™

Map Center & Gallery
2626 W. Indian School Road   Phoenix   279-2323
1334 S. Country Club Drive   Mesa   844-1134

Brown print on brownish parchment; looks old and ·conjures up an image of exploration

Design is like the plumage on a bird. It is specifically created to attract the ones who want what is being offered. The test always comes back to, **does the card work for you?** When a clear message and knowledge of the right "plumage" are combined, you'll have a card that can stand out in any crowd. Designs that attract business aid the bottom line.

Good design is usually simple. To do more overwhelms the card and looks cluttered and busy. Printed material should clearly communicate ideas or information. It may deliver a style that is powerful, chic, clever, trendy, creative, refined, unusual, witty, elegant, full of vitality, intelligent, or technically skilled. But it also needs to be targeted in such a manner that the recipient feels that it is aimed directly at him. Being able to define your target group, and its interests, will help you chose an appropriate style. Then, customers will prefer your business to a company that doesn't understand them.

"The sum total of a person's experience is reflected in his or her taste. With a regular daily diet of graphic schlock and little exposure to the good stuff, it's hard to develop discriminating taste, let alone the ability to imagine better possibilities. And it is even harder to create them."[2] The challenge is getting the elements to work together without hurting the eye or offending the senses. A bad design is painful and makes you cringe, much like a piercing sound hurts the ear. A good card attracts and enhances an image without distracting from it.

Distill a Card That's More than Pretty

Developing a company image or card is a distilling process. Start as broadly as possible and invite opinions about the card's messages and images from as many different sources as possible. Broad participation often finds design details and messages otherwise overlooked. Once these are distilled into a final image, the resulting impression will be more unique and powerful. Egos should not be allowed to intrude; weigh the input of others carefully.

If a card already exists, an important preliminary decision is whether to modify and build on past efforts or to start fresh. Either one demands input and fine tuning. Getting "the look" requires an eye for details and harmony. The effect you want usually comes after trying various combinations and tinkering until it "clicks."

Necessary Steps in Card Creation

- Copy writing
- Marketing strategy and public relations
- Design and logo design
- Layout
- Typesetting
- Make ready and pre-press
- Printing
- Photography, artwork or illustration, if desired

Admittedly, you probably don't need all this horsepower on a business card, but, frequently, the card, letterhead, and envelopes (and maybe other printed material, too) are done at the same time. It is still instructive to understand the process (and hats) involved. The same is true of understanding some of the printing processes, even though they aren't called into play with the typical small business card order.

Card Creation Checklist

- ☐ Gather ideas, opinions, and examples
- ☐ Develop a plan and decide who is in charge of organizing the tasks
- ☐ Set budget and scope of project
- ☐ Hire designer and define the team, which depends on the scope of the project and amount of talent in your organization
- ☐ Negotiate and sign agreement with designer
- ☐ Set deadlines
- ☐ Prepare copy
- ☐ Select images or graphics, colors, paper, special effects, etc.
- ☐ Finalize type and layout; finalize any loose ends with subcontractors
- ☐ Get preliminary approvals from all necessary parties
- ☐ Secure print bids
- ☐ Select printer
- ☐ Check and approve proofs
- ☐ Complete pre-press and plate preparation
- ☐ Print the job
- ☐ Complete any final steps like folding, lamination, die cuts, etc.

A Computer Does Not A Designer Make

Wow! Have you seen all the neat fonts, clever features, and fancy visual effects? Computers provide the power to create infinite combinations of exotic designs. Effects that used to be expensive or difficult to develop are now available with a few keystrokes. The options that used to be the exclusive province of designers and typesetters are now accessible to anyone with a computer and a decent art program.

In the old days, a long apprenticeship was required to become a printer or graphic designer. Almost everything had to be done by hand, and it was time consuming. Minor changes also took a lot of time. The tediousness assured that your "eye" was trained and each little nuance would be mastered through gradual applications. As a result, designers, printers, and technicians had a lot of time and professionalism invested in the finished printed product.

Now, enter the world of the computer. The easy availability of computer-generated graphics and lettering can be viewed as both a boon and a curse. There is much more to making an effective design than mechanical wizardry. For instance, there are intangible elements of balance, spacing, harmony, and aesthetics that combine to make any card, or any image, work—or fall on its face. Technical expertise with computer software doesn't insure that the operator has the illusive "eye for design." Occasionally, you encounter very poorly-conceived cards designed by graphic professionals and exquisite cards created by amateurs. The difference depends on having refined the judgment and discernment to create an image that is a worthy expression of the business identity.

In case you're thinking the book is just motivated to get you to hire a designer, artist, or computer whiz, think again. Sometimes, a person may be trained, yet be unable to create an effective, tightly targeted, and distilled card that's right for the business it was designed for. Since so much information is compressed in a small area, card design is trickier than it looks—and not part of every designer's bag of tricks.

Some business cards that designers, printers, and artists have done for their own businesses are not good examples. Make it a firm rule never to hire someone to assist with your design needs unless they've **done a good job on their own card**. If they're still "inventing their own package," they are less able to assist you in packaging yourself. Also, it is possible to make a perfectly lovely card and still make many of the blunders described in these pages.

Guard Against Card Sins

- □ Over-designed cards and Frankenstein cards (as discussed in Chapter 1)
- □ Beautiful, but doesn't "say" anything or relate to the business
- □ Design elements that are in conflict
- □ A design incompatible with the business, its marketing, or its customers
- □ Dull, uninteresting, cold, old-fashioned impression
- □ Too many fonts, graphics or elements
- □ Inefficient use of white space

A design that you consider clever or creative may be sending an entirely different message to someone else. "Effective design costs no more than ineffective design. Indeed, ineffective design costs more through wasted postage, production, and media dollars. The printing costs are usually the same, but if the design is carefully and completely done, you'll have fewer surprises when you reach the printing stage."[3]* Your responsibility is to figure out what the card should communicate and be clear enough for your designer to express it. Then, before it's done, it's up to you to determine whether the goal you had in mind has been achieved.

Refrain from Cutsie Cards

Be careful about trying to be so clever that your card is "cutsie." Some names or slogans are like the inside jokes on vanity license plates. Although, it may have a personal symbolic meaning, no one else gets it. Genuine cleverness is rooted in a universal image, rather than a private one. If it's an insider joke, print a separate card, and use it for other insiders. A card that elicits perplexed reactions, like

---

* From the book *One Minute Designer*, by Roger Parker. Published by Que, a division of Macmillan Computer Publishing USA. Used by permission of publisher.

"I don't get it" or groans, should make you think again. You want the receiver to say, "Oh wow, that's interesting!" rather than "Oh wow, that's weird!"

So it's back to the delicate dance between being creative and witty and being inappropriate. The best card is outside the norm, yet displays a flair that enhances your credibility. Consider designing a card as a paradox. Break conventions so you stand out in a way that doesn't lead to rejection.

Where Do You Get Help?

- Hire a **professional** artist, designer, or advertising agency
- Appoint a **committee**, either to distill the choices or carry them out
- Let **your kid** whip up something on the computer; hire an art student
- Use **clip art** or a standard software program
- Use **preprinted papers** with matching card kits; use card templates in software programs
- Choose from your **printer's standard options**
- Let your **printer** develop your customized card
- Make only **minimal changes** to what you already have, or decide to make no changes at all
- **Do it all yourself**

Once you are ready to begin, you have to decide who is to coordinate the process, and what services you will hire. You have several options, each with its own pros and cons. Your best choice is likely to be a combination of these options. Budget and time factors may dictate your final choice.

One person needs to be in charge, even when there is group involvement and professional expertise. In a new or small business, that's usually the owner. In a larger organization, that person should be someone who understands the importance of the business's image—irrespective of his role in the company. Keep in mind, however, the old adage that "too many cooks spoil the broth." If you feel strongly about a particular design element or look, don't give in just to have a "consensus." Evaluate the input in light of what you want your card to say. Reject ideas that conflict with your priorities. This holds true whether suggestions come from an "expert" or from Uncle Ned. As with any advice, don't pander. Some suggestions will be in conflict. Remember, advice is like a letter of recommendation; it tells more about the person giving it than the one written about. Still, by asking, you gain other perspectives, so you can fine-tune the combined efforts into a masterpiece.

The creation of any image or graphic symbol is a process, and usually is reached through successive approximation. It involves a series of changes and adjustments, but all the while, you are training your eye to be more discerning. You begin to notice little changes, tiny differences, minor nuances that weren't previously apparent. It may look easy, but it is an on-going challenge.

You'll get better support from whomever you hire if you have a notion about **what you want to say**, and **how you want to say it**. If you are not clear regarding what you want to achieve, your designer starts with a fuzzy idea of what you expect. Provide your designer with as much information as possible, including a list of required elements. Then set her free to do what you've paid her to do—design. My designer has instructed me to say that, although design is a collaborative effort and works best with client input, you should take care not to "tie the hands" of your designer. Every creative person experiences the dilemma of letting someone else (be they editor or designer) massage their ideas.

Of course, it's cheapest to do it yourself, and you're likely to be the best judge of what works for you. Even if you hire all the services done, you have to decide whether to accept and adopt what is offered. Don't settle for something that does not satisfy you or suit the business. Go back to the drawing board (now you see where that phrase comes from) until it becomes a better "fit."

Find Models to Inspire Your Design

"Good design does not depend on money."[4] Go through your collection of cards, and pick out some good ones. Find cards that scream good design and adapt them. You're looking for examples of layout, color, typestyle, overall effect, etc. You'll probably find a variety of things you like—but not all on the same card. Some elements will just pop out; those are the ones that are "talking to you," in the same way you want your card to "talk" to those who receive it. Each part of the card contributes to the total style and should be in harmony. Look at as many examples of cards as you can. Remember the saying, if you copy one person, it's called plagiarism; if you copy many people, it's called research. Don't imitate or infringe on someone else's copyright or trademark; you just want his inspiration. Gather ideas, but in the end, the result you achieve should reflect you and your business, not someone else's.

Don't hold too tightly to your preliminary versions during the design phase. Be open to different ideas, however they may arise. Even if you use a professional designer, go through these steps before you finalize your own card. Every step matters, since you are **training your eye** and increasing your awareness of design elements and their effect on you. You will find this skill useful in the future, as well.

Since computers permit many layout variations with just the click of a few keys, it could save time to be present while your designer tweaks your preliminary design. If you are the one at the computer, have someone else, whose taste you trust, looking over your shoulder. The interaction and reactions to variations provide an instant idea of which effects are getting hotter or colder (remember that childhood game?). As you get "hotter," keep trying similar combinations, and the "colder" ones can be quickly abandoned. Some effort is required, certainly, but there are also inspired moments when all the elements begin to merge together and "look good."

GETTING HELP AND REACHING AN AGREEMENT

Select a Designer Attuned to Your Needs

Even if you hire professionals to assist you, they are limited in what they can do. Your hired hand can only assist in making your intangible business personality more apparent. She is attempting to **express your vision**, your message, and your concept of the business. While trained to help you express a visual image and execute the final layout, she will never have the feel for the business that you do. The card is an extension of your style and priorities, rather than hers. Also, she is not the one who will be harmed if the resulting design doesn't appeal to your customers and express those aspects of your business you wish to make known. Design is a cooperative effort, and you need to play a key part in defining both the message and the resulting image.

Creating a customized card requires a variety of skills. How involved should you be in stating requirements, giving advice, and making corrections and modifications? Only a fool would let someone else determine his business image. This is not to say that you should hire an "expert" and then ignore that expertise. Pay attention to advice (paid for or not), but remember that **you** are ultimately responsible for your card and the image it portrays. You will experience the rewards or penalties of the outcome.

Evaluate a Designer's Portfolio and References

Designers have their own personalities and design styles they do best. That's why, as you collect cards, you are also scanning for a look, a feel, a flavor that "feels good." Those cards that "touch a nerve" are likely to resonate at some personal, non-verbal, emotional level to you. Ask the bearer who did the card's design. If you encounter several such examples by the same designer, pay heed. She could be the ideal one to express your flair.

Even if a designer comes highly recommended, you want to see how she has handled similar projects. Before hiring anyone, you should look at her portfolio and get the names of several clients and printers who have worked with her. Her portfolio displays samples of projects that have been done for other clients.

In reviewing the samples, ask her about:

- What she charged to do such designs
- Whether she created the concept, executed it, or both
- How long it took, and whether it was completed on time
- Her role with regard to the client and the project
- The client's reaction(s)
- How much supervision she received

Check the Designer's References

"Some questions to ask when checking references:

- The relationship—What is your relationship with the designer? Is the designer your client, or a vendor?
- The projects—What work has the designer done for you, and were you pleased with the results? Are samples of this particular project available?
- The designer's role—Ask for specific contributions the designer made to the project. Did the designer work alone, or with the client's staff? Did the designer contribute services beyond graphic design?
- Services—Did you feel the designer gave your project enough time and attention?
- Deadlines—Did the designer meet established deadlines?
- Money management—Did the designer work within budget?"[5]

List used with permission of the Graphic Artists Guild of Albany, a chapter of the Graphic Artists Guild (212)791-3400 or www.gag.org

The Elements of an Agreement with the Designer

- ☐ The **project** and its scope
- ☐ Who is **responsible** for what; define what the client does and what the designer does
- ☐ What **services** will be performed: logo, image, card design only, etc.
- ☐ **Time frames** for each stage of performance and deadlines
- ☐ Rights and **responsibilities** of each party
- ☐ **Budget**—costs, deposits, payments
- ☐ **Breakdown of costs** for services or other types of costs (color separations, photographs, etc.)
- ☐ How **approvals** will be handled
- ☐ Role of **subcontractors** regarding supervision and payment
- ☐ **Form of input and output** (electronic or camera-ready art)
- ☐ **Copyright ownership** explicitly discussed and stated
- ☐ How to deal with **extra work**, corrections, dissatisfaction, termination, or new ideas and changes

Eliminate Areas of Misunderstanding

The client (that's you) usually has only a vague notion of all of the steps that are necessary to take an idea from an abstract concept to a finished work. Discussing the terms of the agreement makes the extent of the work involved more clear. You could both be using the same terms, like "camera ready," (oh, the problems caused just by that phrase alone!) but have entirely different conceptions of what that means. There are many opportunities for missteps if communications aren't precise. Don't leave your design team groping in the dark regarding what you expect; such groping can be expensive.

Establish the price or price range for the negotiated work. Prepayment or a deposit of one-third to one-half of the estimated fee is customary. Usually, the balance is due upon delivery. As with many services, anticipated costs are ballpark estimates. The contract should be specific about how modifications, corrections, errors, or additional work will be handled or billed. Make it clear how much change is permitted before costs start to increase. Always determine how such changes are made (by the hour, design, or what).

If you intend to use color, photographs or special effects, discuss them early, and consider the emotional connotations that will be triggered. (See Chapters 6 and 11 about working with color.) The designer has more things to do when dealing with such effects. Although they increase the design charges as well as the printing costs, they are usually worth it.

The estimate considers the approximate amount of time anticipated. Then the professional usually keeps track of the actual hours spent on project and adjusts the final price accordingly. The designer is selling her time and expertise, so the actual amount of time spent on the project has a huge bearing on the final cost. Take care when defining the project, so that her hours are not spent trying to figure out the project's direction or redoing creative work.

It is best to have the professional provide a series of rough sketches and then gauge the reaction before deciding which ones should be pursued or dropped. Don't underestimate the time it takes to complete a job. There is a learning curve for each project, and time is also required to pull it all together. Just be very clear about the deadlines and delivery of work.

Get it on paper. It is vital that there be a clear understanding of what each party expects. As with other contracts, some wording is the standard of the industry, and should be included in every agreement. A confirmation letter or a contract format work equally well. The form matters less than the clarity it provides. Both parties should know what is expected of them. See the sample agreement in the Appendix, provided courtesy of The American Institute of

Graphic Arts. Count on the negotiation to bring expectations more in line with budget realities (next section). Your best way to keep costs down is to have some clearly defined ideas as a starting point and maintain a realistic understanding of the costs of each of the tasks.

Preparing the contract or letter is usually the responsibility of the design professional. It may be completed at the time of negotiation, in which case it is then signed by both parties and the deposit is paid. Each party receives a signed copy. If the written form is prepared after the verbal agreement and payment of the deposit, the designer signs two copies and sends both to the client for signature. One signed copy is then returned to the designer. In that way, the client can either confirm the agreement or raise any issues that were not in line with her understanding. As with all agreements, good will and a desire to communicate strengthen the written contract. If these simple steps are followed, there should be smooth sailing and minimal disagreement.

Budget for Card Creation Costs

How much can you afford to spend? Let this decision be influenced by whether you consider your business card an effective marketing tool. If you're serious about your business image, you should be serious about how you portray it—professional or amateur, competent or careless. Your business card is the most frequently consulted reference your prospective cutomers use. That is certainly worth consideration when allocating funds.

On one end of the scale you find the "$9.95 Special" offered by some print shops and office supply stores. Balancing this are the multi-thousand dollar cards created by high-end designers and advertising agencies. Oddly, these two extremes are quite popular—and can be equally ineffective. This is not to say that some "$9.95" cards cannot be effective or that expensive designers cannot turn out dynamite cards. They can and do, but the results are not necessarily related to the amount of money spent. Obviously, if one has a worm farm, no amount of design effort is going to substantially change its image. On the other hand, an elegant clothing store cannot afford to have its image tarnished by a card that reeks of poor taste.

A good rule of thumb is to spend as much as you can afford (even if it means cutting somewhere else), but get the most value for your money. If you have a flare for design, you may not need expensive help. If you are somewhat lacking in creativity (be honest with yourself), seek the best help you can afford. Design and "construction" are probably the most expensive aspect of your cards. The actual printing is relatively modest, although printing costs rise as embellishments are added. However, you should always get a few printing estimates since prices can vary greatly.

In considering the amount to spend, remember that your card represents you and your business and speaks both **for you and about you**. Because of the proliferation of printers and "quick print" shops, printing costs are fairly reasonable and competitive. Compared to design or art work, there really isn't much room for negotiation. Money can be saved, however, by controlling the "extras" that make up part of the printing cost, such as foil embossing, raised letters, special paper, color, odd sizes, photos, etc.

The questions you should ask yourself are: What do I really need? Does it enhance the image of my business? Does it say something that cannot be said another way? Is the cost worth the benefit? Consider, if you will, that good taste costs very little, while all the gold foil in the world cannot compensate for the lack of it.

Cost-Cutting Strategies for Designing and Printing Cards

To save money, hire a designer for a one-hour consultation in order to evaluate and critique what you've done (or have had done for you). Ask how to improve upon it. Do a preliminary test with a roughed out version of your new card and note the reactions it generates. (See the section in Chapter 10 on testing your card.) Modify accordingly.

Save on printing costs by increasing the quantity. The larger your order (print run), the less expensive the individual card. Be careful though, you may wind up with 5,000 cards that you belatedly discover are not working like you thought they would.

Also consider package deals. As a matter of course, a printer will usually offer a reduced price if he gets all of your printing business—cards, brochures, letterhead, envelopes, invoices, etc. For printers, business cards are often a loss leader. If you're just printing cards, there isn't a very large markup. The benefit to the printer is the expectation that you'll stick with the shop, allowing it to minimize recurring costs.

Use illustrations that are in the public domain, free of copyright protection.

Art from the public domain; the White Rabbit from Alice in Wonderland; black print on cream-colored stock

Courtesy the Business Card Archives

Just be forewarned, some cost cutting strategies are not a bargain since they can produce a flawed image. Therefore, be especially alert to how people respond to your card. Prices will vary but some effects appear to be expensive, even if they aren't, while others don't look expensive but are. If you're cutting corners, do the cutting where it won't show. You may not be able to afford some of the more labor-intensive options, so delay the special effect for subsequent printings. Design the card in such a way that your next printing can be upgraded with foil or full color.

Michaelangelo's famous contact between God and Adam. Artwork in light brown screen and lettering in black on mottled pink cardstock; folded card

TRADEMARKS
Trademark Your Logo Design

If you are going to the trouble to develop a unique logo, slogan, business name, or design, go to the additional effort of protecting it with a trademark. Federal trademarks protect you throughout the U.S. That protection is secured by filing your design with the Patent and Trademark Office in Washington, D.C.

Trademarks can be secured by submitting:

- ☐ A completed trademark request
- ☐ A drawing of the mark, according to official specifications
- ☐ A registration fee ($245 at this time); must be paid for each class of goods or services protected
- ☐ Three specimens of the mark for each class registered

Assuming there are no problems or conflicts with existing trademarks, you will receive your official notification in a few months. Keep that information in a safe place; it's valuable.

The states also provide trademark registration specific to businesses operating within that state, so you should also file with the Secretary of State's office where your business is located. State registrations are inexpensive but more limited in what they provide. State-issued trademarks only protect a company within that state, and if there is a conflicting national trademark, the state trademark is more likely to have to yield.

The complexity of trademark and copyright law is beyond what can be explored here, but your local library has books on the subject. If you decide to consult an attorney, make sure the one selected is a patent and copyright attorney (trademarks and copyrights are called intellectual property). This area of law is highly specialized and beyond the expertise of most attorneys. Such trademarks contribute to the value of your business, so don't ignore the importance of protecting them.

Rust graphic and owner's name and number; rest of text is black on cream textured stock

Gael Stirler
Owner
602/722-1255
Fax 602/722-1255

7700 E Wrightstown Road
Suite 210
Tucson, AZ 85715

P.O. Box 18904
Tucson, AZ
85731-8904

The Medieval Anachronist
Catalog Company

Show your logo is a registered trademark.

By the same token, be careful that you do not infringe on someone else's trademark or logo. Your business name should be checked **before you use it** to determine whether or not it already belongs to another business. It is a bit more difficult to check out the logo design, but at least, do not knowingly copy someone else's mark.

Legal Protection of Your Trademark

The law of trademarks specifies that the creator owns the trademark. That means that the person you hire will own your trademark **unless you get a release and negotiate your rights in writing**. It is not enough that you paid for the services! Be careful to get this clarified **before you pay for design services**. If you don't discuss it and get something **in writing,** you could find that the original drawing or artwork belongs to the designer. There are ample horror stories of businesses that discover they do not have control over their own promotional designs. Discuss this issue with whomever you hire and get the release signed before you pay. On the other hand, if the design is created by an employee as part of the job, the trademark would belong to the employer.

The U.S. Trademark and Copyright application forms have you specify whether the design is a "work for hire." Whenever you use an independent contractor or free-lancer, (someone who is not employed within your organization), the "work for hire" rules apply. Make certain that your business owns any copyright or trademark that is created (See Appendix for the difference between an employee and an independent contractor).

If you already have designs that could be in jeopardy, contact the person who did them and ask for a letter stating she understands she did not receive the copyright or trademark for work she performed for you. Or prepare a release or assignment and ask that it be signed and returned. Keep these with your trademark registration materials during the life of your business.

DESIGN AND LAYOUT BASICS
The Design Should Support the Message

A card is a paradox. You need to say a lot on it, without it looking crowded. In planning your design, always come back to what you're trying to communicate. What is the most important idea? Then, before you declare the card finished, check to see if you've done it. Don't get so excited about the design that you forget its primary goal. If you've lost track of the single most important message, how is the receiver going to get it?

A card is too small to accommodate more than one primary idea or image. Stay ruthlessly focused! Then have every element of design work toward expressing or transmitting that idea. A graphic designer works with five variables: size, type, color, paper, and images. Each of these has a look, and when they are skillfully combined they represent a style. "The narrower the audience, the easier to identify the style."[6] Then use that style to support the message so it will have the desired effect.

Spacing of Letters and Words

Arranging the open space on the card is one of the primary functions of developing a design. Even if you know exactly what the card will say and the type placement, arranging the space to assist in the readability is very challenging. Tweaking the spacing can take even more time than the other aspects of the design. Spacing is where the impact of a piece shines or comes apart. It is one of those things that goes unrecognized when done right, so if you notice the spacing, or the spaces between the words or letters, there is something wrong.

Spacing between letters and words affects legibility. It is influenced by the weight (thickness) of the type. Light type faces appear to have more white space. Although fonts are discussed in greater detail in Chapter 7, spacing is an integral part of the choices made by the designer. There are thousands of fonts, and computers permit many additional customizations. Avoid using more than three font styles in any design—two is better.

AMCAL

For the Gift of Art™

Scott A. Round
Vice President National Accounts

2500 Bisso Lane • Suite 500 • Concord, California 94520-4826
Phone (510) 689-9930 ext. 250 • (800) 824-5879 • Fax (800) 645-6006

Amcal is in gold foil; the rest is in royal blue on a heavy white stock

White Space Makes the Card Work

- Organizes the blocks of information and graphics
- Helps guide the eye and attention
- Frames the parts or blocks of information
- Creates constraint
- Reduces visual clutter
- Aids readability; but not all white space is good space
- Makes things much tidier; use little white space *within* a block of information, but frame white space *around* it to set the block off
- Leaves room for a hand-written message

Design Tips

- Repeat visual elements to help organize the images; repeats can use color, shapes, size, space, etc.
- Line things up to show a visual connection; don't place anything on the card arbitrarily
- Put related things together and treat as a block of information
- Don't overdo anything
- Avoid making letters too small—can't be easily read
- Avoid busy backgrounds or inconsistent contrast
- Increase contrast, avoid things being similar; if things are not the same, make them *very* different; also, contrast creates interest and attracts the eye, helping to organize information
- Don't use all upper case letters; it's hard for the eye to detect distinctions between the shapes of the letters
- Don't use all italics, bold, or any hard-to-read font; save them for emphasis or accents

- Strive for simple shapes; put things that relate to each other next to each other
- Use bullets to organize information

Design Simplified

Now that it looks like there are a lot of things to remember, let's add some perspective. Just answer a few questions about your proposed card.

- Is it cluttered or confusing?
- Is it inviting and attractive?
- Does it *feel* good to you?
- Is there enough information to reach you?

Stop!! That's enough!! Everything else is secondary.

Designing your card is not a massive effort, but a gradual one—and maybe even a fun one. The result you desire may not appear for a while, but it's forming. You're already becoming attuned to the intangibles that influence a card's overall message. There's no danger you'll ever be blind to those influences in the future. So play with the process of inventing yourself—it can prove even more fruitful than the finished card.

CARD CREATION WITH TEMPLATES
Making a Card With a Template

The following section was written by Linda Strauss to show how a template can assist in the card creation process, and is used with her permission. It is a portion of an upcoming Quick and Painless® book on business card templates. She is "thinking aloud" to explain her thought process.

Template One has many applications. For instance, your logo can reside right inside the black rectangle, as in Example 1A, as large as is pleasing to the eye. The logo would be white or light within a dark rectangle, or the rectangle could be light with a dark logo.

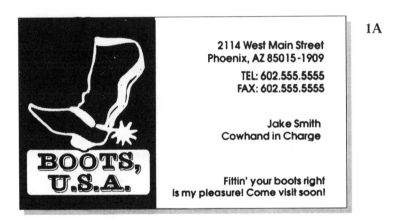

1A

2114 West Main Street
Phoenix, AZ 85015-1909
TEL: 602.555.5555
FAX: 602.555.5555

Jake Smith
Cowhand in Charge

Fittin' your boots right
is my pleasure! Come visit soon!

BOOTS, U.S.A.

Example 1A uses a simple clipart boot, blown up as big as possible to dominate the available space. I also reversed the boot's original colors, so that it would show up on the black background. I placed the word BOOTS, U.S.A. in a white square, since I liked this type for the boot logo and it didn't show up on the black.

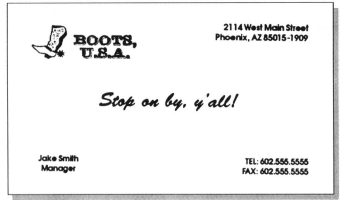

1B

Do you recognize 1B? You've seen it many times before! That's how most business cards come out from a quick copy shop unless you intercede! I used the same boot logo, but kept it small and stuck it up in the favorite left corner that seems to be the standard. I used a slogan too, but which card are your potential customers more likely to remember?

1C

[Note: This is not her actual address; see footnote[7]]

Example 1-C shows a logo that is larger than the black square. In this case, I framed the logo to encase it. Using this technique, you can alter the size of the white square to meet any requirements of your logo. Make the logo as large as you can.

In Examples 1A and 1C, the type for the address, zip code, telephone, fax and slogan are all flush right. This placement of type offers balance for the square and rectangle. Notice also, that I have made my type "anchor" to specific points rather than placing it randomly. The address is level with the top of the square. The slogan is level with the bottom of the square. All of these details make it easy for the reader's eye to move comfortably between elements with no need to jump around.

Template Two

Template Two is a variation of Template One. In this variation, the larger black area and narrower white areas lend themselves to a more sophisticated card. Use a more sophisticated typeface to keep the look consistent. On this card, I used two pieces of clip art—the big party piece is one; the tilted champagne glass leading to Jacqueline Smith is a second.

2114 W. Main
Phoenix, AZ
85015-1909

Tel: 602.555.5555
Fax: 602.555.5555
Email: giftetc.com

Jacqueline Smith
party
consultant

THE
PARTY
PLACE

2A

Type Faces Used: Broadway Engraved Humanist 521 Condensed BT

Notice how the extra champagne glass unites the elements both in and out of the black square. Notice, also, that more distinctive typefaces have been used throughout. Unusual typefaces both create a mood and make a card memorable. The purpose of these examples is to provide easy-to-follow templates for business card designs, not to design logos. Please notice, however, as you examine cards, how an interesting typestyle can add just a little "twist" to really make the card stand out. In this card, I used a typeface called Broadway Engraved for "The Party Place," then I twisted the "a" in "Place" to give it some interest.

Logo designs take designers many hours to create—hence, the high cost. A good logo design is an investment in your business because it has the power to make you memorable almost instantly. However, if you don't have the money for a great logo design, invest time experimenting with interesting type faces to create your own logo. BUT BEWARE! The amateur designer often chooses ornate or elaborate types in an attempt to look "different." Use the KISS principle instead: Keep It Simple, Sam!

Note: Templates One and Two have areas that go right to the edges of the card, called "bleeds." These types of cards cost more to print, but often offer more visibility and excitement. Check with your printer about the additional cost. HINT: Keep the excitement of the card and choose less expensive paper."[7]

Templates are also available in various word processing or graphics programs. Some of them are very sophisticated and can provide a first-class design. The quality of the outcome is still up to the skill of the person operating the program.

MAKE-OVERS
The Evolution of a Business Card

A card for a business is a work in progress. "A new card can be a business face lift. It shows you're new and improved, revitalized, up to speed. And even if your existing card is tops, you may need more than one design. Have a special card just for trade shows. Revolutionize the cold call with a hot card."[8]

Front of a folded (top-fold) card with turquoise and purple on glossy white stock

Before

The new card is also a folded card with a die cut and four-color process

After

Can you tell which Coriolis card was first and what you would count as improvements?

Jeff Duntemann
Editorial Director

jeffd@coriolis.com
CIS: 76711.470

THE CORIOLIS GROUP

Publishers of *PC TECHNIQUES* Magazine & Coriolis Group Books

7330 E. Acoma Drive, Suite 7   Scottsdale, AZ 85260   (602) 483-0192   FAX (602) 483-0193

Both cards have a red swirl in a dark turquoise rectangle and black ink on off-white stock

Jeff Duntemann
Vice President/Editorial Director

THE CORIOLIS GROUP
An International Thomson Publishing Company IⓉP°

14455 N. Hayden Road, Suite 220
Scottsdale AZ 85260-6949
Telephone: (602) 607-2480
Facsimile: (602) 483-0193
E•mail: jeffd@coriolis.com

A Dramatic Change

Geospec Engineered Materials, Inc.

Eva Marie Merideth
Account Executive

1409 East Blvd.
Charlotte, NC 28203

(704) 333-1040
fax (704)-333-1044
pager (704)-518-0384

Black ink on white stock

Green leaf, dark blue wave, the wall and print in black on translucent matte plastic

GeoSpec

ENVIRONMENTAL
RETAINING WALL
SYSTEMS&DESIGN

Gibb Heilman
regional manager

1409 East Blvd/Charlotte/28203
704/333.1040/Fax: 333.1044
800/994.9255

TEST YOUR RESULTS
The Proof is in the Testing

If you want to find out if a different card or feature would work better for you, test it. Try something different than what you now have, and see how well it works. Compare different paper, color or design effects. Incorporate ideas that you want to adapt to your card into your test.

Sometimes, when you test you find answers that are very different from what you had expected. A man in advertising products recently showed me his card and told me that he had experimented with two elements: position and font. The same phrases were present on all the variations, but on half of his cards he reversed their order. He also tested the phrases in plain type and bold type. The results were clear, and he was able to report that in his case bold print **reduced** the impact of the message and resulted in less business than the other variation. Also, he found that one of the lines on top was greatly preferred. All this was discovered for the small price of printing several variations. He achieved a market test and developed a potent new card.

Seek out input and reactions before you actually print. Ask several people (potential users of your services or product(s) if possible) for their input on your "pre-final" card. "Would you mind giving me a reaction?" Make changes, if appropriate, and run them past the person who suggested the modifications. Like all advice, don't pander. Some suggestions will be in conflict, but by asking you get additional perspectives that aid you to fine-tune your masterpiece.

Good Cards Can Come *Free*

Turn your card design effort into an event, a promotion, or a public-relations publicity experience. Ask your customers, clients, suppliers, and employees how they would improve your card, slogan, logo, etc. Design a flyer announcing a contest. Show a sketch of the present version (before). Send the flyer out with your statements, bill payments, newsletters, and post in the store or office. In addition to receiving valuable input from others, asking for advice creates interest in you and your business. Turn it into a two-way dialog. Offer a reward, like a drawing from a pool of all replies, to encourage participation, even if many efforts are off the mark. You're more likely to get a lot of little changes from different people than a total make-over suggestion from a single source.

Who knows you best? Your customers! Involve them in changing or improving your entire image, not just your card. You could even benefit from their insights and concerns on other topics as well. Appoint a committee to sift through the responses. Give recognition to promising suggestions. Consider whether or not to have a vote on the finalists; however, be prepared to handle suggestions contradictory to your ideas.

When you've finished with the new card, trumpet the results. Now, everyone will be interested in how the transformed card comes out. You've created more than a card—a team of boosters who care about your image—because they helped to make it.

Design Should Serve the Business Goals

Never forget that all the parts of the card should be compatible with the personality of the business. A congruent business (See Chapter 3.) runs more smoothly than an incongruent one. Mismatched management makes a business more likely to lurch from crisis to crisis, from patch-up to patch-up. The card merely reflects such business realities. Many related problems can be avoided through intelligent planning and design.

Select every element of your card to express the messages unique to your company and combine them into an eye-catching design. Then ask you customers if you've done it right. They don't have to be trained designers to tell you the score.

Gold raised print on white stock

The Invitation Shoppe

FINE PAPERS & STATIONERY™

DON REYNOLDS   (602) 649-5595
PRESIDENT   FAX (602) 649-5658
1350 SOUTH LONGMORE, #17 MESA, ARIZONA 85202

Yellow boomer-ang; black print on white stock

David Seid

Access Laserpress, Inc.

3502 W. Earll Drive, No. 3

Phoenix, Arizona 85019

602.272.2525

Fax 602.272.4224

Access Laserpress®

Where printing comes back easier.

To Recap

Design makes all the parts of the card work together. It combines many skills, but they work best when tailored to your unique business personality. If you hire a designer, have a contract and trademark your resulting symbols.

Chapter 9

Select From Choices Galore—Infinite Alternatives

Choices Up the Kazoo

Prepare to be overwhelmed by alternatives—too many choices, too may combinations. They can be paralyzing. Here is a chapter about all the varieties of things you could have—the entire candy store. Don't succumb to a sense of too much-ness; it's to make you more aware of the glorious diversity of options and effects. Only a few can be used at a time. Resist the temptation to overdo. Always remember that simplicity and understatement are your best bet. These choices aren't just provided to assist in designing cards for yourself. Awareness of the range of options permits you to better understand all the cards you encounter as well.

Every card has a layout, type, style, stock, color (even if white), ink color (even if black), and a shape (even if the standard rectangle). You can expand the choices of these elements into a whole array of alternatives to add interest and dazzle. As you incorporate new features into an existing card, think about changing only one of the components at a time.

Deviation from the Standard

Figure out what you like, but also be aware of the professional standards in your industry or the expectations of your customers. Ignore them or defy them at your peril. Push the standards so you look unique, but not so far that you look weird or uninformed. If you understand prevailing expectations, you then stretch them in a way that doesn't mark you as a person who "doesn't have a clue." Stand out by your good taste and style, not in a way that offends or marks you as being out of touch—no small task—but that is why a really effective card pays off. It marks you as special. And since your competitors are unlikely to have such a well-tuned device, you'll appear to be the better choice.

This chapter is far from complete, but does suggest many ways to make a card distinctive. If space permitted, several times as many options could be included. The author, too, suffers from being overwhelmed by the over-abundance of possibilities.

Sharpen Your Perceptions and Eye

Maybe you already intended to tackle the card project, but it's gotten out of hand, too complicated—and this book only makes it worse! Step back—give yourself some breathing room. Don't be smothered by the project. Instead, treat designing your card like a scavenger hunt, something that's fun to do. Watch for what you respond to on signs, billboards, or anywhere. Find an image here, a typestyle there, a color and layout somewhere else. Then there is nothing left but experimentation. Your antenna is already helping you locate elements you relate to. Use it. When you sort through your stack of cards (as discussed previously), disregard what they say. Just notice what you are feeling, what your own gut responses are.

Separate the liked (hot, positive, interesting) ones. Sort them into several piles, and keep sorting through them until you start noticing what the "interesting ones" have in common. You're training yourself to consciously register what you're inclined to respond to. After a few shuffles through those piles, you'll be less and less tentative about your preferences. Details emerge. You needn't be the artist or the person who puts it together. By going through this step, you'll be more able to help the person creating your design to develop something on your wavelength. Of course, not all the "picks" can be included on one card, but you now have some tangible ideas to start from.

As with developing any other skill, as you become aware of those nuances, additional benefits follow. You'll also become much more effective in picking features that get the best value for your design or printing dollar. Many of the best cards cost very little and some abominations (really awful cards) are ridiculously expensive. "Good design does not depend on money."[1]

Experiment with Layout and Placement of Type
Justification, either right or left

The number 1, name and title in brick red; the other type and block is gray on white

Centering

First Watch

RESTAURANTS

BRUCE COTTER

9645 N. BLACK CANYON HWY.   61 W. THOMAS RD.
PHOENIX, AZ 85021   PHOENIX, AZ 85013
602-943-3232   602-265-2092

First Watch and bird in bright red; type in royal blue on glossy white stock

Reverse print or reverses

- □ Use primarily for emphasis
- □ Don't use for small type
- □ Avoid serif typestyles, since the "feet" break off
- □ Use sparingly, because they are harder to read

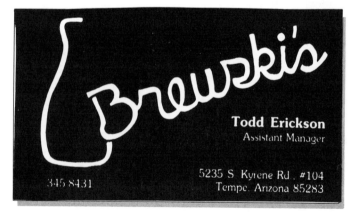

Todd Erickson
Assistant Manager

5235 S. Kyrene Rd. #104
Tempe, Arizona 85283

345-8431

Dark green printed over white stock; bleed on all sides

Bands and Blocks

Dark blue print on white, blue-flecked stock

Apricot circle; print, logo and band in dark turquoise on white glossy stock

Bleeds

Bleeds are areas printed off the edge of the page. The card must be printed on larger stock and then trimmed to achieve the bleed effect. That adds to the cost of the printing. Since it creates a potent effect and indicates quality, it is often worth the extra cost. A bleed should be considered in the early design stage, though, not as an afterthought.

Black Ink on white glossy stock; bleeds on 3 sides

Courtesy the Business Card Archives

Rules (lines) and boxes

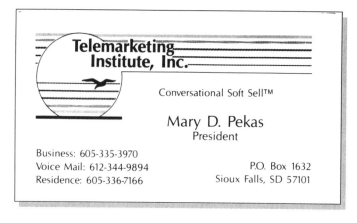

Dark blue on white glossy stock; horizontal lines are screens of various percentages

L I S A
BOISCLAIR
DESIGN
INTERIORS

5738 East Monte Cristo Avenue
Scottsdale, Arizona 85254
(602) 482-5503

*Logo in brown
golden yellow,
blue-green
and rust;
brown border
and print on
white glossy
stock*

Botanical Medicine Store

Darcee Hoffarth
7121 E. 6th Avenue. Scottsdale, AZ 85251 • (602) 970-6157

*Olive green on
heavy light
green stock
with green
flecks*

Screens, Tints, and Gradients

The screen is made up of colored dots, which are stated in the form of a percentage of tint. The lower the percentage, the lighter the screen, so if you are going to print text over a screened color, stick with a low percentage (10% to 20%). This is also a way to have one or two colors look like more colors.

| 10% | 20% | 30% | 40% | 50% | 60% | 70% | | | |

| 10% | 20% | 30% | 40% | 50% | 60% | 70% | 80% | 90% | 100% |

Robert B. Lamishaw

6257 Van Nuys Blvd #101

Van Nuys, CA 91401-2711

phone: 818-782-1587

fax: 818-781-0929

www.scubajournal.com

e-mail: lamishaw@att.net

*The gradient is
in the letters.
Green Cyber Sea
gets lighter
toward the
bottom. Blue
logo darkens
toward the
bottom. Green
and blue on
glossy white stock*

Colleen Dhaoui
Fashion Designer / Owner

Fashion Design
Art Studio & Boutique

Hours: Mon-Fri 9-6 Sat 10-5

3133 S. Mill Ave Suite # A
Tempe, Arizona 85282

(602) 968-9689

LINDA SUE NATHANSON. Ph.D.

E**B**

EDIN
BOOKS
Inc.

102 SUNRISE DRIVE
GILLETTE NJ 07933

908.MIS.EDIN
908.647.3346
FAX 908.580.1008

Hot pink in box, fading to lighter
screens phone number in pink; other
type in black

Light blue and dark blue fading off
the edges on white stock

Watermarks are screened images which are printed over.

QUALITY BOOKS INC.
A DAWSON COMPANY

Jim Hicks
Manager of Vendor Relations
jim.hicks@dawson.com

1003 W. Pines Road • Oregon, IL 61061-9680
Toll Free 1-800-323-4241 • Fax 1-815-732-4499

Gray screened
map; black
print on white
matte stock
with red
bleeds on top
and bottom
edges

Indian Pueblo

Authentic Hand Made Indian Jewelry
Fine Indian Arts & Crafts • Pottery
Rugs and Kachinas
Indian Operated

Phone (602) 947-7504
7142 E. 5th Ave.   1-888-947-7504
Scottsdale, AZ 85251   Fax (602) 947-7547

Turquoise drawing with black ink on off-white stock with blue flecks

Repeats add interest, and add interest, and add interest, and add interest.

Black print on gray screened background which bleeds on all sides on white stock

Borders can echo the mood of the card.

Black print on gray stock

Peach stock with forest green print; fruits are various percentages of screens

Medium blue on textured gray stock

Irregular or torn edge

Dark blue upper right corner fading gradually to opposite corner in heavy cream stock printing in blue and turquoise inks

Silhouettes can be the traditional black on white or a reverse, white on black.

Larry Bram
Director of Marketing

4545 42nd St., N.W.
Suite 306
Washington, DC 20016
Phone (202) 362-7543
Fax (202) 364-7273
E-mail larrytsi@aol.com

Navy blue on textured white stock

PATRICIA J. BELL

9561 Woodridge Circle
Eden Prairie, MN 55347
(612) 941-5053
E-Mail: PatJBell@aol.com

Black on white stock

Curving lines

Full color card on glossy white stock; most print in red; logo in six primary shades

Dark tur-
quoise on gray
textured and
flecked stock

Line drawings or illustrations

Navy blue on
dark tan stock
with bleed on
all edges

*Courtesy the Busi-
ness Card Archives*

Black print on
blue matte
stock

Ruth Kern Books

The Complete Book Service

- OUT OF PRINT SEARCHES
- SPECIAL ORDERING
- BOOK FAIRS
- PURCHASE ORDERS WELCOME
- GIFT BOOKS
- CATALOGS
- NEW BOOK ORDERING

602-943-0738
FAX 602-861-2161
P.O. Box 35366
Phoenix, AZ 85069

*Purple ink on
pink stock*

Cartoons and caricatures

*Black print on
white stock;
red shirt,
name (in
graduated
screen) and
accents on
numbers*

Let Your Card Personify Your Style

A truly customized card was made by an artist who painted an abstract picture. He then cut it into card-sized pieces on which he wrote his name and number. Anyone who got one was, in fact, receiving a sample of a master "piece." Those who are in art or visual-image-rich fields should prepare a card for themselves that is a delight to see—a true expression of a well-developed and unique style.

DECIDE WHAT TO PRINT UPON
Take Stock of Your Stock

The surface you print on should be given serious thought. Texture, color, finish, weight, and type of material can all be varied to reinforce the information printed on it. Each of these factors could play an important roll in promoting your business image. A heavier paper connotes the look and feel of quality. Just as an expensive suit "feels" different than a cheap one, we often sense quality with our fingers.

White stock is the least expensive and most common. Colors vary from mill to mill, and there are no standard paper colors. The amount of color in the stock increases opacity (the degree to which ink does not show through), but decreases legibility because the contrast between the type and background is reduced. (See Chapter 6 on the influence of contrast and legibility.) Nowadays, the popularity of recycling has resulted in a greater selection of recycled papers as well. These stocks often have interesting textures or shades.

Coated stocks (also called enamel paper) have a smooth surface, but come in a variety of finishes: gloss, dull, matte and satin. The coated surface results in better ink holdout, which means ink dries on the surface, without soaking in. That results in colors looking brighter and is important to consider when printing photographs and halftones (photographs composed of many tiny black dots). Coated stocks are slightly more expensive than uncoated ones.

Uncoated finishes can be found anywhere from a rough and bulky finish, to a lightly-textured vellum, to a very smooth finish. These have different optical properties, depending on how much they reflect the light. The properties of paper usually involve some trade-offs since a gain in one trait is often at the expense of another.

Papers can be compared on:

- Weight—either basis weight or substance weight; higher numbers connote heavier paper, which means a higher cost
- Opacity—a paper's resistance to the transmission of light; restricts show through; heavy paper is more opaque
- Brightness—the measure of diffused light reflectance; the brighter the paper, the brighter the colors of ink
- Smoothness—the smoother the paper, the finer the dot-reproduction that can be achieved on it
- Ink receptivity or ink holdout—related to smoothness; tendency of inks to dry on the surface without soaking into the stock
- Gloss—finish of the surface; amount of shine; gloss is often associated with quality, although matte and uncoated surfaces increase readability

Try the Unusual

Non-standard stock may cost a bit more, but the advantages usually outweigh a small price increase. A good printer will have a variety of typical non-standard card stocks in various colors and textures on hand, but he cannot possibly warehouse everything that is available from paper manufacturers and wholesalers. Instead, he'll probably have a considerable number of samples on hand for you to play with and chose from. However, even this seemingly large variety of paper stocks is only a small fraction of what is actually available. If you are not satisfied, keep looking.

Stocks also come in a wide array of finishes or textures

▫ Coarse, rough

▫ Matte

▫ Glossy

▫ Standard textures, like linen or laid

And some finishes are applied after the printing; like laminate or varnishes. These are also available in a variety of finishes.

Reddish brown background with black print and screened edge of back-ground, which does not go to the edge of the card on very rough cream-colored stock

Different stock materials absorb ink differently, and that influences the way the final print looks. Select a stock heavy enough that the print doesn't show through on the back. Take stock into consideration early in the design phase. Darker stock has less contrast with the ink printed upon it. Without sufficient contrast, a card becomes very hard to read.

To be truly unique, forget traditional card stocks. Clear plastic might be appropriate for an ice company, or wallpaper for an interior decorating firm. How about thick graph paper for an engineer, blueprint paper for an architect, a prescription pad for an MD, maps for a tour guide, etc.? There is an infinite variety of material that can be substituted or reproduced for standard card stock—often with striking effect.

Whatever stock you choose, make certain that it will be available in the future for additional print runs. If there is the slightest doubt, order extra, unprinted stock as a hedge against "discontinuance."

Types of Stock for Business Cards

- ☐ Card stock or cover stock
- ☐ Photographic paper
- ☐ Parchment
- ☐ Wallpaper
- ☐ Clear plastic or plastic with eye-catching properties
- ☐ Sheet metal
- ☐ Papers that resemble a profession's characteristic materials: bookkeeping, ledger or graph paper; blueprint paper, prescription pads, maps
- ☐ Wooden strips or veneer
- ☐ Thin metal (such as printer's plates)
- ☐ Cloth (paper backed), printed or embroidered
- ☐ Sandpaper
- ☐ Rubber
- ☐ Chocolate or other edible materials
- ☐ Bamboo
- ☐ Leather
- ☐ Designer papers
- ☐ Cardboard (for a box maker)

Gold logo and black type on thin sugar pine wood strip

Card is white glossy plastic, two sided, yellow face, black print

Use Backgrounds to Enhance Your Stock

- □ Tints and screens
- □ Small all-over figures, particularly if light color
- □ Textures, like marble
- □ Color washes
- □ Watermarks or screens

Metallic Inks Will Make You Shine

For a special effect for little additional cost, use metallic inks. There are hundreds of colors, as well as copper, gold and silver. These inks are high density so they can be used to print over other inks and colors. They work best on coated stock.

Also consider fluorescent inks which come in truly eye-catching colors. They are very light reflective and should not be printed on dark backgrounds.

Special Effects Send a Special Message

Whatever card stock or material you choose as the "foundation" of your card, you may wish to embellish that choice. Card material, no matter how basic or plain, can be greatly enhanced by a variety of methods. Embellishments get noticed and are often remembered, but should not compete with the overall image of your card. Good taste and clarity of purpose should always be the guiding principles in selecting special effects. (See the Resource Section for sources.)

- Holograms
- Foil stamping, reflective inks or finishes
- Embossing and debossing
- Scented inks
- Colorshift inks or papers
- Iridescent papers or inks

"Moonlight" reversed on multi-hued metallic foil, which bleeds to edge and is used for the print as well; on white stock

CLASSIC COACH CO.

AUTO BODY & PAINT ON ALL NEW & OLD MODELS
FINE MOTOR CAR RESTORATIONS
MICHAEL J. JAKL

For Appointment
Bus: 303-279-1543

16015 W. 4th Ave., #7
Golden, CO 80401

Black print on tan stock; gold foiled car

Ronald A. Mazzola
Executive Director of
Marketing/Sales

**(313) 429-5411
ext. 206**

Complete Book Manufacturing

Naturalite
NEON

David L. Glover
602-993-8710
2610 W. Holly Phoenix AZ 85009

Folded; brown on one side tan on the other; front embossed and gold foil

Neon colors on and around the N; red and blue type on white stock

Bright Ring Publishing

Mary Ann F. Kohl

(206) 734-1601

P.O. Box 5768   Bellingham, WA 98227

Black print on beige stock and silver foiled and embossed logo

This is the paper version of a card that was made with edible chocolate. It comes in a plastic box along with a non-edible card.

Non-Printed Enhancements to Cards

- □ Stickers, custom made for you, with phrases like: "We like referrals," "#1 Salesman," "Winner of Best _____ "
- □ Rubber stamps, whether custom made or from the abundant supplies available
- □ Glue-ons, especially objects, like pieces of ribbon or a small sample (scrap) of the product sold
- □ Felt-tip markers or paints
- □ Special effects, like glitter
- □ Wax stamps

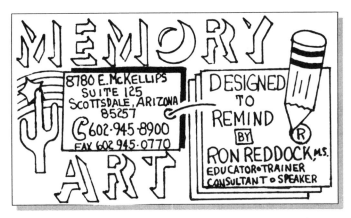

The dynamic art created by this business employs colored markers, so the card also uses markers to make it colorful.

WHEN QUALITY *REALLY* MATTERS
Displaying an Impeccable Business Identity

The word "impeccable" suggests subtle elegance. It is revealed by its understatement and stands out because every element from design to printing discloses high quality. Such details send a message of high class, prestige and substance. It may not matter to everyone, but "those who know" really *do notice*.

Quality is largely conveyed by the sense of touch. In fact, it is transmitted 65 percent by vision and 35 percent by feel. The texture of the paper is noted by the fingers, and a heavier stock provides a reassuring indication of quality (that's why a letter on 24-pound bond paper *feels* more impressive than one on the customary 20-pound bond; you can tell it's important even *before* the envelope is opened). Don't underestimate the value of such perceptions. Patricia Fripp, a delightful and well-known speaker relates a story. A businessman was trying on several suits at the tailor shop. He said, "I can't tell the difference between a $1,400 suit and an $1,800 suit." The tailor paused as he ran his thumb along the lapel and responded, "You can't...but the people whom you want to impress *can* tell the difference."

Clients make value judgment about the professionalism of a business based on its stationery. High quality shines through, and it is assumed that the services are similarly distinguished. Your card often provides the first contact and, hence the first impression of your organization. Some types of businesses need to be of top caliber; their clients expect it. The marks of excellence are clearly recognized by those alert to that degree of professionalism.

A friend told about his experience of meeting Jonathan Winters, the comedian, and giving him a business card. Without first reading it, Mr. Winters turned the card over and slowly rubbed the back. He then looked up, smiled, and said, "If the card isn't embossed, the company is in trouble." Since prosperity can be revealed with such subtle signs, sometimes the card could be felt (pun intended) to be a more accurate barometer than the balance sheet. Fortunately, my friend's card was embossed.

The marks of quality are most valued in such professions as law or finance, which provide services; and often there is considerable money involved. That is a realm where tradition is valued, and traditional methods of producing your stationery are applauded. That means engraving.

Engraved cards and stationery are often printed in combination with other special printing options like embossing, debossing (the stock is depressed instead of raised), metallic inks, and foil stamping. Each of these techniques requires one or more passes through the press (and sometimes other labor-intensive steps), which increase the production costs. Some cards shown in the book have had as many as six press runs, and the impression they make can be quite stunning.

LaDon Henderson
Plant Manager

150 Kingswood Road
P. O. Box 8725
Mankato, MN 56002-8725

Tel: 507-386-7700
Fax: 800-858-8329

Embossed logo with blue "N" and gold, silver, and red eagle; text is royal blue on white stock

How to Recognize Engraving

- Raised print; the letters are embossed, set on top of the paper, but unlike the raised print of thermography (a heated process)

- Fine lines and small letters are very clear and precise

- *Feels* like high quality; on high-grade stock

- Paper is flattened; two forms of engraving: one leaves a depression on the back; the other depresses the entire page, so no depression is evident

- Inks are not glossy but provide a matte effect (water soluble inks are used in the U.S., but engraving abroad is done with inks that are shiny (not water soluble))

- Can use black, colors or metallic engraved printing

- Sometimes combined with embossing or other special effects

ARCHITECTS

JESUS "CHUY" ORTEGA

ROSSMAN SCHNEIDER GADBREY SHAY
8681 East Via de Negocio   Scottsdale, Arizona 85258-3330
Tel: (602) 991-0800   Fax: (602) 991-2623

Turquoise embossed acronym; black engraving on delicate white stock

Engraving Provides Instant Credibility

Engraving is a form of printing which is without peer for fine intricate lines and very small type (after all, that's how they make currency). The process uses an etched plate and a smooth counter-plate on an engraving press, and results in a depressed (as in pushed down) impression. It was the standard method for producing business stationery until recent times, and now other, less-expensive printing methods are readily available. However, in other parts of the world and in the circles of the well heeled and powerful, engraving is still the appropriate choice.

A study was conducted to determine the attitude of executives regarding their corporate identity materials (Yankelovich Clancy Shulman, "Corporate Identity: Image Impact Analysis," 1992). The study considered the most desirable characteristics of the stationery, the method of reproduction, and their perceptions regarding the various forms of stationery. The study found that: "Readability, conveying professionalism, and showing that *the company cares about its clients* are the most desirable attributes of corporate identity materials, in that order"[1]

Executives were given sets of actual stationery (matching cards, letterhead and envelopes) and asked to compare them on a number of questions. The samples differed only in the method of printing:

- □ Engraved
- □ Lithographed
- □ Laser printed
- □ Faxed

The results were unambiguous. Executives preferred engraved materials by a wide margin. Of those executives who preferred engraved materials, 81 percent chose it because of feel; 67 percent chose it for higher quality; 58 percent chose it for paper quality (tactility), and 33 percent chose it for the image it conveys (multiple responses were permitted).

A further study considered only law firms in evaluating their stationery. It compared engraving, laser printing, thermography and lithography (Altman Weil Pensa, Inc., 1994).[2] Again, engraving was the clear choice. More than half said that engraving best represented the attributes valued by a law firm for its stationery:

- □ Easy to read
- □ Makes a positive first impression
- □ Conveys a professional image
- □ Conveys a quality image
- □ Indicates that the firm is successful

The study also determined that engraving best reflects the value of the business and is most important to clients. It instills greater confidence in the company.

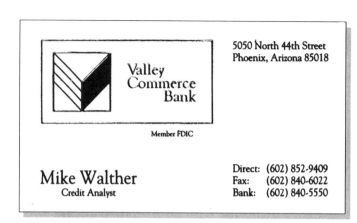

5050 North 44th Street
Phoenix, Arizona 85018

Valley
Commerce
Bank

Member FDIC

Mike Walther
Credit Analyst

Direct: (602) 852-9409
Fax: (602) 840-6022
Bank: (602) 840-5550

*Logo embossed
and gold
foiled; text is
black engraving
on tan stock*

Also Weigh the Stock

When a firm wants to be impeccable, it needs papers that are as upscale as the firm. The weight and finish of fine paper are immediately noted. Stocks of 100 percent cotton are the champagne of papers (the higher the cotton content the better the quality). Such subtle distinctions enhance the business image. Although many paper makers offer 100 percent cotton stocks, Crane Papers are perceived to be the standard of high-end papers (since 1801). Some of them are even hand beveled and gilded (painted with gold).

When you consider the costs that go into the preparation of a letter, the costs for the paper, envelope, and card seem small indeed. Those who opt for engraving treat it as a marketing expense rather than a business supply expense. They know they are communicating value to the receiver in a very tangible way.

Brett A. Shepard

Pacific Ridge, Inc.
1114 E. Leeward Lane
Tempe, Arizona 85283-2053

602.820.9551
602.838.2227 Fax
602.540.7437 Mobile
500.367.2738 Travel
shepco@primenet.com

Pacific Ridge

Black engraving on off-white stock

DOING IT ALL YOURSELF
Using Your Computer to Make Your Own Cards

- Customize or make changes as often as you like
- Treat your card like a resume, which is tailored and kept up to the minute
- Save money by using your laser or color printer
- Use design options like computerized card templates that avoid blunders and guide your steps
- Scan in elements and tweak the layout and proportions
- Eliminate waste; make them as you need them
- Eliminate delay; they're ready right away
- Customized papers and stocks add more color and style capability
- Offers a variety of targeted or unique cards

Be careful that a computer-generated business card doesn't mark you as an amateur. If you go that route, proceed with caution.

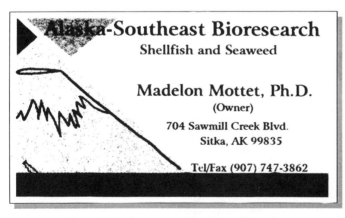

Alaska-Southeast Bioresearch

Shellfish and Seaweed

Madelon Mottet, Ph.D.
(Owner)

704 Sawmill Creek Blvd.
Sitka, AK 99835

Tel/Fax (907) 747-3862

Black computer-laser print and line drawings on pre-printed stock with mauve and dark turquoise figures on white stock

Pre-printed stock has been modified to reflect the mountains and sea critters at the Sitka aquaculture site. The band at the bottom shows seven shellfish.

Pre-Printed Papers and Card Kits

Pre-printed papers and perforated card stock designed to be used in your computer laser printer are available from several sources. They are printed in coordinated sets, so your card, letter-head, and brochure can match. Such pre-printed papers offer the benefits of full color or distinctive accents, without most of the custom design and printing cost. That option saves money when you only need a small volume; however, at some point it's as cheap to prepare and print your own unique design.

Using a preprinted format is better than a vanilla pudding card, but, probably, you'll be wise to develop something that suits you. As with any other how-to concept, you'll see it used both well and poorly. These pre-printed products are not a substitute for developing your image, they're just another way to help you get there. It provides a halfway or temporary answer. Your options are limited to designs on the market, which are already in use by others. "Everyone knows" it's a kit, so it marks you as a newbie or a very small operation. Tradeoffs to consider include convenience, distinctiveness, and per-page costs.

To Recap

Experiment with unlimited option in the design of your card. Pay attention to effects on the cards you encounter, and discover the ones that personify your style. Don't ignore the wide range of materials you can print upon or the high-impact special effects. If you want to appear upscale, engraving and high-quality stock provide the image that gives you instant credibility. And at the other end of the spectrum, you can do it all yourself at home. The important consideration is that you invest the interest to make your card as interesting as you are.

Chapter 10

Discover Even More Ways to Use Cards

Cards Creep Up All Over the Place

Business cards serve many purposes aside from their principal use for generating business. The format is so versatile that it has been adapted for many uses:

- Provide social identity, like family cards
- Inform about your non-career or retired pursuits
- Make statements; support a cause; show membership
- Educate, admonish, and advise
- Promote an event or a special purpose
- Add fun
- Promote networking and job hunting

Business Cards Arose from Calling Cards

Calling cards emerged in Europe in the 1600s, and the practice of leaving them at friend's houses spread from there to America. They were first used by nobility to announce social visits before the telephone was invented. Strict rules of etiquette governed. They are seldom used now except for special occasions. The proper format includes only the person's name and title(s). *Crane's Blue Book of Stationery* provides nuances that are quaint in their careful attention to protocol, but which seem far from the way most of us live now.

"Calling cards are available in several sizes. The sizes indicate male or female, married or single. The following are the correct sizes for use by individuals and couples issuing joint cards.

Child	$2^1/_4$" x $1^3/_8$"
Single Woman	$2^7/_8$" x 2"
Married Woman	$3^1/_8$" x $2^1/_4$"
Man	$3^3/_8$" x $1^1/_2$" or 3 $^1/_2$" x 2"
Married Couple	$3^3/_8$" x $2^1/_2$""[1]

In the East (USA) and some foreign countries the calling card is still to be found. It also shows up to mark special events like weddings and graduations. They are done in very high-quality stock, often engraved (See Chapter 9 on engraved printing when you want to be impeccable.). The edges of such cards may be hand beveled and even hand gilded. They may be either handwritten or printed.

Family Cards

Cards are once again being used for social purposes by those who have no interest in business. "Cards are making a casual comeback to the ageless Tarzan-meets-Jane game. And we're not just talking about recycling the tired by-the-book cards used for work. 'Here's my card' isn't what most would expect to hear on schoolyards, but schoolchildren said they are discovering that business cards are great ice breakers for the sometimes awkward immersion into the dating world. So important, many say that they are often among the first things they pack for school, alongside homework and lunch."[2]

Alber Group

Robert & Marilyn
Ren & Roz

16614 S. 36th Place
Phoenix, Arizona 85044

H-602.706.0254   W-602.965.1441
ALBER@ASU.EDU

My niece, Geneva, started carrying her card while in kindergarten, long before she could read it.

Alaska-Southeast Bio-Research

Geneva Mottet
Research Assistant

704 Sawmill Creek Blvd.
Sitka, AK 99835

(907) 747 3862   Fax: (907) 747 3862

Michael Jeremiah Payne
(602) 555-0123

Mail: 957 E. Grandview Rd. #17, Tempe, 85283
Residence: 1134 E. Desert Dr., Tempe, 85283
Mom's Office: (602) 555-1234
Dad's Office: (602) 555-2345
Mom's Pager: (602) 555-3456
Our Fax: (602) 555-4567
My pediatrician: (602) 555-5678 (Dr. Watkins)

And even a card for a cat

*Black print on
dark gray
textured stock*

**B U S I N E S S
M A R K E T I N G
S E R V I C E S**

Lito Gitomer

Corporate Mascot

705 Royal Court
Suite 100
Charlotte, NC 28202
office 704/333-1112
fax 704/333-1011

Retired Cards

All these cards are black on white stock

Marie G. Wallace
Life in Progress

Swimmer   *Law Librarian*
Speaker   *Trainer*
Storyboarder *Writer*
Wearable Art

3233 Selby Ave., L.A. 90034   310-837-0839

NO PHONE   NO ADDRESS

                    RETIRED

NO BUSINESS   NO MONEY

Jerry Dombek
Project Manager

RETIRED

Projects
- Women
- Fast Cars
- Scuba Diving

Availability
- 24 hours
- 7 days/wk

Experience
- All play
- No work

Qualifications
- Ph.D. of Play

'Good Happens'

- Traveling
- Camping
- Photography
- Treasure Hunting
- Ecstasy

(Mobile) 531-5094 • (Pager) 271-6888 • (FAX) 381-8350
(Play Room) 955-9660

Les & Mary Mahugh

U.S.F.S. Retired   U.S.O.C. Retired

(406) 755-6703

4575 Mont. 35
Kalispell, MT 59901

Cards to Mark Special Events

Purple print on lavender stock

Courtesy the Business Card Archives

BRETT HARVEY
COMMUNICATIONS DIRECTOR

212-791-3400 x104

90 JOHN STREET
SUITE 403
NEW YORK, NY 10038

FAX 212-791-0333

WWW.GAG.ORG

Orange, rust and navy logo with text in navy on white stock

Cards to Educate, Admonish, or Advise

Are You
Handicapped?

IF NOT - PLEASE PARK ELSEWHERE
IN THE FUTURE.

Red print on white stock

Courtesy the Business Card Archives

Hi, My name is ONYX
and I have AIDS.

**_NO_ AIDS IF YOU
KNOW AIDS!**

"GET THE FACTS"

Contact
THE ONYX
BLENDING and MENTORING
CENTER FOR LIFE
P.O. Box 62524
Phoenix, AZ 85082-2524
(602) 264-6333
FAX - (602) 230-1991
Melissa Teasley
Jacqueline Mayfield
MSW / MPH

Black and white photograph...   *...Black printing with red ribbon*

Courtesy the Business Card Archives

GREAT FALLS, MT 59406

BOX 6146

**GREAT FALLS
REPRODUCTIVE
FREEDOM
COALITION**

WHO DECIDES?

*Turquoise on
white stock*

Courtesy the Business Card Archives

Are You Making Any Of These Common Marketing Mistakes?

1. Not having a unique selling proposition (that which makes you special).

2. Failure to utilize your customer list.

3. Forgetting to recognize that you have to both sell and educate.

4. Running image advertising.

5. Failure to determine and address what your customer really wants.

6. Not testing for results.

7. Failure to make doing business with your firm . . . easy, appealing and even fun.

8. Forgetting to tell your customers the reasons why.

9. Abandoning marketing campaigns that are still working.

10. Forgetting to focus on the customer and no one else.

MARKETING GENIUS'   602 423-1246

Inside of folded card; black print on white stock

Interests and Hobbies

BUD ANDREWS
Professional Bass
Fisherman

PHONE (904) 726-1272
1025 HWY. 44 EAST
INVERNESS, FLORIDA 32650

Brown print on glossy beige stock

*All black type
except the
name in
purple on
white stock*

Jack Gurner

BUSINESS CARD
COLLECTOR

116 DUPUY ST.
WATER VALLEY, MS 38965
(601) 473-1154

*Black print on
white stock*

(619) 232-9555

Mid-City Theatre

Loch David Crane
Publicity

548 Fifth Avenue • San Diego, CA 92101

Cards For Fun

All cards this section are black on white stock

OUR RUSH JOB POLICY

IF YOU WANT IT BAD...YOU GET IT BAD,
AND
THE WORSE YOU WANT IT -
THE WORSE YOU GET IT!

COMPLIMENTS OF BUTTONS & BADGES, PHOENIX, AZ

MY CARD

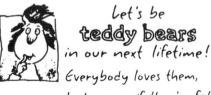

Let's be
teddy bears
in our next lifetime!
Everybody loves them,
nobody cares if they're fat,
and the older they get,
the more they're worth!

COMPLIMENTS OF BUTTONS & BADGES, PHOENIX, AZ

I Am The Father Of The Bride

NOBODY'S PAYING MUCH ATTENTION TO ME TODAY, BUT I CAN ASSURE YOU, THAT I AM NOT BEING IGNORED. THE BANKS AND SEVERAL BUSINESS FIRMS ARE WATCHING ME VERY CLOSELY TO SEE THAT I DON'T LEAVE TOWN.

COMPLIMENTS: BUTTONS, BADGES & TROPHIES, PHOENIX, AZ 846-1626

Learn from the mistakes of others— you can never live long enough to make them all yourself.

Compliments: Buttons, Badges & Trophies 602-846-1626 Phoenix, AZ

HUG LICENSE

_____
name

is hereby licensed
to give and receive heartfelt hugs.
Everyone participating in this warm, loving gesture
will experience one of life's simplest and most
enjoyable pleasures.

4 HUGS A DAY KEEPS THE BLUES AWAY

*Two-sided
card with dark
red print on
pink stock*

Courtesy the Business Card Archives

HUG PRESCRIPTION

DAILY : **4 HUGS** FOR SURVIVAL

8 HUGS FOR MAINTENANCE

12 HUGS FOR GROWTH

FOR HUG ABUNDANCE
SEND $1.00 FOR HUG CATALOG
HUGS UNLIMITED
P.O. Box 4041
Huntington Beach
California 92605 ● (714) 530-9918

Dr. Feelbetter

Membership Cards and Admissions

Living To Be Free On Three
-An Organization Dedicated To Trikers-

BROTHERS OF THE THIRD WHEEL

You Have Just Met

Triker _____

Int'l Hdqrs.   P.O. Box 345, Coal Valley, IL 61240-U.S.A.

*Logo in brown
screen; type in
black on white*

Subject to the rules on this card please admit to

The Magic Castle™

7001 Franklin Ave. • Hollywood, CA 90028

MAGIC CASTLE™

_____

and party (total of eight people maximum) for dinner. Reservations required.

IMPORTANT CLUB RULES

1. Absolutely no one under 21 admitted. Photo I.D. required.
2. Strict dress code. Coats and ties for men, evening wear for ladies (i.e. cocktail dresses). No casual wear (i.e. jeans, tennis shoes, etc.).

(Over)

Print in dark maroon on glossy stock

BOWL FREE!

At Bradenton's finest bowling center!
GALAXY LANES BRADENTON
4208 Cortez Rd W • 758-8838

Good for one FREE GAME OF BOWLING
when lanes available, not valid Saturdays after 6 pm.
One Free Game per person per day.

Red print on white stock

Courtesy the Business Card Archives

PROVIDE ADDITIONAL BENEFITS WITH CARDS
Keeping Your Card Around

Whenever possible, provide a reason for someone to keep your card. Do something to make receivers want to hang on to them. The more prominently "kept," the more mileage your card is getting, for each sight of it serves as a tangible reminder of you. Each encounter gives added mileage to your marketing.

Useful Information (see following list supplied
by the Business Card Museum)

- Conversion tables, reference information, tide tables
- Calendar—which lasts for exactly one year

- Magnets attached to the card
- Dates, events, schedules
- "Keepers"—things you want to remember
- Checklists
- Recipes or food preparation tips
- "How to" information, instructions, and definitions
- Ordering information, mini-catalog, products, training, etc.
- Maps and illustrations
- Tools like a scraper, bottle opener, or luggage tag
- Competitions, meetings, events, special upcoming dates
- Interesting and useful facts

Reward or Bonus

- Bonus to person who makes referrals
- Coupon, discount offer, hole punch for series of purchases: a dozen bagel card, buy three and get one free, free dessert with dinner
- Ticket, special promotion

And people do hang onto special offers. One restaurant owner told me of giving a card promising a free steak dinner. It was redeemed ten years later by someone who had kept the card around all that time.

Interesting, Amusing, or Fun

- Sayings, quotes and aphorisms
- Poetry and inspiration
- Cartoons, jokes, humorous lift
- Puzzle, riddle, game, illusion or trick
- Self-test or survey of some sort

101 Things You Can Put on the Back of Your Business Card to Make It More Effective

Additional Locations
— Advertisement
Amortization Table
Anniversary Gift List
— Appointment Reminder
Bible Index
— Biography
Blood Alcohol Chart
Branch Offices
— Calendar
Calorie Chart
Car Accident Procedure
Car Care Reminders
Cartoons
Chemical Emergency
    Information
Childhood Immunization
    Chart
Cholesterol Chart
Clothing Sizes
Concrete Calculator
Conversion Tables
— Coupon
Decimal Equivalent Chart
Distributors
Emergency Phone
    Numbers
— Endorsements

Envelope Sizes
Fire Safety Tips
First Aid Procedures
Flag Etiquette
Favors
— Free Trial Offer
Frequent Buyer Card
Geographic Directions
Guarantees
Hazardous Material Tips
Heimlich Maneuver
Helpful Hints
Home Bar Checklist
How to Sell Your House
Illustrations
Important Holidays
Important Phone Numbers
Instructions
Internet Information
Joke/Anecdote
Language Translation
— List of Products
— List of Services
Loan Payment Schedule
Lock Combination
    Information
Map
Membership Card

Menus
Mileage/Destination Chart
Mini-Book Review
Mini-Resume
Miranda Rules
Mission Statement
Money Conversions
Monthly Payment Schedule
Mortgage Principal Interest
Mouth to Mouth
    Resuscitation Instructions
Nail Sizes
Organization Affiliations
Paper Sizes
Periodic Table
Philosophy
Phone Card
Photograph
Poem
Poison Information
Political Campaign
    Information
Postal Rates
Prayer/Psalm
Price Bid Chart
Price List
Product Benefits
Product Specifications
Program Descriptions
Quality Policy

Recipe
Referrals
Reservation Call-Ahead
Riddle
Safe Deposit Inventory
Safety Hints
Screw Sizes
Service Centers
Slogan
Sport Schedule
Survey
Tax Deadlines
Telephone Number Index
Tip Table
Train/Bus Schedule
Translation (into a 2nd
    language)
Travel Distances
Viscosity Comparisons
Voting Instructions
Weight & Measures Table
Wind Chill Index

Courtesy of **The Business Card Museum**
402 Bethlehem Pike, Erdenheim PA 19038
(215) 836-0555

Give Objects with Value

A really effective way to get much more visibility and longer life for your card is to incorporate the information and graphics from the card onto a promotional product. In most instances the card can be copied exactly and used as an imprint on the product. Almost any promotional product with imprinting space sufficient to accommodate a business card will work.

Promotional Items That Can Sport a Business Card Imprint

1. Letter opener
2. Coaster
3. Tape measure
4. Mug
5. Magnet
6. Ruler
7. Address book
8. Calendar
9. Phone card
10. Chocolate
11. Key chain
12. Note pad
13. Seed packet
14. Ice scraper
15. Pin or button
16. Bookmark
17. Box
18. Magnifier
19. Wallet
20. Compact mirror
21. Luggage tag
22. Sponge
23. Jar gripper
24. Matchbook
25. Computer diskette
26. Napkins
27. Box of crayons
28. Business card case
29. Coin purse
30. Clock
31. Coupon holder
32. Manicure kit
33. Playing cards
34. Notebooks
35. Desk pen holder
36. Calculator
37. Golf bag tag
38. Paper weights
39. Hunting/fishing license holder
40. Glassware
41. Decorative jars
42. Sewing kits
43. First aid kits
44. Ash trays
45. Binders
46. Litter bags
47. CD Rom cases
48. Cosmetic case
49. Coasters or cup holders
50. Photo albums

List provided by The Three Marketeers (See Resource Section)

The order of popularity of premiums items (in this order)

1. Wearables   24.0%
2. Writing   11.9%
3. Glass/Ceramics   9.4%
4. Calendars   7.7%
5. Recognition awards, trophies   6.4%
   and emblematic jewelry

Premiums, however, are never a substitute for a card. Always provide a cardboard one along with the premium so that it will get filed with the others. The value of the premium is to reinforce your image and to help the recipient think of you fondly. Your card also needs to be in the card file so it won't be overlooked.

People also hang onto special offers. One restaurant owner told me of having a card that promised a free steak dinner. One was redeemed ten years later by someone who had kept the card around all that time.

Gold foil, teal blue and purple on glossy white stock.

An effective use of cards was demonstrated by Strathmore Papers, which makes coordinated papers for cards and letterhead. The sample business cards demonstrated paper in humorous ways. These were not just paper samples, but about 50 actual cards arranged in a clever display. Who could resist keeping them on hand? The following two cards are fictional businesses supplied courtesy Strathmore Papers.

Planning to move?

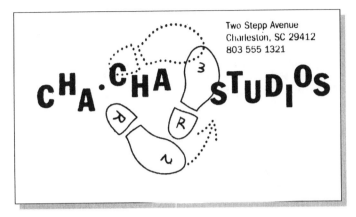

Two Stepp Avenue
Charleston, SC 29412
803 555 1321

*Stock with
woven pattern;
black feet and
the rest is in
purple*

Can't get your idea to fly?

*Blue sky on
light blue
paper; black
letters*

Make a Sequence of Cards

Several cards can operate together as a very brief catalog (each card showing different products). Put part of the information on one card, with different information on other cards. People end up wanting them all. Make certain that each card contains enough information that any one of them can help them reach you if the other cards are gone. If they are interesting, people will be eager to see what you've got next. Artists can develop a mini-gallery by periodically bringing out new cards with a recent work of art.

Two different versions of the card in full color, each showing two book covers. Both versions have the same back.

Or Show a Sample of Your Wares

U.S. GAMES SYSTEMS, INC.

Lee Stockwell
Special Sales & Promotions Manager
Extension 307

U.S. GAMES
SYSTEMS, INC

179 Ludlow Street
Stamford, CT 06902 USA
(203) 353-8400 • Fax (203) 353-8431
E-mail USGames@aol.com
(800) 544-2637

*Black print on
white stock*

Full-color actual Tarot card by a company that produces them is on one side of the card and echoed in the silhouette logo on the back

THE FOOL .

©1997 USGAMES

Things to Do to a Card to Increase its Longevity

- ☐ Apply a magnet to the back
- ☐ Laminate it
- ☐ Make it a toy, like a hologram, on pressure- or heat-sensitive stock
- ☐ Use peel-away adhesive, so it can be stuck in a visible place
- ☐ Attach it to something that is likely to be kept, souvenir or premium item
- ☐ Turn it into a luggage tag

Ways to Use Your Card

- ◻ Affix it to your corporate literature
- ◻ Use as a name tag; tape it over event name tags; customize a name tag you take with you use as a promotional piece at all events
- ◻ Use your card as a gift tag when presenting a small gift or flowers

This is a *very* brief list. We're looking for your creative ideas and will be giving prizes for your unusual and effective uses for cards. Enter the contest in the back of the book.

TECHNOLOGY ALTERS WHAT YOUR CARD CAN DO

Electronics Devices Re-invent the Business Card

Up to now, the book has discussed the exchange of business cards as an aspect of sharing personal data and impressions. But in this age of information, it should not be surprising to learn that there is a new term for that, Personal Data Interchange (PDI). And those at home in the world of electronics have not been idle. They have harnessed all manner of technology to improve our ability to communicate and collect each other's vital data, and to do it easier, faster, and more accurately.

Are such enhancements likely to replace the traditional business card? No, you still need to have a rectangle of cardboard that provides a visual reminder when the computer doesn't happen to be on. Also, not everyone feels at home on the Internet or eager to visit your website. Many people have no interest in gadgets. Your business card is still an important link. It does its work in the vital initial contacts, then helps to strengthen a lasting interpersonal bond.

Electronic Business Cards On Disk

For a while, electronic business cards (placed on diskettes) were popular. However, simply transferring information that could be shown on paper to a diskette was not powerful enough to engage the recipient. The disk-based information needed to include animation, sound, interaction—elements that could not be put on paper. The other problem involved with disk-based business cards was anticipating what type of computer the recipient might have.

In the final analysis, a combination of formats is proving to be the most productive. For instance, hybrid business cards are designed to act as mini-brochures. Your Internet site address on your business card directs interested parties to a much more media- and information-rich location than is possible with just a card. They can later review it for more details about you and your firm. Or consider even more elaborate multimedia brochures that can be placed on relatively inexpensive CD-ROMs. These can usually be viewed on a variety of computers and, perhaps, include links to your Internet site for up-to-date information.

Your *Sig* Is Your On-line Business Card

At the bottom of an e-mail (That's electronic mail, which is delivered to your electronic mailbox by exotic on-line methods; it is very fast and almost everywhere in the world can be reached with an e-mail address.) message, there is a place for the sender's signature (called "sig" for short). The information in the signature is automatically added to every message as it is sent. The file that holds the customized information which goes out with every e-mail transmission is called the *sig file*. The sig should not be longer than four or five lines long or more than seventy characters wide (so it does not waste bandwidth). Do not abuse the receiver by making your sig too long. Long sigs get flamed (punished).

Everyone who communicates with you by e-mail will see your sig, so it operates as a potent self-promotional tool. As with your cardboard business card, you need to transmit your information succinctly and make it clear what it is you offer. It will contain much of the same information that's on your card. Some sigs are very amusing or clever, imparting a sense of the personality behind it.

A sample sig:

```
John Jacob Jingle Heimmer Schmidt  (222) 123-2345 (voice)
1234 Main Street, Suite 333        (222) 123-2330 (fax)
Smalltown, OH, 34345           jingle@aol.com (e-mail)
Way To Go Travel; Book: How To Take a Vacation Every Day
When you want to go, see Way to Go
```

"Some companies let employees write and design their own sig files, so outgoing Email messages all are different. Other companies define a style or a few rules that all Email signatures must follow, but allow employees creativity within those limits. Other companies make all sig files follow an exact format, with no personalization allowed except the sender's name and phone number. In most ways, sig file content decisions are marketing decisions."[3]

Also, those in academic circles, who use e-mail a great deal to communicate with colleagues can use a sig file to indicate their affiliated field, university, and department. They may also provide a quote, which they change often, to stimulate discussion, like: "The logic of the world is prior to all truth and falsehood." Ludwig Wittgenstein.

Faster than Drawing Your Business Card

Be prepared for technology to alter the way we share our basic data. At the 1997 Consumer Electronics Show, IBM introduced a device that sends the kind of information usually provided on a business card. "You extend your arm to a potential business client, grasp his hand and squeeze it firmly. Instantly, tiny electrical impulses carry your personal business card data through your body tissues and into your client's body, where it is captured in a credit-card-size device in his pocket."[4]

Virtual Business Cards

The new entry as the electronic business card is the vCard, a product that is used for "Internet mail, voice mail, Web browsers, telephony applications, call centers, video conferencing, PIMs (Personal Information Managers), PDAs (Personal Data Assistants), pagers, fax, office equipment and smart cards. vCard information goes way beyond simple text and includes elements like pictures, company logos, live Web addresses, and so on."[5] It is more than the mind can handle, and it intends to revolutionize the way we communicate.

Features of the vCard:

- Carries directory information
- Contains graphics and multimedia: photos, logos, audio clips
- Provides geographic and time zones when you can be reached
- Supports multiple languages
- Is independent of transport and operating systems
- Is Internet friendly

Plan for Plan Files

Plan files are a method of retrieving information about people. The technique depends on a program or protocol called finger. Finger performs searches for data on individuals, so why not decide what will be found when you are fingered? The information to be displayed is kept in two files located in your project directory: ".project" and ".plan" (The period that precedes the file name indicates a Unix system file.).

You determine what information is in the directory, but let it be open to outsiders, who can view the contents that have been made available. For example, you can display your publications or other credentials, as is often done in academic circles. Plan files can be used as your personal billboard or another on-line form of business card.

So, do these kinds of electronic monikers signal the end of business cards as we know them? Do they open the door to other wizardry that will replace the tried and true business card? Don't hold your breath! Technology may transmit the information, but not the mood of a business in the way that your card does. Look at such devices to augment, but not to replace your card.

To Recap

There are many, many ways to use a card besides generating business. These can be social, educational, to make a statement, or for fun. Add something to your card that makes the receiver keep it around. Technology is enhancing the way we transfer our personal information, but isn't ready to eliminate the card as we know it.

Chapter 11

Extract the Best Printed Piece from Your Printer

A Printer is a Partner

You're almost there—your new, dynamic can't-be-beat card is nearly a reality. Having done the soul searching necessary to define your message, and then weighed the limitless design options, you have it figured out. Now, to the printer...

Not so fast—you should have involved your printer much earlier. The time to talk with him is at the point when you are still exploring a variety of options. He's in the best position to provide practical advice that will simplify (oh yes, they can be simplified) your remaining steps.

Your printer is your partner in preparing your new business image. He can enhance your intended product—or leave it a near miss. Involve him early enough in the design process to clarify the practical issues. Look at the print shop's display of examples that it has done for others. Not only will they show features that can be modified for your needs, they also provide clues to the quality of the work done by the shop. Are they examples you'd be proud to use yourself? Inquire about effects you like, and whether they would work for you.

Invite the printer's reaction to several of the styles and options you are considering. If you've already collected model cards, take them along. Often, there are several ways to achieve similar effects, at very different prices. Here is the person who knows the tricks of the trade, who can give the intended card a high-quality look. With a few words he'll provide precise information that will make you rethink some possibilities or consider new ones. For example, he may be aware of promotions for full color printing for no more cost than a one- or two-color job would be. A dose of practical, press-related advice can ground the concepts that have been floating through your head.

Your printer sees a lot of good and bad cards; it's part of his job. Get him to talk about traits of good cards or suggestions on ways to improve yours. Even if he's not directly involved in developing the design, he's usually glad to point out potential errors that may lead to problems or unnecessary costs at the production stage. If you're only making minor modifications to your present card, the printer's staff can execute revisions very reasonably.

As with your designer, your printer's job is to help you look good. And he can do that better if you develop an on-going relationship. The printer wants a long-term, repeat customer; you want an expert who understands your needs. Think of printing your card not as a simple printing job, but as a step toward establishing your business identity. You will find that there are abundant payoffs from building a working relationship with your printer. Such collaboration will eliminate haphazard or duplicated printing costs and lead to more "bang for the buck." Also, "regulars" routinely receive preferred treatment.

CONSIDER PRINTING COSTS
Talk Dollars Early

The initial contact is the time to bring up expense, even though you're only talking ballpark figures. Find out how much various combinations of options would add to your printing bill. Figure out which of the choices you're considering provide the best value.

With your printer's advice, you're more likely to find cost-effective methods to achieve the eye-catching effects you want.

The more your printer understands your goal or image, the more his involvement helps you get your pieces assembled as part of a coordinated program—even if it is being achieved one project at a time. Some of the costs incurred for the card (like logo design or custom dies) are reused in many other ways, and should not occur again. So, don't think only about what the card is costing, but consider the reusable elements of identity you've captured.

The expense of having a unifying style is not great, but the impact is impressive! Whatever the design style (theme, motif, logo, slogan, etc.) you've developed, it should reappear on all your printing. Continue using the unifying elements of design, color, typestyle, paper, and texture for everything you subsequently print. Printing all of the pieces at the same time minimizes extra color charges, as well as some of the set-up costs. Economies of scale further reduce the overall expense to the point that a dramatic effect often costs no more than piecemeal printing. Careful planning and collaboration with your printer is sure to provide extra benefits at little or no additional cost.

Your printer can be anything from a quick copy shop or one-man offset operation in your neighborhood to a multi-million dollar press with a staff of hundreds. Each type of printer has advantages and disadvantages, from personal and handy, to complex and sophisticated. The costs of operating the different kinds of equipment dictate what a particular printer does most effectively. That's part of the reason why an early discussion with him regarding costs and other matters is so important.

Understand the Bidding Process

By the time your card design is complete, you have made a variety of decisions regarding the appearance of your intended card. These are then translated into specifications, which tell the printer what you require, and are used to determine the steps and costs for your job. Good specifications are stated clearly, accurately, and completely. They will be used for getting bids and, later, to verify that the job is complete.

Your specifications should:

- ☐ Be specific and precise
- ☐ Be used for getting bids, and provide a basis for comparing them
- ☐ Show all the things that the printer needs to know to make a bid, and be identical for each printer who bids (compare apples to apples)
- ☐ Be given to more than one printer since costs of services vary greatly
- ☐ Permit a breakdown of cost components
- ☐ Stipulate quantity, color (number of inks, paper weight and color, maybe state a specific brand) and any special needs
- ☐ Specify approximate time frames and delivery date
- ☐ Eliminate misunderstandings by being clear and using terms that printers relate to
- ☐ Reduce surprises or eliminate unintended extras
- ☐ Permit accurate budgeting of costs; avoid cost overruns
- ☐ Track changes, if made during the job
- ☐ Simplify payment when job is complete
- ☐ Provide a checklist for what is delivered

Ways to Keep Printing Costs Down

Since you're planning a long-term relationship, talk to your printer about other upcoming printing needs and your budget restraints. Count on him to save you money in a variety of ways:

- □ Print larger press runs that dramatically reduce the per-piece rate
- □ Select options that require fewer press preparation stages or are less labor intensive
- □ Schedule your projects during slow or low-volume periods
- □ Eliminate some set-up charges; avoid duplication
- □ Schedule projects when it can be part of a press run that includes similar projects
- □ Schedule your project when you can benefit from specials or discounts
- □ Secure paper or other components when they are discounted or discontinued; query about your printer's house stock or odd lots
- □ Help to get the best rates for design or sub-contracted services
- □ Use new technologies to reduce labor or pre-press costs—like printing directly from disk
- □ Print and store materials, masters, and portions of projects until they are customized or needed
- □ Do as many things with the printer's in-house staff as possible
- □ Print blanks, complicated or costly parts at one time, to be customized as needed

When you adopt a paper and cardstock as part of your business image, do not just think about the printing to be done now. Paper manufacturers change their stock from time to time, and you may be unable to match the paper you have been using. If you can, stock up on matching paper, envelopes, and cardstock, so it will continue to be available for printing projects down the road. If your antici-pated needs are great enough, you might even be able to negotiate a volume discount.

TAKE TIME INTO ACCOUNT
Budget Time as Carefully as Costs

Printing a card order is actually a series of steps, and they take time. Even in the optimal situation, where the job comes to the printer truly "ready to go," the cards will seldom be ready as quickly as the customer had hoped. Few customers understand all that must be done between the time the order comes in and when it goes out the printer's door.

Negotiate the time frame for completion as carefully as you did the bid options and cost calculations. Make sure your expectations are realistic. Start the project before you're in a "gotta have it right away" mode. If there is an upcoming event, begin weeks rather than days ahead, so there is less stress on everyone. If you're still involved with a design professional, allow even more time for her to com-plete her part and bring all the assembled elements to the printer. When you and your printer work together within a realistic time frame, you'll have less anxiety, and probably fewer mistakes.

In a process called pre-press, printers convert camera-ready copy to printing plates. In a simple job, like most business cards, prepress may only require one step. However, in a complex job, pre-press can encompass assembling type, making negatives and color separations—and then making the plates for the press.

A recurring frustration for printers results when customers don't do their part when they agree to, and then lean on them to make up the time lost. There are many details required in preparing a printed piece. Give yourself a checklist that includes your own timeline, so that all of the parts you're responsible for arrive at the printer **before the time crunch.**

What "Camera-Ready" Means

- Everything is there, ready to be photographed and turned into printing plates
- All the graphics and text are in place, with size and layout finalized
- Instructions are clear and specific
- The printer does not have to do anything except make the necessary plates to have the project ready to print
- Colors are indicated
- Everything is straight and precisely placed

The camera-ready boards and any dies used belong to the customer. They can be returned to the customer or the printer can store them for you. The plates used in the job usually belong to the printer. Depending on the job or the equipment used, the plate can be metal or a less permanent material. Metal plates are able to be used on future printing jobs, but cost more to generate. Other materials are not retained, and must be re-generated when there are reprints.

Steps That Take Time at the Printshop

- Getting the project to "camera ready," unless it arrives that way
- Getting any custom input from the designer (or anyone else involved)
- Performing prepress activities—stripping, camera work, making plates, etc.
- Ordering special paper, stocks, or inks
- Getting ink colors matched or mixed
- Preparing dies for embossing, hot stamping, die cuts
- Scheduling the project with other jobs (sequence often dictated by the limits of the equipment or the complexity of a particular job)

- Adjusting for poor planning, whether the customer's or the printer's
- Preparing proofs and getting approvals, permissions, or releases
- Incorporating any last-minute changes
- Correcting any errors caught at the proof or color match stages
- Printing the job; press time
- Changing plates if a split run (cards printed for more than one person)
- Allowing inks to dry between press runs
- Waiting for work to come back from subcontractors for stages not done in-house (like lamination or foil stamping)
- Additional press runs for special effects, two-sided, multiple colors, etc.
- Folding or scoring
- Wash up, ink changes
- Doing special effects, like embossing or foiling

Watch for Problems That Cause Delays (submitting computer files)

Time gremlins lurk in any project, causing complications that throw it off track. Such delays are frustrating for both the customer and the printer. The Graphic Arts Technical Foundation researched the most frequent problems that arise when digital files (computer input) arrive at the printer. They found that a remarkable 57 percent (based on a thousand cases) had problems that caused production delays and/or increased costs. Of the 27 potential problems often encountered, they identified the ten worst offenders.

Ten Most Frequent Problems with Computer Files Supplied to Printers

"1. Missing or incorrect fonts (22.2%)

2. Missing or incorrect trapping (11.5%)—[relates to the way colors overlap]

3. Files defined with incorrect color—e.g. RGB [red, green, blue] versus CMYK [cyan, magenta, yellow, black] (10.9%)

4. Scans supplied in wrong file format (7.8%)

5. Incorrect page settings or page setup (7.4%)

6. Graphics not linked (5.2%)

7. Incorrectly defined or undefined bleeds (5.2%)

8. No laser proof supplied (4.6%)

9. Missing graphics (4.5%)

10. Resolution too high or too low in customer-supplied scans (3.2%)"[1]

Changes in technology may reduce some problems, but are responsible for causing others. Be careful that you or your card designer avoid such pitfalls. A camera-ready layout sidesteps these problems, but may not be suitable for all your input. Many projects include some computer files (since designers frequently use them for visual elements and layout), and they reduce required steps at the print shop. For example, some equipment permits the card to be printed directly from computer disk, without the expense or delays of color separations and printing plates. Most of these delays won't arise if you provide careful specifications and verify the printer's parameters prior to submitting the project.

Avoid Imposing Unrealistic Expectations on Your Printer

☐ I need this tomorrow; I'm sorry I couldn't get this to you when I said, but the time got used up

☐ I'm in a time bind! This is a crisis! My job is on the line! But the conference is tomorrow!

☐ Can't you just put my job at the front?

- But, I only need a few cards
- Sure it's camera ready—can't you read my sketch?
- You mean you can't just touch it up a little?
- What do you mean, that's gonna cost extra?
- Just add a little artwork here and there to fix it up
- Oh, I don't care—just jazz it up
- I'm on a real tight budget, but I want it to look like this (a very expensive effect)

Take Care in Checking the Proof

Between the time that you bring the job to the printer and it is put on the press, the printer will prepare a press proof for your approval. This will show **exactly** what your completed printed piece will look like. You will be notified to come examine the proof, and the job will be held until you have **approved the proof in writing**. This is your last chance to catch errors or make adjustments. Anything not caught at this stage could require reprinting the entire job—at your expense. When a card arrives for printing truly camera ready, a proof is usually unnecessary.

Steps to Check a Proof

- Take your time; don't hurry, even if a deadline is looming
- Carefully check every word (letter by letter) and each number (digit by digit)
- Compare the proof with the original and with a list of your addresses and phone numbers
- Make sure that any graphics are the right size and orientation
- Check each feature, line, and symbol
- Check placement, size, and alignment
- Notice the percentages of screens, bleeds, borders, and any special features

- Make certain photographs are in focus, scaled and cropped correctly, and facing the right direction
- Check your colors; if the exact shade of color is critical request a match print or a progressive (with 4-color process); notice how colors line up to each other (gaps or overlaps)
- Write any corrections on the proof in a bright color; circle any flaw, broken letter, or errors; be explicit about changes
- Compare with the prior proof and comments, if this is a correction of a prior flawed proof
- Confirm direction of folds or cuts, back printing or finishing steps
- Clarify anything that is not the way you wanted or expected; questions now avoid errors later
- Determine whether there will be additional costs for changes or corrections, and who will pay for them
- Only after you're fully satisfied that it is totally correct should you sign the proof

PRINTING PROCEDURES

Types of Printing Processes
an * indicates those most in use for business cards

- Thermography*—raised printing; heat sensitive inks
- Offset lithography*—flat printing
- Digital printing—direct from a computer disk
- Silk screen—artistic effects
- Engraving—depressed plate printing; shows fine details
- Lasergraphics—computer printers; self-designed and printed cards

- Photocopiers

- Photo process—not printed on a press, but is really a photograph printed from a computer design (See Chapter 7 on photography options.), permits full-color cards

Most small print shops use offset lithography as the primary printing method. Thermography (raised printing) has become very popular, but such orders are usually sent out to firms that specialize in it. Lithographic presses handle illustrations and colors easily. Plates are inexpensive (but are not kept for future jobs).

Most business cards are printed by offset lithography, which permits various colors to be used. Lithography is based on the simple scientific principle that oil and water do not mix. The non-image area on the printing plats is kept wet. As the printing press turns, the rollers "ink" the image area, then transfer that image to the stock.

Printing Procedures that Require Additional Attention
Screens

Screens are always designated by a percentage of ink. (See information in Chapter 9 on the table of screen percentages.) These are often used as backgrounds, or with some other pattern dominant. Use screens of your basic color and vary the percentages so the printed piece will look like more colors. By overlapping screens of two colors, more colors can be created. For example, overlapping red and black creates burgundy. Please note, the screen angles must be carefully planned to avoid moiré patterns. Ask your printer how to handle this.

*Black on
white textured
stock*

Close Register

Whenever two colors or effects touch, careful printing adjustments are required to avoid overlapping images or gaps between them. Close register can increase the printing costs. The way close register is handled is part of the planning with color, duotones or overlays.

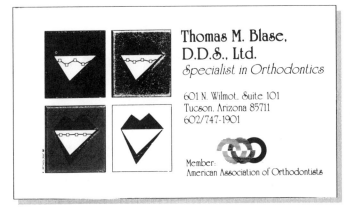

*Four color
process (full
color) and
each square
and mouth is
embossed;
black ink on
white stock*

Courtesy the Business Card Archives

All the flags
are in their
appropriate
colors; four
color process
(full color);
text is black
on glossy
white stock

Engraving Is in Its Own Class

Engraving is unsurpassed for precision and character definition. The art and type are embossed into the paper with a recessed etched plate, which results in an embossed printed image on the surface of the paper. It is no longer the common method of printing, since it uses metal plates and labor-intensive printing procedures. Although there in an initial cost for dies, these can be used over and over. However, it leaves an impression of high standards and refinement, which makes it the proper choice when quality is critical. (See more on engraving in Chapter 9, when you have to be impeccable.)

THE CLUB AT LAS CAMPANAS

JEFF RAU • HEAD GOLF PROFESSIONAL

LAS CAMPANAS SANTA FE
132 CLUBHOUSE DRIVE • SANTA FE, NEW MEXICO 87501
505 995 3535 • FAX 505 995 1032 • 800 241 9400

Gold logo and
black engrav-
ing on heavy
white stock

MICHAEL BEAN   INTAGLIO PRINTING

3609 TODDSBURY LANE
OLNEY, MD 20832   (301) 774-7672

Engraved card in black on off-white stock

Courtesy the Business Card Archives

Note the really fine details on the image

Bleeds

As mentioned in Chapter 9, when printing goes to the very edge of the paper, it is called a bleed. The printing equipment requires a small edge to carry the paper through the print path. Therefore, when there are bleeds, the printer must print on slightly larger paper, so that the edge can be cut away, letting the image "bleed" off the edge. Bleeds add to the printing expense because more stock is required and more trimming must be done.

Two-Sided Cards

When there is printing on both sides of the card, it must make at least two passes through the printing press. Colors or special features may increase the number of press runs further. Inks have to dry between the stages, lengthening the time for completion.

Specialty Inks

Specialty inks, like metallic inks or scented inks, (excluding colored inks, which are discussed below) usually must be secured especially for your project and will require set-up and wash-up charges. The effects are likely to be dramatic enough to warrant the additional expense.

Iridescent purple ink on lavender stock

Folded, Glued, Die Cut Cards, or Other Special Effects

Such options are infinite, so require careful planning and communication from the beginning of the project. If these are integral to the effect you want, they should be thought through from the first step. Careful coordination of all production details will require extra attention.

CONTINENTAL CIRCUITS CORP.

3502 East Roeser Rd
Phoenix, Arizona 85040
Phone (602) 232-9190 ext.1156
Nabeel Jawlani   Fax (602) 268-0208
Manufacturing Engineer   Pager (602) 450-9699

Bright purple ink on embossed logo, crossed with foiled copper lines; company name is embossed and foiled; text is engraved in black on heavy white stock

This card took at least four press runs: colored ink, embossing, foil stamping and engraving, but the effect is stunning! It looks like a circuit board, just the thing for a circuit manufacturer.

Embossing, Debossing, and Foils

Special effects are signals of high quality because they require specialized design services, the purchase of customized dies, plus added production costs. (See Chapter 9 on special effects.) Since these techniques are not provided by most print shops, you need to allow extra time for die preparation, as well as contracting the services out. However, the effects are usually worth the additional expense and scream "Notice me!"

COLOR PRINTING REQUIRES EXTRA CARE
Every Card Has a Color—Even If It Is Black

When no color is specified, that means the job will be printed in black, the standard default ink color.

Color choices for your card include:

- Black printing only
- One color card, but that color is not black
- Two color card—black, plus one other color (which you specify)
- Two color card—specify each color
- Full-color card—four-color process (CMYK) or photographic process
- Specific shade of color—PANTONE MATCHING SYSTEM or other color system
- Special inks, like metallic ink, which can be in addition to any of the above

Use the PANTONE MATCHING SYSTEM® for Specific Shades

Most color printed on business cards is spot color, with the color providing an accent or focal point. It makes the card more interesting. Contrast that with a full-color card, showing all the shades provided in real life. The printer uses different methods of achieving these different effects. These alternatives should be addressed at the initial design stage and their respective costs considered.

Some printers offer simple color options and a set rate for them: green, red, blue, brown, etc. In such cases, you select the color offered, but get no choice of the shade provided. Alternately, you may specify a particular shade of color or attempt to match an existing color. In those cases, you are likely to be handed a PANTONE Color Formula Guide. It contains a thousand shades and permits you to designate a particular shade, which will be indicated with a specific number. Even with a number specified, some shades fall between the colors shown, so sometimes colors must still be mixed. Also, the inks will look different depending on whether they are printed on coated (glossy) or uncoated (textured) stock.

MoneyCreek

Internet Web Development
Virtual Mall/Site Management

D. McGuire, Managing General Partner
602-954-7966 Voice/Fax
http://www.moneycreek.com

Yellow circle on horizon graduating to caramel; black silhouette and text in black on white

PANTONE MATCHING SYSTEM shades are widely available through your printer, and will be identical through any printer you select. Therefore, having a consistent color is not a matter of hit or miss. As part of the selection of your business image, include a color that will be consistently used on all future printed materials.

Full-Color Printing—Four-Color Process

The four-color process method of producing full-color illustrations depends on creating an image out of tiny dots. If you look closely at the pictures in a newspaper, you can see that they are made up of small dots. Color images are created the same way, but the dots are of different colors. The colors in four-color process are cyan (medium greenish blue), magenta (hot pink), yellow, and black, which can be printed in various combinations to create almost every color. Black provides detail and shadow. Together these shades provide a full-color effect.

In order to be printed, the original image is photographed through a filter, which changes a continuous image into a series of dots. For a full-color image, the image is photographed four times. Each time uses a different filter, and creates an image of one of the four colors. The resulting four images are each in a different color, made up of a series of dots. These are called color separations. The images are printed on top of each other, and the resulting combination of dots looks very much like the original image. When this method is used, it is critical that the colors be carefully balanced.

Likewise, duotones are produced when the image is black and one other color (for the lighter tones). In that case it is really a two-color process, which offers greater depth and richness to the design.

THE FRENCH PRESS
The Finest in Specialty Foods

Réjane Jehano

PO BOX 408
RUTHERFORD, CA 94573
(209) 394-2944
FAX: (209) 394-7622
DIRECT LINE: (707) 963-9220
FAX: (707) 963-6021

Full color picture of man primarily in shades of orange and brown; black text on light yellow stock

Flowers are full color with black print on glossy white stock

Printing Customs

Printing Industry of America (PIA) a professional organization, has developed eighteen printing guidelines, which are widely used throughout the industry. Printers are not obligated to follow them, but most do. These guidelines are often printed on the back of the quotations and they are summarized below.

Custom 1:   Prices are valid for sixty days.

Custom 2:   If you cancel an order, you must pay for the goods and services to the date (preferably in writing) of cancellation.

Custom 3:   Experimental or custom work will be charged at prevailing rates and may not be used until the applicable charges are paid.

Custom 4:   All creative work done by the printer, and not expressly identified and included in the selling price, will remain as the printer's exclusive property. To use it at any point thereafter, you need to pay for the rights (unless you previously negotiated for them).

Custom 5:   New quotations will be submitted if the original art or copy varies from the description in the original, signed quotations.

Custom 6:   All preparatory materials, like production artwork or plates will remain the property of the printer.

Custom 7:   Alterations will be charged at current rates.

Custom 8: The printer is not liable for any errors unless you identify those errors on a signed pre-press proof; verbal instructions do not count.

Custom 9: Unless specifically provided in the quotation, charges for press proofs will be at the going rates. Press time lost due to customer delays or customer changes will be charged at current rates.

Custom 10: A reasonable variation from the color proofs to the press sheets is acceptable due to a variety of production factors like equipment, inks, paper or printing operations.

Custom 11: Overruns or underruns will not exceed ten percent and the actual quantity delivered will be billed for.

Custom 12: The printer will carry insurance to cover all the customer's property while it is in the printer's possession.

Custom 13: Unless otherwise specified, the price quoted is for a single shipment, without storage. Special shipping arrangements will be billed for. Materials delivered from the customer or designated suppliers are verified with delivery tickets regarding cartons, packages, or items shown only. The printer will not be liable for the accuracy of quantities of materials based on tickets from the customer or designated suppliers. The title for the finished work will pass to the customer upon delivery or full payment, whichever comes first.

Custom 14: Production schedules will be adhered to by the printer and the customer unless affected by actions beyond the control of either. The final delivery date will be re-negotiated if the customer does not adhere to the production schedule.

Custom 15: Customer-furnished materials (i.e., inks, film, paper, artwork) must be manufactured, packed and delivered to the printer's specifications. The printer can charge for specification deficiencies.

Custom 16: Payment must be made according to the terms of the quotation or invoice, unless otherwise made in writing. Claims for defects, damages, or shortage must be made by the customer in writing within fifteen days or the job will be deemed acceptable.

Custom 17: The printer is liable for losing or damaging a customer's property, but liability is limited to the selling price of the damaged goods and not consequential damages, such as profits or losses. As security for payment, the printer has the right to put a lien on the goods held, including work in progress.

Custom 18: The printer is not responsible for violation of copyright, libel, invasion of privacy, or other problems with materials provided by the customer. The customer is responsible for defending a printer being sued over the reproduction of originals or copy provided by the customer.

Print Blanks or Shells If There Are Numerous Employees

Every employee should have a *current* business card, but it isn't easy to keep up with personnel changes. Every promotion is important for the employee who receives it, and is often accompanied by a new title or a change of department. The promotion should be symbolized by an updated card. Then consider all the other employee changes that can occur: new employee, marriage and name change, divorce and name change. As more contact information is added to a card, like pager or e-mail addresses, more frequent card reprinting will be needed. Only about half of the people will be using the same card a year from now.

Print blanks or shells in large numbers, that will be customized with a single press run as such changes are required. Shells are cards printed with the company name and logo. They include any expensive or time-consuming special effects that are used regularly on the company's business cards. Later the individual's name and title can be printed, enabling a quick turn-around time. Blanks are cost effective and time saving, especially when it involves a complex card requiring numerous colors or extensive press time.

Lamination and Special Finishes

Lamination is achieved by putting a plastic film over a surface. It makes the card waterproof and impervious to normal wear and tear. It's also impressive. There are a variety of weights of laminates. Some companies put one kind of film on the front of the card and a different one on the back, which permits the receiver to write on it.

REPRINTING YOUR CARDS
Preparing to Reprint Existing Cards

As you get down to the bottom of your box of cards, you need to make a decision. Will you reprint exactly what you have or make some modifications? If you keep the identical card, it's just a trip back to the printer. Whether it is the same printer or another, you need to determine whether the prior artwork is still available. Assuming the prior printer kept your materials, you only need to inquire about the availability of the prior stock and get a current price quote. Even if nothing has changed, consider if the same card can be improved with spot color or addition of foil, for example. Such changes will change the look, while keeping the layout unchanged.

If modifications are minor, the printer is equipped to make alterations or set new type. Usually the costs for such services is small. Don't expect a major redesign, however. Most print shops are limited in their scope of design services. However, they are "in the business," so will be able to make appropriate referrals or sub-contract some services on your behalf.

To Recap

Your printer is an important part of your card design team. Get printing feedback before you finalize the design. Allow enough time for the printer to do all that is required to get your card done "right." Develop a relationship with a printer who understands your needs, and think beyond a single print job.

Section III

Put Your Card to Work— Make Your Ambassador Hustle

Now you're ready! You've figured out the images and messages to make you both unique and desirable. You've waded through the dismaying process of developing a card and considered more options than you would ever have suspected. So, it's time for the payback.

Not so fast—you've got a freshly-printed stack of exquisite cards, but they still have not found their way into the *right* hands. This final section puts the emphasis on getting your card out to contacts of all sorts. Don't ignore all the cards you received from others; they're valuable contacts. After all, you've gotten one card back for almost every one you've handed out. Since a box holds 1,000...

Chapter 12 explores ways to give cards more effectively, and the next chapter discusses what to do with the ones you accumulate. Chapter 14 considers ways to use your card in the international arena. Other countries place great value on business cards and the experience of exchanging them. To deal with foreign countries requires an awareness of what is expected and, especially, what should **not** be done.

The emphasis shifts from the individual businesses to the largest possible perspective (Chapter 16). Both the Business Card Archives and the Business Card Museum chronicle the impact of our culture upon business cards—and vice versa. Our history, whether individually or collectively, is reflected through the business cards we use. But businesses cards also have a history of their own, as shown in Chapter 15. So, the humble business card becomes a lens through which we view the ongoing changes in printing and marketing, messages beyond those that that the card creator had intended.

Section Table of Contents

Chapter 12

Get Your Cards Out There—Sales, Networking, and Trade Shows

A Business Card Is a Sales Tool

Every business or organization needs to make sales or generate income in some way. Unless money changes hands, a company cannot stay in business. That is even true for non-profit organizations or those in the public sector. Whether or not there is a profit motive at work, keeping up a flow of funds must always be a concern. Each of them must influence someone to "buy" what they provide, because without enough money, the operation will flounder and eventually founder.

Ways businesses generate money

- Stores sell products to their customers
- Consultants sell services to their clients
- Government agencies must sell their operations to the legislature or funding authorities, and (sometimes) to the public
- Charities must sell a vision coupled with services to its contributors

So the business (in whatever form or arena) needs to do all the many things to encourage people to vote for it with their dollars. Somewhere in that equation, getting the business card into the "right hands" becomes important.

The card helps to sell the business, but it also sells the one who bears it. If someone reacts positively toward the person named on the card, it is reflected in their feelings toward the business, and vice versa.

Rules for Giving Your Business Cards

- ☐ Consider every business encounter as an opportunity to create or reinforce a strong positive impression, and offer a card when appropriate

- ☐ Don't run out of cards; carry plenty, with an extra supply in your briefcase or car

- ☐ Don't give dirty, worn, dog-eared or crossed-out cards

- ☐ Men should not leave their cards in their billfolds, where they sit on the cards (which adds a characteristic curved or a crushed appearance)

- ☐ Don't hesitate to give a contact another one of your cards from time to time

- ☐ Never give a card without taking the time to make a positive personal connection: a few warm words, a firm handshake, and eye contact

- ☐ Make comments about your card or something on it—draw attention to the card; write on it

- ☐ Remember, your card does you no good in your drawer or pocket; pass it on

- ☐ Don't wear an outfit without two pockets, one with cards to be given out and the other one for cards you receive

- ☐ Have a follow-up strategy—and follow it, and follow it, and follow it

- ☐ Treat the other person's card as a reminder of them; write an impression or comment on the back as soon as you have a spare moment

There are two schools of thought, give your card to everyone you meet, trusting that some will find their way into the "right hands." The other is to be discerning about how and to whom you impart your card. Indiscriminate passing out of cards may be perceived as overzealous or unprofessional. There are merits to both of these approaches, but you need to form your own strategy and decide what works for your business. Again, it's a matter of finding a suitable balance and knowing what is appropriate.

Include your card whenever you send sales literature or correspondence. It is likely to be filed in another filing system than the letter files, so could end up doing double duty for you. Letting the card drift free in the envelope often means it gets overlooked. Although staples, paper clips, tape or glue will all work, be careful how they are attached. They may deface your card. There are those who swear by a drop of rubber cement, since it can be rubbed off when the card is removed. Using Scotch® Brand Removable Tape also lets the receiver detach the card without mutilating it. Yet another option is the Card-It®, which cuts two diagonal mounting slots to hold your card in place. It will work on any size or weight of paper or cover stock (See the Resource section.), so you can attach your card to almost anything.

Don't Just Give Your Card—Bestow It

Cards are seldom given or received without some personal contact. The experience of exchanging cards is important for establishing or reinforcing a concrete personal relationship. The fact that you give your card out personally makes it the most targeted of marketing strategies. Take the time to make it a true exchange—of yourself, of words, of time. Whenever you give a card you are making a gift of yourself. Make it significant.

Such social rituals are important to establish trust and a personal awareness of each other. If you do not find positive ways to connect to those who could matter to your business, your card will be unable to re-establish them later. Americans are usually quite open and friendly in meeting new people, so we are often careless about such rituals of recognition. However, they serve a variety of purposes, and are far from "small talk." They set the tone and basis for further relationships. (See Chapter 1 on making impressions.) Other cultures consider these preliminaries so vital that they will not commence business unless they are satisfactorily completed. (See Chapter 14 on using your business card when conducting international business.) Don't look at such niceties as obligations or conventions, but rather enjoy them as pleasant encounters.

A colleague once advised, never just hand out your card. Instead, turn it toward the other person and s-l-o-w-l-y **bestow your card** upon them, as you would convey a gift. And indeed you are doing so. It works even better if you use both hands. The delay removes the experience from the rushed pace of life. The carefully paced exchange creates an island of calm, and allows you to connect in a refreshing way. Even if the entire experience is fleeting, the sense of ceremony makes it memorable.

Use an Attention Getter to Give Your Card

Even an "ordinary" card can become memorable if presented in a noteworthy way. If you want to attract attention, present your card in a fun manner. Busicards® (a folded humorous carrier for your card, illustrated below) were developed by Walt Hendrickson, a well-known cartoonist. They create a positive impression and provide room for a personal note. (See Resource Section.)

Your card inside

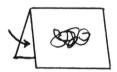

If you really want to get attention, consider card carriers that make a sound: applause, ringing phone, trumpet fanfare, drumroll and more from Clegg. (See Resource Section.) These carriers also can have flashing lights.

Jot/a/Card®

Another way to adapt your card to a note is by using a Jot/a/CARD, which is a perforated card and note that can be separated once it is written on. It's just the thing to show you're attentive to details. (See Resource Section.)

The

Plus

a collection of products from Business Cards Plus

MIKE KEMPLE
QUALITY SERVICE / SALES

(616) 327-7727 • MI WATS 800-875-7727

business cards plus

Jot/a/CARD® International & US Patents Pending

·   *Perforation*

"A Service Oriented Company Specializing
In Thermography, Foiling & Embossing"

MIKE KEMPLE
QUALITY SERVICE / SALES

8938 SHAVER ROAD
KALAMAZOO, MICHIGAN 49002
(616) 327-7727 • MI WATS 800-875-7727

business cards plus

Building Referrals Builds the Business

Every kind of business can benefit from referrals and word-of-mouth dialogue. Nourish your referral sources. (See Chapter 4 on the reasons why people refer business.) Keep track of the ways your customers and clients find you. Acknowledge and reward those who sent them; and give them every incentive to continue. Provide feedback, so they know that you were able to come through.

If you aren't getting referrals, explore ways to get more. In some businesses, nearly all the clientele come through referrals. By the same token, part of your expertise, what you have to offer to your clients and customers is your insider knowledge about who they should go to for what you don't provide. When you can tell them, "Here is someone who can provide what you need," they will trust that person to the extent they already trust you. That means they seek her out confidently—she comes recommended.

You gain reflected glory if the company where you send business is really good, but may get burned if it isn't. It is with that sense of responsibility that we tend to trust the people who have treated us (or those we know) right. Making referrals is one of services that increases your expertise and trustworthiness. Talk to those to whom you make referrals, and see how to make it a two-way street.

With a Little Help From Some Friends

Constantly think of ways to get your card into the hands of more people who need what you provide. Think not only of those who can use your services, but those who are in a position to pass your cards along to their contacts. Then broaden their exposure as you pass their cards on as well.

Ways to get cards into more hands:

- ☐ Card dispenser for your own card at your place of business
- ☐ Card carrier on your person (pocket or purse) always filled and ready for any occasion

- Random display of cards at your business; includes all sorts of businesses
- Affinity display at your business where you provide cards for related businesses as well as your own. For example, a person in the wedding business has a photographer, printer, disc jockey, caterer, and anyone else who you would need for a wedding; it shows only one provider for each category, and they all have a similar display promoting each other
- Affinity display for businesses that are located close to each other, like within a shopping center; can be tied to other cross-marketing activities like sidewalk sales and shared advertising
- Cards inserted in everything that you send out with postage, figuring that at least some of them will get passed along; include an offer, bonus, etc. on the card to bring people in
- Organizations where you place your card at every place or seat, so everyone in attendance leaves with a card from everyone who is there
- Networking, card exchange groups or leads organizations that gather specifically to refer business to each other; make a flier of all the member's cards so everyone knows who is involved, as illustrated on the next page.

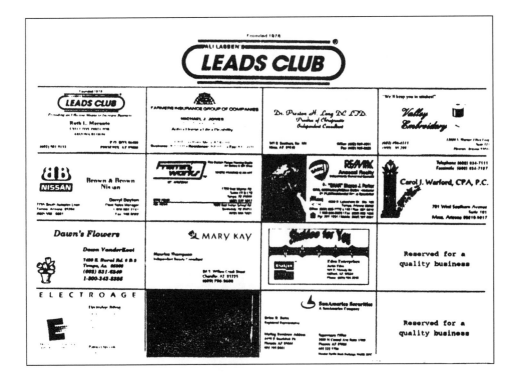

Turn-Off Cards and Ignore Me Cards

A businessman showed me a lovely, well-designed card. After receiving a favorable reaction he pulled out his "other card." He explained that one style was for the people he cared about developing a relationship with, while the other style was for those he didn't care about. He was deliberately using a vanilla pudding card to become invisible.

Sometimes, people do not want to be noticed or prefer to discourage certain business contacts. They may *intentionally* use a card that makes them appear to be unattractive (with a bland or negative message). With such a strategy, they make an evaluation of their contacts and decide who gets the good one and who gets the kiss-off card.

"When You Want To Eat
Your Competition Alive"

Piranha Marketing, Inc.

Joe Polish, President
Tony Policci, Consultant
Eunice Miller, Consultant

1801 S Jentilly Lane Suite C-20 • Tempe, Arizona 85281

Tel. (602)858-0008 • Fax (602)858-0004 • E-mail polish@joe polish.com

*Two-sided
card...*

WARNING:
5 Things You Need To Know About Joe Polish and Piranha

1. Joe Polish is blunt, straightforward and may NOT tell you what you want to hear.
2. Only those very serious about making money, utilizing unusual and exceptionally effective marketing strategies, and those really ready to change should contact Joe. His time is extremely valuable and much in demand. Please do not waste his time or yours with casual curiosity.
3. The best ways to initially communicate with Joe personally are via FAX or e-mail. He rarely takes unscheduled calls. However, he does have an excellent staff in place, they can be very helpful, and you are welcome to call them.
4. In many cases, staff or Joe will recommend books, courses or tools that best address your questions and needs. Individual consulting requires substantial investment, however many situations are well served by the products Joe has developed or obtained.
5. Do not be disappointed or frustrated by Joe's refusal to dispense free advice. Free advice is rarely a bargain for the recipient nor a fair return on investment and experience for the giver.

*...black print
on bright
yellow stock*

MAXIMIZE MEETINGS AND NETWORKING
Different Styles of Meetings

- Working a room—networking and mixer prior to a set program
- Organizational meetings—networking at scheduled events
- One on one—anywhere or any time
- Elevator meetings—strangers, brief random encounters
- Social situations—formal or informal
- Professional conferences, conventions, and training activities

❑ Corporate meetings with only employees in attendance—if the organization is large or has several locations, they may not know each other

Attend Events for the Business

How much money does your company spend on professional luncheons and meetings? It can add up quickly. Although such events can be a good investment for your company, the value increases sharply when you *use* the meetings intelligently and pursue a system that maximizes the benefits of being there. Track the benefits you and others on your staff receive from attending. Take every opportunity to be interesting to *all* you speak with. Even ho-hum events begin to sparkle because you attended and were there to show your business in the best light.

If you attend with a co-worker or friend, **never, never, never** spend your time together while you're there. Don't visit with each other—spread out to increase the number of contacts you each make. Don't sit at the same table or with old friends either. You're there to "do business" as a professional, not to pursue your social life. It is amazing to see how often all the people from the same business spend their time together, creating an impenetrable club that prevents anyone from relating to them. That sends the wrong message and a negative impression of the business, to boot.

Each event you attend has to compete with all the other organizations, seminars, and training sessions that are offered, not to mention preferred recreational activities. Each of them also takes time away from the office and competes with getting the real work done. Therefore, it is necessary to be selective about which organizations to join and how many events to attend. The unavoidable inconvenience, travel, and unavailability at the office are even more costly than the registration expenses. Make sure your company is getting its money's worth.

Once you decide to go, go with a determination that it well be worthwhile—and it will happen just that way. These events can be very cost effective, so use each event to broaden your circle of contacts. However, it is **not** enough just to show up—you need a plan for using those contacts. (See Chapter 13 on follow-up strategies.)

Identify Yourself at a Meeting

Stand up and state clearly and proudly: "Hello. My name is Pat Green, with The Way to Go Travel. You can count on us to get you there with a smile." Sparkle with personal warmth. Make a habit of stating the whole thing without hesitation. This is your moniker, your **verbal business card**. Follow through with your actual business card to reinforce the image you've just instilled in the minds of your listeners.

Your Self-Introduction Should Include:

- ☐ A greeting
- ☐ Your name
- ☐ A smile
- ☐ Your title, if relevant
- ☐ The name of your company and, if it is large, your department
- ☐ A slogan or tag line about the business, its location, products, services, etc.
- ☐ Any elaboration that time and circumstances permit about yourself, the service, philosophy, location, a special offer, etc.

In a one-on-one situation or small group, also add:

- ☐ A few words related to the others present
- ☐ A handshake
- ☐ Restate the person's name and react to his or her input
- ☐ Your observation of their reactions to what you've said

Jazz Up Company Cards

Stuck with generic, poorly-designed, one-size-fits-all company cards? Rarely is such a card ideal for everybody on the payroll. On the other hand, the company can't be expected to custom design a business card specifically for each employee. The card has a history reflecting the company's past, image, corporate culture, promotions, logo use, and philosophy. Further, the company may have invested a considerable sum of money and thought in its card design. Messing with the company image is usually considered bad form. There are, however, steps that an employee can take, often in the form of "suggestions." (See also Chapter 4, Personalize the Impersonal.)

If your company is large enough to have several departments, it might prove beneficial to suggest a "department card" that would more accurately reflect what the division or department does. Such a card would also extol the company image/mission/purpose by incorporating important parts of the company's generic business card. To be successful in this endeavor, your proposal should include the benefits that might accrue to the whole business through a department card. If this doesn't fly, try to get approval to slightly modify your company card—a simple addition such as a border, personal symbol, credentials, awards, etc. Most companies won't object if one adds, for instance, "Salesman of the Year," or "Member of such and such professional organization."

Some companies are so attached to their card design that they simply won't allow any tampering with what they feel best represents their image. It's probably neither wise nor conducive to lengthy employment, to inform the boss that you, the new hire, think the company card stinks and that you can design a better one. Discretion being the better part of corporate ladder-climbing, your purpose would be better served by leaving this book lying around where "they" (that hazy, vague, nebulous body of corporate decision-makers) can find it. Eventually it will wind up in the right hands, and *voilá*, a new, better card will emerge!

If all else fails, you can always personalize your generic, one-size-fits-all, company business card by simply writing on a personal message, home phone number, extra product or services information, or even a "10 percent off with card" offer. Your imagination is the only limiting factor in personal messages to be added to your company card. Just be sure that it's in good taste and appropriate for the occasion.

Never forget that *you* are the representative of the company and the one who happens to be present at the moment. You are creating the impression for both yourself and your company that will influence the course of future business contacts. Make it a strong one so that they remember you despite a ho-hum card. In spite of all has been said about your card's importance, it is ancillary to what you do for yourself through the sheer force of your personality.

Have Several Different Self-Identifying Scripts Ready

- The 7-second introduction
- The 15-second introduction with a hook
- The 30-second self-promotion
- About 5 minutes for extended social situations

These "scripts" should always be accompanied by your business card. Your time is brief, so this is not when you want to be impromptu. Create a sound bite about you and your company beforehand. Always be ready to deliver it on a moment's notice, because that's all you may have. Tailor it for the audience or circumstances. Practice each until your delivery is polished. It is very hard to estimate how long it takes to say something, unless you have actually timed several versions. As you do so, you also will find a natural and comfortable rhythm that will eliminate being at a "loss for words." You are trying to convey a sense of confidence that increases audience interest in you and your business. Seek out opportunities to speak up.

Prepare another type of sound bite. Start by stating a problem or issue, and then state how you or your product have solved, improved, or dealt with it. "You know what a problem exists about such and such. Well, we have been able to solve it." Their reaction will tell you whether you should go into further detail. For example, "You know how hard it is to eliminate bad checks. Well, we provide a check reader that eliminates bad or counterfeit checks at the time of purchase."

Capitalize on Face to Face

Use props, especially if you can tie it into yourself, your business, your slogan, etc. Having a prop on your person reminds them that you personify the business. It also makes you memorable, since you appeal to more physical senses and represent a coherent, multi-faceted image. Note and reinforce the reactions you receive. A person with a very effective card commented to me, "We know it's a great card because people always respond with surprise and appreciation." That's the kind of reaction you could get, also.

I always take the opportunity to make a comment about something on my card. Some capable salesmen say that they always write a personal note on the card, because then the other person feels you've given them something special. "Let me write my home phone number (back line number, etc.) on the card so you can call me any time." This is one argument for leaving your home phone number off the card, so that it becomes something personal, which you can offer selectively.

Patricia Fripp, a dynamic and well-known public speaker tells about how she built her business when she was a men's hair stylist, at a time before most people had heard of it. She would give each of her clients three cards along with specific instructions about what to do with them, "This card is for you; pass these others along to the next two people who tell you how great you look." It works. A friend credits following that piece of advice for the growth of her custom wedding gown business.

Seal It with a Handshake

A handshake is not just a social nicety; it establishes a sense of physical connection. A firm handshake is an essential sign of trust and acceptance. It acts as a very tangible body language where you touch, in reality, as well as symbolically. You're saying that you're sincere and friendly (in the historic sense, that you are unarmed, which may be more relevant in these violent times than we'd care to admit).

Don't offer a timid or wishy-washy handshake! Confidently thrust out your hand. Connect firmly with the other person all the way to the web of the thumbs. Then hold hands firmly, and shake up and down several times. Don't try a bone crusher, but also, don't waffle. Look the person in the eye, and say something such as, "It's pleasure to meet you" with total sincerity. I find it difficult to have confidence in a person who lacks a direct handshake—which puts him off to an uphill start.

Men sometimes avoid taking a woman's hand and just shake the fingers. This is inappropriate, unless cultural factors dictate otherwise. Treat women the same as men; your handshake should confirm an equal footing. The handshake is important even in the brief span when people pass each other. When the other person's hands are full, some other body part will have to do. Even shaking "hands" with a shoulder or a pinkie can still be symbolically effective.

Have a Strategy

- Experiment; try different cards and then track new business
- Treat other people's cards like you think they are important; cards are only "triggers" to remind them of you (and you of them), so make both memorable; don't expect the card to do all the work

- Have a parallel flyer handy to say the rest of the stuff that didn't fit on the card. Think of the card as the excerpt and the flyer as the expanded version, so make them complementary
- It's a two way street; show the other person what you want them to do: offer a referral or related information; look for an opportunity to cross market each other's products or services
- Tie your card to another service: call our 800 number to _____; fax us your _____; bring in this card and receive _____
- Bulletin boards are free put your card in appropriate places; also speak up when you are at a meeting that invites you to introduce yourself or tell what you do
- Leave a stack at relevant businesses; get extra cards to share with your customers

Code Your Follow-up Steps

It is easier to follow up with contacts if you have a system which helps you remember what you need to do for them. Aldona Ambler, a national consultant and trainer, has developed a method of bending the corners of cards as she receives them. Her system tells her what follow-up steps are required once she returns to her office. Through frequent speeches and consulting work, she encounters people in ways that make it inappropriate or inconvenient to make notes. Also, she doesn't like to break eye contact with people while they are talking with her.

While holding the person's card so that the name is horizontal and facing her, she folds a corner (or more than one corner) down as a reminder of what action the person wanted from her.

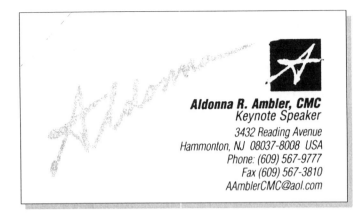

Two-sided card with baby blue signature and dark blue print on white stock

Aldonna R. Ambler, CMC
Keynote Speaker

3432 Reading Avenue
Hammonton, NJ 08037-8008 USA
Phone: (609) 567-9777
Fax (609) 567-3810
AAmblerCMC@aol.com

1. Upper left corner—requested appointment

2. Upper right corner, also—wants the appointment right away. If they are waffling about an appointment, she <u>un</u>bends the right corner.

3. Lower left corner—send them something

4. Lower right corner—problem, confused, miscellaneous requests

Occasionally, something serious or a threat to the business is encountered. In that case, she folds the card in half and deals the problem without delay.

After an event, she sorts the cards by the folded corners, and is able to take the next step smoothly. Since her staff knows the system, she can hand off the cards so they can provide the appropriate action. Consistency is critical (she's used the same system for over ten years). The method works best if you are undeviating about what the folded corners mean and then follow through on the encoded information promptly. It is even possible to tell later what steps have already been taken simply by looking at the way the card was folded.

The folded corner method can be adapted for other types of messages (mental prompting) that are relevant for your operations. The key is in the follow up. If you devise and maintain a folded-corner system, don't be surprised that people will be impressed by your memory.

If You Don't Provide a Card…

There are only three safe reasons for not using business cards. In one case, the person is such a powerful presence everyone knows who he is. Unfortunately, such notoriety only applies to a handful of people. The second strategy is to provide something much more significant than a card, like a book, package of useful material or product samples, which will be valued and kept.

The third reason for not offering a card is to maintain control. With that method, the person doesn't offer a card, but says, "Let me take *your* card and send you mine along with some relevant information." In that case, follow-up is essential! Those who use that system only send a card (along with whatever is appropriate) to someone who gives them one. If the prospect hesitates to give a card, that signals their lack of interest. Therefore, some preliminary screening has already been accomplished.

Any other reason for being caught without your card makes you seem to be unprepared or a newbie. Since you may not be taken seriously without a business card, even a poorly crafted one will serve you better than none at all.

Network Marketing Organizations Replicate Sales Skills

Network marketing, also called multi-level marketing (MLM), can be expected to continue as an accelerating trend, with an increasing impact on the economy. The wide variety of products and services distributed through network marketing companies creates millions of enthusiastic new salespeople. The ease of enrollment gets new members involved quickly. Usually, training is provided right away, so the newly enrolled member knows enough to promote the products while recruiting other participants. Because so many sales associates lack prior sales or small business experience, many are unaware of the many useful ways a business card can help to build their businesses.

To succeed in any network marketing program, it should be treated as your own small business—because it is. The word "network" means you sell initially to those who know you or to those who know those you know. Word-of-mouth advertising is vital! A business card helps to reinforce those links and reminds friends and relatives of what you provide. Improve your visibility among those who already see you often. Involve them in helping you to succeed, and remind them that you are serious about building your business. This is an arena where team-building skills are eventually rewarded. Make the best-looking card you can, and work diligently to pass lots of them along. As you make a determined effort to give your cards out unstintingly, you'll see the virtue of going through a boxful quickly.

MLM companies vary in their policies about business cards for associates. Some companies provide cards (for a charge) that are all alike except for the person's name and phone number. Personal deviations from the official card are not permitted. Other companies provide company logos and slogans that the salesperson may use on cards and flyers, but it's up to each person to design and print their own cards. Still other companies have no specific policy regarding cards or flyers.

Find out what your company's policy is regarding business cards, then strengthen your card in additional ways. For example, "We like referrals" or "Sales Leader" stickers can add color to your card, along with a specific call for action. Put your cards everywhere, from bulletin boards to inserting them with your bill payments. Anything that can be said about promoting network marketing companies also applies to franchise operations. Build your business by capitalizing on contacts that you already have. Constantly gather more contacts—and their cards. Organize them and follow up on them. (See Chapter 13 on following up.) Those stacks of cardboard are as important as your product line to the success of your MLM enterprise.

Consider Why People Ask for Your Card

- ☐ Do people ask for your card just to get rid of you? Are they trying to force closure?
- ☐ Evaluate the situation and your intuition as to whether the person really wants your card
- ☐ Trust your interpretation of the body language you are receiving; become aware of what level of relationship the person wants with you or your business; observe carefully
- ☐ If you know the card is going directly into the trash, politely pass on and avoid the charade of exchanging cards

Document the Event to Keep the Memory Fresh

Develop a short report form and complete it right after the event. By taking the trouble to note important contacts, you'll soon develop a sense of what meetings or strategies are most productive. Establish a practice of having a form completed by everyone from your company who attends. Follow up on any leads which may have been cultivated. You'll be surprised at the amount of business generated by networking at events, once you start keeping track. Just the act of paying attention increases the diligence of your staff—and thereby increases the quantity of such leads.

Information for event checklist:

- ☐ Event and sponsor
- ☐ Date and location
- ☐ Who attended: your company, general attendance
- ☐ Program, speaker, purpose of activity
- ☐ Cost to attend; distance, travel time, meeting time
- ☐ Follow up required
  With person met at the event
  Pass information from event to other employee(s) or contacts

- ☐ Suggestions; other action steps
- ☐ Benefits; resolutions
- ☐ Other relevant information

NETWORKING CARDS
Job Hunting and Resume Cards

Anyone who has need of a resume, should also prepare a business-card sized mini-resume. Considerable emphasis is placed upon developing a resume that can secure the "right" position, yet more jobs are found through networking than in any other way. I often attend professional meetings and luncheons where people announce that they are looking for work. Seldom do they leave me something that I could be pass along on their behalf or which could help me to contact them later. Even if a resume is offered, it is too much for such casual contacts. Unless the person is already known, a contact is unlikely to be able to track them down when a hot lead arises. Such events are the perfect opportunity to provide a resume card.

Consider job fairs and trade shows where you visit with many contacts without a clue about which ones are warm. A resume card is a small taste of what you offer that you can pass out broadly. Of course, you'll still need your full-scale resume in reserve, but it can be saved for those cases where there is a higher probability of success.

Make it clear what you are looking for; state an objective. "The objective, or job target, is important because that's how people know you're looking for a job. Remember, this isn't a normal business card. Choose a few of the best highlights from your resume—qualifications taken from your profile and/or one or two achievements. This card is intended to get people to remember you and call you. Don't pack the space with text—make it easy to read"[1] This is one occasion when a homemade computer-generated card is adequate and appropriate.

JOHN KILMER, seeking a position in
Hotel, Restaurant, and Nightclub Management
602.483.7072 • pager 602.578.9876

- Keen ability to develop profitable business ventures
- Increased one restaurant's annual revenue from $500,000 to $2.6 million
- Over ten years experience directing successful high-volume hotels, restaurants, and nightclubs

Black print on white stock[2]

Steffen Bundschuh [boond'shōō]
Mechanical Engineer (M.S., Dipl.-Ing.)

4400 Memorial Drive #2139   *Phone:* (713) 868-4926
Houston, TX 77007   *e-mail:* steffen@seas.gwu.edu

Experience in:
- energy conversion & storage technologies for HEVs
- EV/HEV system design & simulation   - tri-lingual (German, French)
- energy system design (e.g. HVAC, PV)   - multi-cultural
- biomechan. engin. & ergonomic dsgn   - European work processes
- finite-element method (FEM)   - economic sensitivity analysis
- virtual reality & neural nets   - 3D CAD/CAE (*I-DEAS*)

Black print on white stock

Linda Bowers M.A.
NCC Board Eligible Counselor
Trainer and Consultant

(602) 749-2108   P.O. Box 64807
(602) 297-7309   Tucson, AZ 85728-1807

Black print on white stock

"Keep your networking cards with you at all times, and hand them out to everyone you meet. Give them to your friends and relatives to hand out. Mail one or two with every letter, thank-you note, and resume you send out. These cards really work, because they're easy to give and easy to keep. Make them interesting to read while getting your point across, and it will be easy for people to call you with job leads."[3]

To really make a distinctive resume card, use the colored and folded-over version called NetCards®. (See Resource Section.) They are too elaborate to show here. (Folds out to $3^1/_2$" x $7^1/_4$", both sides.)

TRADE SHOWS, CONFERENCES, AND CONVENTIONS

Trade Shows Let You Show Yourself Off

Eighty-Three Billion Dollars—that's $83,000,000,000! That is the amount of money spent on conferences, conventions and trade shows in 1995 in America (figure supplied by the Convention Liaison Council).[4] While that number includes such expenses as travel, hotels, registrations, exhibits, etc., it does not include the promotional literature, products given away or the salaries of those participating. There were about 4400 trade shows alone in the U.S. and Canada in 1997.[5] Consider that an estimated 140 million people participate a year (many people attend more than one event), and you can see that a lot of time, energy and money is at stake.

Attendance at conferences, conventions and trade shows offers considerable benefits for almost any kind of business. Whatever you could name, there is an organization holding an event for those who care about that subject. In the U.S., there are more than 138,000 organizations. Events they conduct account for at least two-thirds of that 83 billion dollar (and increasing annually) figure, above. They conduct thousands of special interest and professional activities all over the country.

There is a daunting selection of events just within any single industry. The question should not be whether or not you will participate, but only which events and how often. If you're going to be involved, make it worth your while. Be selective; choose those activities which will best serve your staff and your organization. Since your competitors will be there, don't put yourself at a competitive disadvantage by staying away. Find out what industry leaders are up to and what you can do to become a more effective operation.

Don't forget *why* you're attending a show. Whether you're an exhibitor, a presenter, or an attendee, you have to make the most of the limited time you spend there. The money and energy invested to attend are high, yet the fortuitous contacts that often develop can turn them into a real bargain. Events require an incredible amount of planning, which starts months, or even years, in advance. The event planners have worked hard to bring all the elements together with enough variety to make everyone glad they've come. The typical conference or trade show involves a cast of hundreds or thousands, with each part demanding careful coordination. Likewise, your own planning should start early and involve anyone in your company who will be effected by attending or exhibiting.

Pay Receptive Attention

There are so many things going on in every direction and at the same time it's easy to get distracted. Sensory overload (and tired feet) are a temptation to tune many otherwise useful things out. After a few hours, so many people are just walking around in a daze. Whether you're walking the show or manning a booth, you are there to connect quickly in a variety of ways with many kinds of characters. Although you need to prepare a game plan before you arrive, an inflexible strategy will disregard some of the true delights and payoffs of taking part. No matter how good the event's program and structured activities, often the unexpected encounters, the never-to-be-anticipated coincidences supply the true value of attending. What happens in the halls or over a cup of coffee can be a long-term reminder that your professional colleagues are invaluable assets.

Those Who Come to the Show

- Exhibitors
- Buyers
- Your competitors
- Curious people
- Customers
- Industry partners
- Those who influence others
- Job hunters
- Market researchers
- Mates of attendees
- Media representatives
- Meeting attendees
- Problem solvers
- Speakers
- Students
- Vendors[6]

Remember, at most such events almost everyone who attends is an "insider." They are already committed and knowledgeable; they are there because they want to stay informed, see familiar faces, test out new products, and be involved in emerging trends in their industry. They're looking for new ideas and contacts, just like you. You'll have a chance to spend time with people who are usually difficult to reach—their gatekeepers have been left behind. They're downright eager to relate to you in the flexible, open, and temporary circumstances that events provide. There are few settings where you can make as many first-rate contacts (or deals) as quickly.

Why Come to Shows and Conferences

- ☐ Promote yourself and your business; pursue sales and networking
- ☐ Travel and an opportunity to get away; a change of scene
- ☐ Celebrate a good year, campaign, or specific success; reward team members
- ☐ Enjoy the excitement, high energy, novelty; and fun
- ☐ Check out the competition's products and methods
- ☐ See colleagues and customers in a new setting
- ☐ Renew friendships and relationships
- ☐ Gain easier access to those whom you're trying to reach
- ☐ Cultivate and strengthen face-to-face relationships with people you already do business with
- ☐ Attend the educational opportunities; increase trend awareness
- ☐ Get away from the office and its distractions
- ☐ Make appointments with customers, suppliers, peers
- ☐ To see and be seen
- ☐ Prepare for buying decisions

Get the most leads from your trade show:

Key: Spend less time with each visitor to see more visitors.

Connect: Attitude – Approachable – Active
Q ualify–"What's your responsibility?"
U nderstand–"What are you looking for?"
I dentify–"Here's how we can help you."
C reate an Action Plan–"I'll call you Monday."
K ick them out–"Thanks for stopping by."
The Valence Group • 800 488-0780 • © 1993 Mark S. A. Smith

Two-sided card; rust and black on cream stock; laminated for repeated use...

...*rust on back*

Your Trade Show Success Checklist
- ☐ Lots of business cards
- ☐ Comfy shoes or foot pads
- ☐ Show guide
- ☐ Have a great attitude
- ☐ Eat breakfast
- ☐ Drink lots of water
- ☐ Take pain reliever
- ☐ Pens & contact pads
- ☐ Small mints/breath spray
- ☐ Date book to schedule action plans
- ☐ Badge up & to the right
- ☐ Double check visitor's phone numbers
- ☐ Thank-you note cards
- ☐ Follow up now!
- ☐ Get weekly tips from the Trade Show Maximizer Hot Line 719 471-6685

Bring Plenty of Cards

It's a hard choice deciding which events to attend, but once you've marked an event on the calendar, consider what you will be taking for promotional materials. Whether you're walking the show or manning a booth, take a good look at your business card. Consider whether it needs a face lift or special customizing. Do you have enough or should you reprint? Is there sufficient time to avoid a crisis before you're ready to leave? Some exhibitors print special cards just for a show with their booth address or show specials. Such cards promote their presence as well as their products.

```
Come by
Booth 626
and visit the
Story Angel™
Entertainment with
Positive Family Values

Drop your business card
by to register to win a
signed & numbered
limited edition print of
illustrations from the
book
"Coco's Luck"

Miracle Sound
Productions, Inc.
Toll Free: 888/892-7375
Check out our show specials!!!
```

Full color drawing of angel on the front with black print on the back; on white stock

Over a several-day period, you are going to give out many cards and collect many others. Prioritize their lead potential. Follow up and treat these cards as little treasures you've mined—there's gold there. The Center for Exhibition Industry Research (CEIR) made a comprehensive study of the costs of closing a sale. The cost of closing a sale that begins with a trade show lead is $550 versus $997 for closing a lead from any other source.[7]

Proper Conduct while Working a Trade Show Booth

- ☐ Be ready organized, attractive, and trained
- ☐ Be welcoming; treat each person as an interesting individual, not just a body; smile a lot
- ☐ Be knowledgeable and informative about the company's products or services
- ☐ Qualify prospects and find out their needs in a personalized way

- Send the kind of body language that makes you seem professional, confident, and approachable
- Respond to attendee's concerns and questions; make them glad they inquired
- Take orders and get information for follow-up after the show
- Let people take their time in the exhibit; find the balance between being available and remote, responsive and hovering
- Don't keep people waiting; "58% will not wait more than one minute; 28% will wait three minutes; 14% will wait five minutes" [8]
- Dress and appear to be professional in every way
- When there are several employees, don't socialize among yourselves; visitors feel that they are intruding and irrelevant
- Prepare an inviting and interesting space, which feels like a sea of calm in a flurry of competing impressions; encourage people to pause and enjoy it
- Exude a sense that you're enjoying being there and want them to feel the same way

Six Tips for Successful Trade Show Exhibiting

The following list is provided courtesy of Dr. Allen Konopacki, Incomm Center for Research, and is used with permission.

"1. **The Opener**. Salespeople should not ask, 'May I help you?' when greeting visitors. It prompts a response of 'No, just looking' from attendees. A more effective greeting like, 'Thank for visiting our exhibit. What prompted your interest in our products?' encourages conversation. It prompts the customer to answer with more than a 'No' response or 'I'm just looking' reply.

2. **How to Get Prospects to Notice Your Exhibit**. Always present a smile when looking at prospects. People respond to a smile and it's the best and quickest way to invite the individual across the carpet line. Over 90% of prospects will have a positive response to a salesperson who smiles at them.

3. **Getting Your Message Across**. The old cliché 'a picture is worth a thousand words' is very true at shows. Prospects comprehend only 10% of a verbal message but when photographs are used they will understand as much as 35% of the message. The best way to assure that your message is getting across is to use some type of interaction. This practice can guarantee that as much as 65% of your message is being understood.

4. **Asking Smart Questions**. To find the best prospects at trade shows, ask smart questions. Ask questions that zero in and focus on the customer's needs, like 'What created the need' or 'What would you like to achieve?' People who can describe a need are more likely to be Power Buyers versus individuals who can't identify a specific goal or need.

5. **Leads that Turn into Sales**. A lead is really a message from the prospect to the sales rep who will be following up in the field. Good leads will contain key comments abort what the prospect said while visiting the exhibit. Avoid generic remarks like 'hot prospect' or 'send brochure.'

6. **Avoid Radar Vision**. Radar vision is the process of scanning the show aisles looking at the different name badges. This action makes prospects feel uncomfortable and looks as if you're trying to qualify them before they get into the exhibit. Instead, glance at the person's badge and introduce yourself by stating, 'Hello, I'm Allen Konapacki, and you're _____ ' Follow up by using smart questions to determine what prompted the interest."[9]

Business Cards at the Trade Show

- ☐ Make sure your card shows your state, zip code, and area code
- ☐ Bring lots of cards, as well as other promotional literature
- ☐ Include your Web address (see below)
- ☐ Print show specials or other attention getters
- ☐ Print your booth address; start handing them out even before the event starts

- Give out cards which can be used for admissions and passes or to get additional bonuses
- Don't horde your cards at your booth; have stacks easily available at several booth locations so an attendee can take one even if you're not free

Your Web Address and Trade Shows

If your business card and other materials do not show your Web address, reprint immediately. A principal benefit of being at shows is to get people to check out your on-line information, which is available 24-hours a day. Your Web site is a potent sales assistant, which should include information about the company, products, services, prices, ordering information, etc. (Also see Chapter 2 on the implicit messages sent by having an electronic presence.) It will support the efforts of your sales staff before and after the event.

A recent survey by Allen Konopacki discovered that fully 22 percent of attendees visit the Web address of companies they intend to see at the show **before** the event. That means that they arrive informed about what you provide. The number of visits to the Web site goes much higher right after a show, as people check out details about what they saw at the event. People are getting the details they want without relying on sales presentations. And it is no longer teckies who are the primarily users of the Internet. Many of the people who visit Web sites are middle and upper-level managers, who rely on such information as part of their decision process.

Some companies are experimenting with handing out business cards with only the company name, logo and Web address (that means no address or phone number) to encourage visits to their Web page. Of course this strategy is risky unless you have the other person's card or a way to maintain contact with them. However, it is another type of specialized card you may want to have on hand for suitable circumstances. It's too early to tell if this daring card style of providing only a Web address, will develop into a trend.

Errors that Exhibitors Make

"1. **Pitching instead of Listening**. Attendees complain that reps want to demonstrate the equipment before clearly determining their real level of interest. It gets down to programmed communication. The booth representative has a perceived program. So when an attendee gets close, the rep is going to demonstrate and pitch the product or equipment.

2. **List Building**. Prospects dislike it when a rep simply wants them to sign up for something, give them a premium or run an imprint of their card—all with the intention of putting them on a list. Of course, companies need to obtain information to qualify a prospect. But there's a difference between qualifying and list-building. Qualifying means letting the prospect set the agenda for the conversation. List-building is getting the name, rank and serial number for solicitation. That's really detrimental.

3. **Selling to Individuals rather than Groups**. There is a big annoyance to prospects. They walk into an exhibit, and all the salespeople are occupied. And when they try to listen to a rep's presentation from off to one side, the rep makes no effort to include them. So prospects never really feel welcome in the exhibit. What the prospects recommend is that the rep should try to deal with them as groups, rather than as individuals. They say 'All they need to do is glance at us, nod, smile, throw a question or increase the volume of their voice loud enough so that it indicates we're welcome.'

4. **Asking Trap Questions**. Typically, this means asking a question such as, 'If I could show you a way to improve your company's productivity, would you be interested?' This type of question traps the prospect into saying yes. People dislike sales language that is manipulative."[10]

5. **Being Uninformed or Unprepared**. Anyone manning an exhibit should have basic product knowledge; pre-event planning and training shows. Target and customize your message and materials for those who will attend.

Large and small gatherings are unparalleled opportunities to see and be seen, to learn, to start and strengthen relationships of all sorts. Whatever your reasons for participating, it is a smorgasbord from which you can glean unlimited benefits. Attend with a sense of adventure, looking for those priceless and unexpected contacts that make you say, "I can't imagine having missed this! I got much more than I'd expected."

Welcome Foreign Attendees

Every gathering, whether it's a conference, a seminar or exhibit, draws people from near and far. More and more participants come from foreign countries, where business practices differ. Take the time to be gracious to the foreign visitor. The true bridges between cultures are established relationship by relationship.

The universal language is a smile. Be warm and inviting in ways that transcend language. Speak slowly and watch for understanding. Those from foreign countries will appreciate your thoughtfulness. Respect their differences by following the card conventions that are important *to them*. See Chapter 14 for ways to relate to those from other countries.

For example, take time to read their card and then acknowledge them. Don't write on their card itself. Treat it with the same respect you'd show to the person. Don't shove the card into your pocket; they will notice. In many parts of the world, such details are vital before business can proceed. You won't be taken seriously (or get to first base) otherwise.

To Recap

Your card is a valuable asset, but only if you can put it to work. Develop strategies where you make more contacts with potential buyers. Strengthen your networking skills and participate in conferences and trade shows routinely.

Chapter 13

Organize and Follow Up with the Cards You Receive

Up to My Ears

Help! I'm up to my ears in cards! Now that you have gathered these cards, you are faced with this all-too-common dilemma. And almost no one is comfortable with how they're handling it. Many a New Year's Resolution has started with, "I'm going to find a better way," or "As soon as I can get around to it." But time goes by, and nothing changes. The combination of guilt and annoyance turns into something you prefer to ignore. There is an element of embarrassment because you've so long promised to "deal with it," yet it's still not dealt with. Even if you've got a bit of a system, it doesn't work too smoothly or consistently. It isn't kept up.

No matter how successful you've been with the exchange of cards (See Chapter 12 on distributing cards.), you face the sometimes overwhelming task of organizing your collection. After taking your precious new cards out of your pocket or purse, you are ready for the next step. And then... And then...what *does* come next?

Having a clear plan coupled with an efficient system for follow up yields the best benefits from your stash.

Start With the First Step

The first step entails using a simple method to organize your cards as they arrive. This initial sorting should not to be confused with later, more specific categorizing.

Initial easy sorting methods:

- Random piles or boxes
- Rubber band groups—sorted by various criteria
- Alphabetical files or boxes
- Plastic pockets in folders or notebook—organized in general order
- Stapled or attached to files or other system
- Filed in slots in a card holder
- Combination of these

Retrieval is the goal. Whatever system you devise, it is so you can find information that you need on a particular person when you need it. You are putting the cards (or the information on them) into a system that permits you to retrieve it when needed. All of your choices should aid you in that end. This chapter offers alternative methods for storing and retrieving vital information. There is no best method. In fact, any method will fail if it is too complicated or doesn't fit your way of functioning. You already have at least a make-shift method; these are additional methods, and you're likely to use a combination of them. Also, organization evolves, and you're likely to use one method until you adapt it to another system later. Don't lose sight of the fact that having an organizational system is to help you get access to these contacts, not to be just another niggling thing you've got to get around to.

Of course, no system is very good unless you keep it up to date. Put your cards away when on "hold" while on the telephone, or whenever you have a free moment. Don't let them stack up (now that's an appropriate term for this discussion) until organizing them has become a big job. Otherwise, you'll still be shuffling through your stack, looking randomly for someone's information.

Also, no system works if you don't replace the old contact information with more current data from time to time. Keep the latest information you can for those in your system, and remove the dead stuff.

Cross Reference Your Information

The brain works in strange ways, and each of us has quirks that influence how we remember things. To compensate, we have mental devices that we develop to help recall what we've filed away. Whatever your quirks are, recognize them; build them into your method of organizing your contacts. You may not be able to remember a person's name, but it comes to you after you remember something that sets him or her apart: very tall, bit of an accent, married to a blond dancer, is available on weekends, etc. If you don't reliably remember that person's name, don't file his information by name alone. Set up several categories, and file his contact information in several ways that relate to the ways you connect to him. Then cross reference to the other information topics. For example, George Bloom may be filed under "Writer" or "Writer's Organization" (where you met) or under the area of his specialization, "Military History" or the name of his employer or publisher, "Battlefield Press," etc., as well as according to his name.

Put people who have something in common together, so when you need a service, your options or contacts are already grouped together. For example, all the plumbers you know may be filed together, irrespective of their individual names or the companies they work for. When you are looking for a plumber, you'll find someone to help you quicker than by recalling and looking them up individually.

Not All Cards or Contacts Are Equal

Since not all cards that come your way are equally important, they need to be sorted, prioritized and culled. It doesn't hurt to remember why you're getting all these cards in the first place. These are vital links to fulfilling your goals. These cards represent living, breathing people who have their own agendas—and are, likewise, wondering how well you fit into them. It is one thing to file a card, it is another to form a relationship, so, you're considering which of these contacts may be nourished toward a longer-term alliance. Of course, it's too early to tell, but you're scanning for potential. So it is enough to decide a person **might be** high priority.

It is just as important to decide who really isn't a prospect for special handling. Life being so demanding, we have to develop rationales about where we invest our energy. If there is a "snowball's chance" for further collaboration, let it go now. On the other hand, be sensitive to your own prejudices or areas of pre-judgment.

Simple Ways to Organize Cards

◻ Alphabetical
  Person's name
  Business name
  Type of business
  Type of contact, i.e. client, vendor, colleague

◻ Color Codes
  Divisions; dividers
  Highlight with felt-tip markers or stickers
  Tabs

◻ Priority or Importance or Type
  Primary contacts
  Secondary contacts
  Short-term contacts
  Long-term contacts
  Future contacts; upcoming contacts

Near or far contacts; local, out of state, out of the country, etc.

Past contacts; prior or closed contacts

Personal contacts; household versus business matters

GET SERIOUS WITH AN ORGANIZATIONAL SYSTEM
Choose the Product(s) that Works for You

Boxes

This is a simple, self-explanatory system. We recommend that cards be arranged alphabetically **within** categories, which are themselves arranged alphabetically.

Examples: Carpenters

Smith, John

Carpenters

Hammers and Nails

John Smith, Contractor

Products

Can be homemade or purchased, such as an actual shoe box or other small box outfitted with cardboard dividers. Office stores carry a variety of supply 3" x 5" card files and alphabetical dividers.

Pros and Cons

Pros

- Easy to re-sort cards
- Easy to add or discard cards or move them from one to another category
- Easy insertion or deletion of categories
- Infinitely expandable by the addition of more boxes
- Inexpensive
- Person can see and handle the cards themselves, so the cards trigger memories of the giver
- No learning curve; anyone can update the system

Cons

- Bulky and awkward
- Not as portable as other systems
- Sometimes unsightly
- Old fashioned; provides no benefits of technology or ability to access card information by electronic means

---

Files

Although not the appropriate size, cards can still be filed in the standard letter or legal sized filing system. Again, they should be placed in folders labeled according to category and grouped by rubber bands.

Products

Choices consist of: portable file boxes (plastic or cardboard), expandable or light-weight files, file cabinets, or office furnishings such as desk drawers.

Pros and Cons

Pros

- ☐ Easy to re-sort cards
- ☐ Easy addition and/or deletion of cards and categories
- ☐ Portable files are inexpensive

Cons

- ☐ Bulky
- ☐ Not very portable
- ☐ Wastes precious office filing space
- ☐ Individual cards not readily accessible

Rotary Card Systems

Rotary systems use light cardstock with a distinctive cut on the bottom edge designed to slide on a track. You will recognize the distinctive shape, although tradmark restrictions prevent its name being used here. They are available in several popular sizes. Business cards can be attached to the cards by tape or slots; or the information can be written onto the card to be filed (then you do what you want with the person's business card). Such a system does not, however, have a way to deal with vertical cards or two-sided or folded ones. (See Chapter 6 on various card shapes.)

This is generally a desk-top system. Cards can be directly inserted into tracked filing boxes or onto specially designed rotation devices.

Products

Included are open rotary files, covered rotary files, portable card files with snap-lock covers and handles, V-files, mini-files, refill packages of cards and tabs, card protectors, or card sleeve conversion kits, and conversion adhesive tabs. Another device cuts the bottom of the business card with the characteristic shape. It is inexpensive, but often cuts out critical information.

Pros and Cons

Pros

- Easy to re-sort cards
- Easy addition and/or deletion of cards and categories
- Appropriately sized products
- Designed to be used as small office furnishings, hence variety of colors and choices
- Cards anchored, so they can't fall out or get lost
- Easy to move cards around within system
- System commonly used and understood by most office personnel

Cons

- ☐ Less portable—generally a desk-top system
- ☐ The large and small cards are not interchangeable; two different systems

---

Notebooks

With the use of pliable, plastic inserts similar to picture sleeves in wallets, business cards can be arranged and carried in various sized notebooks or can be stored on books shelves.

Products

These include simple three-ringed binders with inexpensive customized divider tabs, packages of three-hole-punched clear, plastic sleeves holding eight to ten business cards each, address-book-style notebooks designed professionally to carry in briefcases or as an accessory to other planners.

Pros and Cons
Pros

- ☐ Portable
- ☐ Easily re-organized
- ☐ Easy addition and/or deletion of cards and categories

- Different sizes and designs available
- Inexpensive
- Easy to coordinate cards between the office and carry along notebooks

Cons

- Uses valuable shelf space as the collection gets larger; may be hard to find a particular card
- Need a system for organizing binders, or you can lose people (cards)
- Does not expand infinitely

Planners

This system is similar to notebooks. The difference is that the cards are placed are placed in a specific section inside a larger notebook system. Organizing your cards is just part of being organized. For example, plastic sheets with appropriately spaced punch holes are added to an already existing day-planner notebook. This method allows you to keep many things "under one roof" (i.e., calendar, phone and address pages, reference information, etc.).

Products

This includes various binders ranging from the inexpensive to those of custom quality, specially designed plastic card holding pages, and appropriate divider tabs.

Pros and Cons

Pros

- Portable
- Easily reorganized
- Easy addition and/or deletion of cards and categories
- Different sizes and designs available
- Easy to coordinate cards between the office and carry-along notebooks
- Some are designed to correspond with computer office management
- Makes a professional and organized appearance
- Keeps cards themselves handy without re-copying the information
- Keeps your card visually present as a reminder, not lost in a large system

Cons

- Because of limit space within sections, needs to be coordinated with one of the other systems for contacts needed less frequently
- Quality binders may be expensive

Computers

Computers are the most comprehensive of all the organizational systems and permit uses other than the retrieval of cards. It is a common component in today's workplace. Tomorrow's office will most likely house a computer management system devoted to superior communications efficiency. This system enhances the ability to access the data and collect statistics for demographic analysis. More than just the typical business card information this system allows for additional, more specific data to be entered and stored for future reference. All on-line information can be transferred to a hard-copy form.

Even when you use a computer to capture the information on the cards, you have to make a decision about what to do with the cards themselves Some people throw the cards away and only treat them as a source for data stored within the data base. Since that eliminates the visual and tactile cues, the card itself ceases to serve as a reminder of the giver. If the cards themselves are kept for later reference, then one of the other methods of organization is still necessary. I personally favor keeping the cards around for occasional perusal, even if they aren't organized.

Products

For maximum efficiency, this system requires a computer with adequate memory capacity, appropriate software programs for office management, and often related devices like a scanner, a modem, a printer, and printer forms matching the software specifications.

Pros and Cons

Pros

- Comprehensive office management
- Can be coordinated with other off-line organizational systems
- Expected component of most effective office management systems; can be used for a variety of tasks
- Easy to re-organize data
- Easy addition and/or deletion of data
- Can re-group data according to evolving needs

Cons

- High start-up costs for both the computer and the specialized software for it
- User may require software training; long learning curve
- Limited portability—may require additional equipment (i.e., lap-top or palm top computers)
- Requires use of another system for storage of original cards

Other Electronic Devices

- ☐ Card Scanners
- ☐ Contact Management Software
- ☐ Electronic Personal Organizers

Who knows what is looming on the technology horizon? But you can be sure that there will be innumerable devices for the collection, storage and transmission of personal data coming forth on a regular basis. It's impossible to conjecture which will survive or capture the interest of the everyday, card-carrying businessperson. (Part of Chapter 10 is devoted to just such devices.) Rest assured, none of them will be a serious threat to the traditional business card. They may augment the face-to-face exchange of cards, but it is the warm, living, human, responding, and bonding interaction that occurs at that time that they cannot replace.

What To Do with the Unusual Card

Occasionally you will receive odd-sized, two-sided, vertical, or folded cards which require special consideration. Fend for yourself! None of the systems are designed to accommodate such cards, except the computer, which treats all cards in the same way— blindly ignoring everything except the data on them.

PUT THE CARDS TO WORK
Follow Up on Following Up

Now that you have organized your cards, it is time to decide how to proceed with your contacts. Once you have made acquaintance with someone whom you regard as a potential customer or client, you will want to respond right away. This timely and thoughtful communication will remind the contact why he is glad to have made your acquaintance.

I have a special place on my desk where I put such new cards, and they don't get moved until I have followed up. Whether I'm efficient or not, they stay right there until I've determined what needs to be done and taken that step. The card is as tangible to me as the person or organization it represents. While I am "on hold" or shuffling papers about, I continue to notice those cards and am reminded that follow up is pending.

There are many ways to follow up. They are dictated by your type of business, your budget, and your style of interaction. If you are attempting to move from a casual contact to a business relationship, it's still too early to know what will develop. At least, you have made an overture. If nothing happens, try again. Don't assume that the other person will contact you, even if that was the specific understanding. If you don't take the initiative, in all probability, the contact will be lost. If it sounds a lot like dating, in some respects it is. You're looking for those people who connect with your needs and vice versa. Following up is a ceaseless activity, similar to courtship, and is as necessary to sustain a business as cash flow.

You actually need two follow up systems. One is to **evaluate** your contacts or customers and take the appropriate next step. Call that **lead development**, since those contacts could turn into new customers or clients. Second, you also need to have a way to organize all your contacts, whether or not they are leads, so that they end up as part of your resource network. Call that your **database**.

Information Gets the Job Done

Don't cringe at that word, "database." Say it out loud; it is a reality, whether or not you're comfortable with it. Processing information is part of the world we all have to live in. The information explosion impacts everyone, and recognizing business cards as part of your database is just another example. Don't resist it, but obtain the benefits that come from intelligently making use of the available information. Even if your business is not computer-based, you have some method to organize the data (which are simply facts) already, however haphazard it may be. (By the way, data is a plural word; one of them is a datum).

Remember the old phrase: "It's not what you know but who you know." But your contacts do you little good unless you are aware of whom you know, what they mean to your business, and you find a way to sustain those connections. These connections are the most important resource of your business; they will determine whether or not you survive. And they will become more valuable over time. Harvey Mackay, a well-known writer, speaker, and envelope manufacturer is an enthusiastic missionary about what can be accomplished by collecting and using information on the business contacts in your file. (See his book, *How to Swim With the Sharks Without Being Eaten Alive.*)

Ten Follow-Up Strategies

- ☐ Call to pursue a topic that arose in your conversation; propose what you want to happen next
- ☐ Send information about your business
- ☐ Request information about their business or products
- ☐ Share appropriate referrals, your contacts; continue to offer more leads or resources
- ☐ Send or fax news clippings or relevant information
- ☐ Make an appointment, visit their location, or invite them to yours
- ☐ Invite them to various related events or meetings
- ☐ Send a thank you note or small gift
- ☐ "Do lunch" or coffee at some public place
- ☐ Arrange a conference call or meeting with contacts they need, and include yourself

What you choose to do is less important than the fact that you have followed-up and will continue to do so. Develop your own strategies and **stick to them!** Like your card and everything else about your business, your follow-up should be compatible with your prevailing business style and personality. They are an integral part of your comprehensive marketing plan.

Treat It as Data From Data

Once the data is gathered, you will be able to glean more from it than just the obvious information. There are common characteristics to be found. For example, grouped by zip code, your data may reveal special areas of activity. Finding correlations (a fancy word for relationships) and percentages may offer valuable clues to the strengths or weaknesses in your marketing plan. For example, it has been unexpectedly discovered that there is a high correlation between disposable diapers and beer purchases. Why, since babies don't drink beer? (Husbands sent to the store to buy diapers to stock up for the weekend figure out that they might as well stock up on beer for themselves, also. The figures also show the social changes which make men more involved in parenting activities.) There may be similar correlations between your products and services (or someone else's products and services) that you can tap into in perusing your own database.

As you ponder the possible meanings of your statistics, you will be unconsciously improving your overall business plan. You will be able to use dollars and other resources more wisely and will catch erroneous assumptions before they can do much harm. You will see patterns as they occur, like those that are cyclical (i.e., high sales in the summer, low in the winter).

My experience as a statistician showed me how much demographic savvy can contribute to overall success. When attempting to make changes, be careful not to alter too many variables at once. By making one adjustment at a time, you will be able to clarify which actions are responsible for improvement.

I encourage you to enjoy the many contacts you will make as you pursue your business venture. Value a two-way communication process with your acquaintances. Be open to their suggestions and feedback. These ideas can and should be added to your database as an extension of their business card. Other sources of data can include trade show lead forms, or event attendance forms, which are mentioned in Chapter 12.

To Recap

Once you have gathered cards from your ever-expanding contacts, you need to organize their information so you can stay in touch with them. There are a variety of methods for arranging cards, but each of them has advantages and disadvantages. How easy is it to retrieve current information on the people you meet? The important consideration needs to be how well any system suits you and how easily it can be kept up.

Chapter 14

Launch Your Card in the International Arena with Style

As the World Shrinks

The world continues to shrink, and national boundaries no longer impede the flow of trade. It is now common to encounter customers, suppliers, and colleagues from far-away countries. You will increasingly exchange cards with people whose business and social conventions are very different than those we are familiar with in the United States. Whatever your type of business, it is time to think bigger and consider the impact of the world arena.

Dealing with other countries can be good for business, but it is can also fraught with pitfalls. Americans are too often blind to other cultures and assume familiarity where it doesn't exist. We must avoid reinforcing the stereotype of Americans being overbearing, insensitive or self-centered. Many attitudes accepted here as truth are seen very differently abroad. For example, change is not as readily accepted in other countries. "In Confucian and Islamic societies, history and tradition far outweigh change. In these societies, reputation and reliability are more highly valued than the idea of new and improved."[1]

Traveling alerts you to many differences that are rooted in unfamiliar religions, geography, social customs, and traditions. Whenever dealing with someone from another country, be aware that any assumptions you bring with you are risky; so are stereotypes. Avoid them! You will need to get advice from a native so you can avert mistakes that could arise in an unfamiliar setting.

Start with Your Name

Remember, when you are abroad **you are the foreigner and may appear strange to them**. (Why do you think you're called a "stranger?") Although the international language of commerce is English, you cannot assume that you will be able to read or pronounce some of the cards you receive. Your name is likely to be unusual and hard for them to remember, so pronounce it distinctly. The company name, which may be so apparent and clever in English, might make no sense at all once it has been translated. Sound every syllable out clearly and slowly. If necessary spell it. Have them say their names carefully also, so that from the beginning you are saying each other's names correctly. Sounding out the words can be part of the bonding experience. The struggle to speak without error is very humanizing—it's certainly a cure for pomposity.

Since your name is likely to be unfamiliar to non-English speaking people, the written form (on your card) helps the receiver to both see it and understand its spelling. Also, it is easier to understand a name and other vital information if it can be seen and then fully translated at a later time. Even before you go abroad, it is advisable to find out whether or not your counterpart is comfortable speaking English. Even when a translator is present, you should inform yourself regarding the appropriate behavior for the country while you are visiting.

Find out what your company's name or slogan means in the other language. When the business was named, you probably did not consider how well the words would translate, or whether the business name would have any negative connotations. (See Chapter 3 on business names.) Before doing much business in a particular language or country, find out if there are any negative associations with the words or other aspects of your design (like the color of your logo). We know that in the US a "lemon" is not something we want associated with a vehicle, but in France, for instance, their biggest car company is Citroen, which translates to "lemon." Nor do you want to depend on a "chicken," by which we mean a fearful person, not a bird or a meat. Yet, products can fail when we are unaware of similar innuendoes in another language. Also, avoid abbreviations unless they are universally recognized and accepted.

Give Respect to Business Cards

- Show the same respect for a person's card that you would show toward that person
- It could be taken as an insult if you don't handle cards carefully
- Pay attention while reading it; take your time; don't write on it or sit on it
- Don't give cards casually or to everyone you meet; be selective
- Arrange cards you receive in front of yourself on the table in the same order that people are seated, so you can match their placement to their names and aid your memory
- Never forget to take the cards you've received with you when you leave
- Keep enough cards with you so you're prepared, whatever happens

Business cards have exalted significance in many foreign countries, where they are treated with greater formality. By contrast, Americans tend to be very casual about their own cards as well as the ones they receive. Abroad, being casual is not considered appropriate for business, whether in attire or manner. Always appear to be professional so you don't convey a mixed signal.

The business card is a tangible statement revealing your status and identity. In fact, it is unlikely that you will be taken seriously without it. Dr. Braaten, a professor at The American Graduate School of International Management (also known as Thunderbird), who specializes in bridging cultural differences in the business arena, said, "A business card won't necessarily open up new business to you, but it shows an appreciation for the other person's home customs. It enhances the relationship and starts you out on a positive footing."

Whenever you are playing in the world arena, extra care must be taken to understand how to relate to those from other cultures. The business card is a form of communication that reveals many cultural differences. Dr. Braaten also indicated: "Everything you do communicates—so your card is one way you can show your cultural understanding (or at least display an effort to understand)." Consider it an aspect of business preparation to build your cultural competency.

Avoid International Blunders

- Being too familiar
- Inappropriate touching
- Using first names, improper names, or nicknames prematurely
- Offensive body language or gestures
- Failure to recognize dietary strictures
- Failure to abide by time strictures
- Superstitions—whether theirs or yours
- Failure to use titles or show proper respect

Most blunders are unintentional. They may be tolerated, but do not build trust or further a spirit of cooperation. An innocent mistake can instantly undo the possibilities brought about by considerable effort. In the same spirit that you want to be careful not to offend, do not be too quick to take offense when the other party transgresses.

Subtle signals matter. The feel of a card also communicates about your rank. Since some cultures place such store on their cards, they are quick to notice signs of high quality. An understated card works best, with paper and printing of superior quality. Although engraving is rare in most circles in the U.S., it is preferred and relatively common in many countries abroad. The feel and texture of top-quality stock and a superior design are recognized as signs of elevated status. Don't compromise your image by ignoring such broadly recognized measures of class.

Also, note the emotions you display. Be sensitive to non-verbal communications that you send or receive—they won't mean what you're accustomed to. "To be warm and friendly is relatively acceptable in the United States (although hugging in the business arena is questionable under any circumstances). In Asia (and Japan, in particular), any form of physical contact is absolutely unacceptable. Furthermore, speaking in a loud tone of voice is viewed as unsuitable and indecorous. In Asia, the lower the tone of voice, the higher the rank."[2]

Business Cards Establish Your Identity

The business card is your shingle and your identity. It also reveals your place in the power structure of your company. Your title should be on the card, as an indication of your place in the "pecking order," which signals whether they defer to you or vice versa. It can be very awkward when they don't have enough information to know how to proceed. Some types of positions are difficult for foreigners to relate to, since they do not have comparable positions where they live.

Always have plenty of cards and be ready to exchange. However, countries differ as to whether or not the exchange of cards is appropriate in social situations. If you are not dealing with an official English-speaking country, get your card's text translated and printed on the back. In that case, you will need different cards for the various languages and countries encountered. Don't cut corners on a cheap or free translation. Obtain reactions from natives of that country to make sure your translation is appropriate and free of unintended meanings.

The rules for exchanging cards differ widely from country to country, but you should be alert to the important role cards play in the entire business relationship. Arrange for extra coaching from a native so you can participate smoothly. Think of these initial greetings as ceremonial occasions, and give them the attention that they deserve. After all, you're being watched to see if you are indeed deserving of a business relationship. Follow their lead. The cultural nuances are fraught with meanings and must not be rushed. Other cultures place great emphasis on proper etiquette—they prefer to do business with those who sustain long-standing relationships. Such rituals are not just preludes to doing business; they are an integral part of the business occasion.

Welcome Foreign Visitors

Whenever your foreign counterparts come to visit you, do not assume that they must do all the adjusting to our ways. It is a sign of respect to show that they, too, are bringing valued traditions and expectations. Reach out with sensitivity, and do not treat their differences as irrelevant. Many a story can be told of the appreciation and strong bonds forged when such respect is shown (and the opposite horror stories can have equally decisive effects on the business relationship).

A colleague in the industrial spice field described how they would welcome foreigners who visited their plant. Outside the plant the U.S. flag and the flag of the visitors country fly at the same height. At the entrance was a bulletin board with a welcome posted in the visitor's native language. Inside, smaller crossed flags of the respective countries further emphasized their inter-relatedness. By the time that the meetings began, the visitors were all smiles. The marketing director's card showed his name and title in four different foreign languages.

Brown print on tan stock; gold foil on the F

International Cards Are Not a Standard Size

The United States is the only country with a uniform card size. Here, business people are accustomed to the standard sized, $3^{1}/_{2}$" by 2" (88 mm. by 52 mm.) card, which is often illustrated and colorful. (It is conventional to state the horizontal measurement first and then the vertical measurement.) Cards from other countries are usually simpler in design, but do come in a variety of sizes. Even though the sizes used abroad are not standard, some of the most frequent sizes are shown. So, consider not only the appropriate language to put on a card, but also inquire about its appropriate size. Increasingly, the credit card size ($3^{1}/_{4}$" x $2^{1}/_{8}$"— 85.5 mm. x 54 mm.) is becoming the standard for cards around the world. The following information from "Crane's Global Guide" is provided courtesy of Crane Business Papers and is used with permission.

Business Card Sizes in Other Countries	
3$\frac{1}{2}$" x 2" 88 x 52 mm (millimeters; metric) U.S. standard business card	Also found in: Brazil Canada France Mexico Russia Switzerland
85.5 x 54 mm 3$\frac{1}{4}$" x 2$\frac{1}{8}$" Standard credit card	Germany Italy Switzerland
85 x 55 mm	Germany United Kingdom
74 x 52 mm	Netherlands
90 x 55 mm	Australia Brazil Hong Kong Japan Spain
90 x 50 mm	Australia Finland France Israel Norway Russia Spain
110 x 72 mm	Spain

Courtesy of Crane Business Papers[3]

COUNTRIES AROUND THE WORLD HAVE DIFFERENT BUSINESS CARD CUSTOMS**

Asia

Those from the Far East are characterized as reserved. They don't hurry, gush, or display enthusiastic emotions. They are maddeningly slow with social rituals until you have established trust with them. All the while, you're being tested as to what kind of person you are. The culture is rooted in an emphasis on the value of the group or family over the value of any particular individual. Consequently, independence is not encouraged and group consensus is the norm.

Many Asians prefer face-to-face contact, so many letters go unanswered. Keep conversations general and impersonal, because safe topics differ between cultures.

Never use sarcasm because you are likely to be taken literally. Disagreement must be very subtle, if you want to avoid giving offense or embarrassment. Loss of face must be avoided since it is a grievous event.

---

*   Unavoidably, the following information is very general. Differences do exist within cultures and countries. Also, there is no uniform treatment of the countries mentioned, and too many are omitted. A *Quick and Painless*® book on this topic is in the works.

Japan

No other country places as much emphasis on the card as the Japanese. The business card is always exchanged as a ceremonial event, known as *meishi*. Print your text in Japanese on the reverse side; get a good translation. The highest ranking person should present cards first. Then the exchange proceeds in the order of descending status. The Japanese company is likely to have a whole entourage, each of whom will proceed through the ceremony in their appropriate order. It is vital that you have enough cards so that each member of their delegation receives one of yours, and vice versa. Always have ample copies of your card with you. You may end up exchanging cards with a particular person more than once.

The exchange of cards occurs after the person has introduced himself and bowed. It is a necessary prelude to successful business negotiations. The card establishes the hierarchy of each of the participants, so they know their relative status. The card must show the company, your title and position in it, as well as any special awards, degrees, or titles that would reveal your relative status. They will not know how to treat you without such roles being clear. They often have difficulty with positions or titles that do not have corresponding positions in Japanese companies. Status is not determined primarily by your position, but by the relative importance of the company. For example, it is higher status to be a department head at General Motors than to be the president of a less prestigious or powerful company.

畢費　杯頭鷹　石版　65×50cm

梵谷藝術中心
故鄉畫廊

版畫原作 ● 水彩 ● 國畫
複製名畫 ● 藝術海報 ● 油畫

Two-sided card; blue sky, tan owl,
black print on glossy white stock...

梵谷藝術中心 · 故鄉畫廊

葉 明 佳

高雄市五福一路162號TEL: (07) 271-4163

...black print
on back

The card must be presented with the type facing toward the recipient, and with the Japanese-printed side facing up. The receiver should not need to turn the card over to read it. (In their turn, they will present the English side up for you.) Cards are held between the thumbs and forefingers of both hands and presented with a slight bow. They are received in the same manner. Using both hands is a display of humility toward the other person. Both parties give cards. Take time to read the card and acknowledge the person. If they bow at any time during the exchange, do likewise. Only then do you shake hands. Until such formalities occur, the negotiations do not begin.

Don't shove the other party's card into your pocket, fold it, or write on it. The card represents the person, so it should be treated with respect. Don't put them in a wallet or a rear pocket. Use a card holder and carry them in a front pocket, briefcase, or purse. Don't put the card away until you leave. Instead, hold it in your hand and close to your chest (heart), like you are holding them in your thoughts.

Gender is an awkward issue, since Japanese businessmen are unfamiliar with women in positions of authority, and do not defer unless the person has unquestionably high status. A woman in authority should have some male underlings who will defer to her status in order to show that she is not there in a serving role (like a secretary). Any women who is planning to represent American companies in Japan should be carefully coached on how to act to maintain respect and avoid being dismissed as less than an equal. On the other hand, Japanese women are known for their deference, so any foreign woman is perceived primarily as a foreigner (unaccustomed to behave as a Japanese woman) and only secondarily as female.

Two-sided card; black print on glossy white stock...

ピーター・デ・ヤガー

コンサルタント、 講師

カナダ、 M3J 1P6
オンタリオ州 ダウンズビュー
シャープクロフト ブルバード 133番地
TEL. & FAX (416) 638-9336

コンピュサーブ ID: 70611,2576

*...black print
on glossy
reverse*

China

China is the world's most populous country, having over 1.2 billion people. Because of the Communist political priorities, the country has been very isolated in its commerce until recent years. Now it is beginning to encourage economic trade and development, so will play an increasing role in world trade. American companies are scurrying to get into place to benefit from the influx of new consumers.

Most Chinese have three names: surname, generational name and given name. The surname (family name) comes first, although the other two names can be written with a space or hyphen between them. Western first names are sometimes adopted, which can provide helpful gender clues (Henry Wang). Also, others identify themselves by their initials (H. L. Wang).

The biggest problem with names in China is that there are so few of them; mistaken identities are hard to avoid. According to an article in the *Los Angeles Times*, "The nation's top five family names cover nearly one-third of the population or 350 million citizens— the equivalent of every man, woman and child in the United States and Mexico, combined, sharing just five last names."[4] By comparison, there are 2.4 Americans named Smith. The 1982 Chinese census showed 87 million people named Li, followed by 80 million Wangs, 78 million Zhangs, 60 million Lius, and 50 million Changs.

In the entire country there are only 3,100 family names, and a mere 100 of them account for 90 percent of the Chinese population.

Adding more variety of names seems logical and desirable, but any change encounters numerous cultural snags. China is a "culture in which names contain enormous significance—even, many believe, the seeds of a person's destiny. Parents are reluctant to deviate from the tried and true, afraid of forever jinxing their offspring."[5]

Titles and status are very important, so if they have titles and degrees use them (Director Chang). Since women usually don't take their husband's name at marriage, they should be addressed by their maiden name. Have your card printed in English and Chinese, showing your business titles plus academic degrees and awards earned.

Although the practice of presenting a card with both hands is less frequent, they will appreciate the respect shown if you do it. Write your hotel and room number on your card before presenting it. Give your card to every member of their team. It is discourteous to read their card quickly. Take some time; then look at the person and smile. Place all the cards on a pile. Always address the leader first, then address those lower those down in ranking order.

- Expect foreign businessmen (yes, they will usually be men) to be highly qualified for the positions they hold
- The Chinese don't like to say "no," so avoid questions with yes or no answers; also, avoid saying "no" yourself
- Don't touch—they prefer a smile to a pat
- Be modest in dress and gestures
- Send the same representative for every trip or contact; trust is placed in the individual as much as the company
- Meetings start with tea and conversation; don't rush to talk about business; wait until they ask you what you would like to discuss; developing an atmosphere of trust and sincerity is important

- Print cards specifically for mainland China—the character style is different from those used in Hong Kong and Taiwan

Hong Kong

- Business cards are essential—English on one side and Chinese on the other
- The many years of British colonial rule have developed an efficient and bustling system of commerce; it's too early to tell what the Chinese takeover may alter
- Print cards specifically for Hong Kong—the character style is different from those used in mainland China and Taiwan

Cheng-Lam ANG BSE (Hons) ASU

Regional Marketing Manager, POS Systems
Hong Kong, Indonesia, Malaysia, Singapore, Sri Lanka, Thailand, Vietnam
(e-mail ang @ obs. omcp omron sg)

洪振南

OMRON BUSINESS SYSTEMS SINGAPORE (PTE.) LTD.

1 Marine Parade Central #13-04/05/06
Parkway Builder's Centre
Singapore 1544
Tel: (65) 440-3933 (5 Lines)
Fax: (65) 440-3868

OMRON

At work for a better life, a better world for all.

Two-sided card; dark blue company name and slogan, the rest in black ink on white stock for both sides

Cheng-Lam ANG BSE (Hons) ASU
Deputy Managing Director

洪振南

- Point of Sales Systems
- Retail Information Systems
- Hotel Management Systems
- Card Readers/Pre-Paid Card Systems

OMRON BUSINESS SYSTEMS (MALAYSIA) SDN. BHD.

No. 6, Jalan SS 21/35,
Damansara Utama,
47400 Petaling Jaya, Selangor.
Tel: (603) 7187118 (5 Lines)
Fax: (603) 7188852

OMRON

At work for a better life, a better world for all

South Korea

- Card even more important than other oriental countries—lots of rituals

- Don't ever hand a Japanese card to a Korean

- Like China, Korea has very few family names (three names account for 45 percent of the population) so be careful to avoid mistaken identities

DONG-HWA CORPORATION

YONG-SUCK, PARK

CHIEF OF SALES DEPT.

RM. 606, KOREA BLDG.
44-12, YEOEUIDO-DONG,
YEONGDEUNGPO-KU,
SEOUL, KOREA

YEOEUIDO P. O. BOX 520
PHONE: 783-4055~6
TELEX : K26830 DHCORP
CABLE: DHCORP, SEOUL

Two-sided card; black print on white stock...

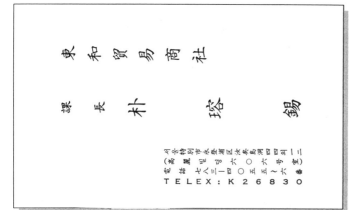

...black print on reverse

Taiwan and other Asian countries

▢ Business cards essential

▢ Look at it, and remember the name and title

▢ "Yes" means yes or I understand; "maybe" means no

▢ Frankness is not appreciated

▢ Cards are exchanged in both business and social situations

Russia, Belarus, Ukraine and other Former Russian States

The poor service in Russia is legendary. Under the communist regime full employment was the goal, so no one would be fired for poor performance. Therefore, sloppiness or indifference were never punished. The result today is still rude waiters and sales clerks, poor-quality goods, tardy responses and unhelpful service providers. In fact, customer service simply doesn't exist. In some places this is starting to change. The need for foreign currency is so great that some enterprises are seeing the wisdom of providing improved service.

Foreigners are not trusted. Discrimination and racism are widespread. Women seldom are in key business positions, although they are often well educated in science and the arts. Foreign women are not respected in higher level positions.

Russians tend not to be punctual, but the foreigner should be. A professional appearance is very important. An exchange of business cards is becoming increasingly important. The card is placed on the table in front of the person receiving it until the end of the meeting. Because the phone system is unreliable and telephone books are rare, people depend more on business cards for contact information. You, too, should be careful to get cards from your counterparts, since you won't be able to dial "information."

Two-sided card; lime green band and "O" in name; the rest is black print on white stock both sides

India

India was a British colony for many years. Therefore, bureaucratic formality and business organization were highly developed. The system of English common law was also in place so the trapping of business are respected.

- □ Hindus, Moslems and Sikhs are greeted differently—though their religion may not be apparent if they are wearing Western clothes

- □ They are reluctant to say "no," or prefer to respond with vagueness

- □ Indian businessmen are so prone to back-slapping and touching that Westerners find it excessive; they consider it friendly—but men should avoid touching women

Australia

Since Australia was a colony of the British Empire, language should present few barriers. Almost everyone speaks English, although be aware of British spellings and pronunciations of various words. Since they are easy-going, direct, and casual, it is easy to do business with Australians. They do not like to mix work and social events, so keep those distinctions clear. Informality is the norm. Have your business card ready. However, since not all businesses use them, you may not get one in return.

J. Saunders & Sons Pty. Limited
15 Salisbury Road
Castle Hill NSW 2154
Australia
Telephone (02) 680 4566
Home (02) 634 7640
Facsimile (02) 899 1353

Helmut Wick
Production Director

SAUNDERS
Engraved Stationery

Gold Saunders, red script; the rest black engraved type on white stock

John S. Price
Managing Director

Consultants to Management

Level 1, 18 Rodborough Road, Frenchs Forest, NSW 2086.
A.C.N. 002 315 988
Telephone: (61-2) 452 0822   Facsimile: (61-2) 971 0678
SYDNEY • MELBOURNE • CANBERRA • BRISBANE

*Black print on
white stock*

Europe: East and West

Be prim and proper, and do not take any familiarities; show respect. Suit coats are worn; women do not wear pants to work. First names may only be used if invited. Use their academic titles and degrees to show respect. Business cards are *de rigieur*. Use a weaker handshake, and be punctual in business and social events.

Status is important, so some cards include other types of information like gross revenues or number of employees. It often includes the school you graduated from, along with all degrees awarded. Education is esteemed. Some cards almost look like a mini-press release. The card is often larger than our standard card, so there is room for a note. Because of the close proximity of many countries, each with their own language, most Europeans are fluent in numerous languages. Few Americans can match them. Fortunately, most business occasions will be conducted in English or a translator will be provided.

*Red car; red
and burgundy
type and
border*

UELI EISENHUT

*BACKOFENGASSE 486, FL-9493 MAUREN
LIECHTENSTEIN VIA SWITZERLAND
TEL. 075/33356   FAX 075 33358   TELEX 889125 EIAV*

Spółka z o.o.

mgr inż. ANDRZEJ
KONCEWICZ
Prezes

ul. Grzegórzecka 10
31-530 Kraków
tel/fax: (12) 21-76-20
tel: 21-41-22 w. 40, tlx: 032-6389

Red band and "soft," the rest in black on glossy white stock

*Blue ribbon;
the rest black
on white stock*

Albrechtstraße 14 · D-8000 München 19
Tel. (0 89)12 68 06-0 · Fax (0 89)12 68 06-60

Rainer Hoffmann
Consultant

Privat: Zelterstraße 2
6370 Oberursel
Tel./Fax: 0 61 71/5 79 30

Guillermo Calleja Pardo
Vicerrector de Relaciones Internacionales

Universidad Complutense
Pabellón de Gobierno
Ciudad Universitaria
28040 Madrid

Tels. *(34)(1) 544 57 82*
(34)(1) 549 50 50
Fax *(34)(1) 544 57 82*
Telex *22459*

Black print on white stock

England and Great Britain

England and English-speaking countries still have many cultural differences from those in the United States. These include different spellings and pronunciations of common words, as well as social conventions. Not only is England's English different from ours, but it differs from the other countries of the British Islands: Wales, Ireland, and Scotland. They have many differing traditions and guard them intensely. Numerous historic grievances have strewn this whole area with minefields, and as a newcomer you won't know when you're on dangerous ground. So don't assume that just because you understand the language that you're home free.

TONY BALDRY, M.P.

House of Commons
London SW1A 0AA

Telephone: 01- 219 4476
Messages: 01- 219 4343

Engraved black print on white stock

CARDS
LIMITED
3 NEW PLAISTOW ROAD,
STRATFORD, LONDON E15 3JB

Paul S. Beck
Director

Tel: 0181-221 0033
Fax: 0181-221 0044
Mobile: 0956 552364

Gray fan and black engraved print on white stock

Moslem Countries

In Moslem countries (Near East and Africa) do not present a card with your left hand. The left hand is considered unclean and should not be used for such purposes. Likewise, it is an insult to give gifts or eat with the left hand.

There are very stringent rules regarding the way women are to be treated, so be sensitive to their gender rules. Think twice before sending a woman for conducting business in such countries.

محمد عبدالعزيز الأشهب
ممثل خدمات التسويق

مجموعة   صنـدوق بريـد ٦٥٤٩
إدارة   الريـــــــــاض ١١٤٥٢
الفـروع   المملكة العربية السعودية

تلفون : ٤٧٧٤٧٧٠
تلكس : ٤٠٧٨٤٤ آر بي جي سي بي سي إس جي

البنك السعودي الامريكي
Saudi American Bank

Two-sided card; black print on white stock...

Retail	P.O. Box 6549	Mohammed A. Al-Ash'hab
Banking	Riyadh 11452	Sales & Service Rep.
Group	Saudi Arabia	

Tel. : 4774770
Telex : 407844 RBG CPC SJ

البنك السعودي الامريكي

Saudi American Bank

Two-sided card; black print on white stock...

SECOND SECRETARY

Brian L. Goldbeck

CHIEF
ECONOMIC/COMMERCIAL SECTION

U. S. EMBASSY	TEL. EMBASSY: 271950-8
BOX 1088	COMMERCIAL OFFICE: 272417
SANAA, Y. A. R.	TELEX: 2697 EMBSAN YE

Two-sided card; black print on white stock, gold foiled emblem...

الملحــق الاقتصادي التجــارى

براين ل. جـولدبيـك

السكرتير الثـاني

سفــاره الـولايات المتحــدة الامريكية

تلكس : ٢٦٩٧ امبسان   تلفون { السفارة : ٨-٢٧١٩٥٠   ص. ب : ١٠٨٨
                                { المكتب التجاري ٢٧٢٤١٧   صنعــاء - ج. ع. ي.

...black print on reverse

Africa

Hennie Erasmus

Consul (Trade)
South African Consulate-General

9107 Wilshire Boulevard
Suite 400
Beverly Hills, CA 90210

Tel. (213) 858 0380

Black print on white stock

AVI BLANKROTH

2025 Pennsylvania Avenue, N.W.
Suite 1124
Washington, D.C. 20006
Tel: 202-828-4155
Fax: 202-828-5114

MADE IN USA
SOUTHERN AFRICA TRADE EXPO '93

WASHINGTON, D.C. · JOHANNESBURG

Two-sided card; red and blue logo; black print on white stock...

AVI BLANKROTH

Export House   1st Floor
71 Maude Street   Sandton
PO Box 651525   Benmore 2010
Johannesburg, South Africa
Tel: +27 (11) 884-5417
Fax: +27 (11) 884-5418

MADE IN USA
SOUTHERN AFRICA TRADE EXPO '93

JOHANNESBURG · WASHINGTON, D.C.

...red and blue logo; black print on reverse

Central and South America

Spanish is the prevalent language, although you will encounter English, Italian, German or Portuguese. All cards and other literature should be translated into Spanish. Educational degrees and other titles are very important, and in some case used to give a person exaggerated importance. Present the card with the Spanish side up, facing toward the recipient.

The practice is to have two surnames (Jose Gomez Garcia). The name from their father is listed first a (Gomez) and is the one commonly used in an address (Senior Gomez). The second is the name from the mother (Garcia) and it is not stated.

Family is very important. Always begin a conversation with a discussion about their family. Express interest and don't rush it.

In Latin America, a business card is treated as a form of identification. People look at the card you give them, and assume it is yours. Because that assumption has been abused, businessmen often given their cards with the corners folded down or torn off, so it can't be used improperly.

Be careful about referring to the United States or yourself as American. We are North Americans and they are Central or South Americans. They are sensitive about us northerners usurping the term "American."

Black engraved type on white stock

EDUARDO LEÓN-PÁEZ H.
TEL. 222-8747 FAX 223-0531 APDO. 4379
SAN JOSE 1000, COSTA RICA

PRESIDENTE
INTER·CONTINENTAL
ALL INCLUSIVE RESORT
Puerto Vallarta

Cecilia Reyes
Ejecutivo de Cuenta
Account Executive

Carr. Puerto Vallarta - Barra de Navidad Km. 8.5 C.P. 48300 Puerto Vallarta, Jal.
Tels. (322) 80191 y 80507 Fax. (322) 80116 y 80609 E-MAIL: intercon@pvnet.com.mx

Gold foil logo and medium blue type on textured cream stock

Canada

Canada is our large neighbor to the north, which shares many thing in common with our own country. However, Canadians are proud of their country and do not want to be treated just like a suburb of the United States. Its history is very much identified with its dual French and English roots, and in 1931 it gained independence from England. However, the country is still a part of the British Commonwealth.

Canada has two official languages: English and French. By law, all products must be labeled in both languages. Political issues have been intense as Québec (the predominantly French province) has pushed for recognition of its unique culture. As a consequence, the two cultures are struggling for political advantage and have heightened the areas of sensitivity. There is a high degree of tension between the English-speaking provinces and Quebec, which could result in Canada being broken into several autonomous nations before long.

Print your card with English on one side and French on the other, and be careful to get guidance from those familiar with the areas of controversy. The values and business styles are very different, with the English-speakers being more reserved (like those from England) while the French are much more animated and emotional.

GOVERNMENT OF **Alberta**

CANADA

*Red flag, blue
Alberta, black
type on white
stock*

Allan L. Shields

Director, Investment Promotion

MINISTRY OF ECONOMIC DEVELOPMENT AND TRADE

12th Floor, Sterling Place, 9940 - 106 St., Edmonton, Alberta T5K 2P6
Telex 037-2197 • Telefax 403/427-0487 • Tel. 403/422-6236

To Recap

Opportunities to do business with companies from abroad will increase. Those from other countries have very different priorities and customs in the way they transact business. These differences are reflected in the use of business cards. Be sensitive to such cultural differences if you wish to develop lasting relationships.

Chapter 15

Explore the History of the Business Card

This entire chapter was commissioned by the Business Card Museum and is reprinted with its permission (with only minor editing changes).

The History of the Business Card
by Jennifer McNulty

Business cards are used today by virtually every business person around the world. These 2" x 3" pieces of stock paper are exchanged constantly during business meetings and relations. Some meetings are held for the sole purpose of business card exchange. In certain countries, Japan, for example, a business card can determine the success or failure of a business transaction. How did these cards attain the importance they have in business? The answer to this question goes back almost four hundred years, starting with the emergence of the first tradesman's cards in the late 1600s. The story continues through the eighteenth century, with the development of the calling card, entering the nineteenth century with the advertising trade card. Finally, evidence of the first business cards can be found in the last two decades of the nineteenth century.

Tradesman's Cards

The fifteenth century marked an important milestone in the history of modern communication. With his invention of movable type in the 1440s, Johann Gutenberg moved society toward a new level of communication—mass communication. The development of the first printing press made possible the transmission of uniform messages and information to large groups of people.

Due to the widespread illiteracy of the time, however, the only people who were able to use printed matter were the educated upper class. It is no surprise, then, that the earliest predecessors to the modern business card appeared in the 1600s among the skilled tradesmen of the upper class. Tradesman's cards performed an important advertising function—providing information about a proprietor's location and line of wares. They were aimed at the upper class, who were the only people who could afford to be customers. And, actually, the skilled craftsmen were the only ones who had the money for the printing which was extremely expensive at that time.

The term" trade card" was never used in the seventeenth century. Instead, printers referred to these cards as shopkeeper's bills. This was due in part to the wide variety of stationery uses the card had. They sometimes served as impromptu receipts or bills, or even labels or wrappers.[1]

There are few remaining cards from the seventeenth century. But those that do exist follow a similar format—they list the name of the shop and then there is an illustration of the shopkeeper's sign. Again, it must be remembered that during this period, the majority of the population knew little, if anything, about written language. Instead, they relied on pictures and illustrations to aid them. Also, most cities were not developed to a point where they had formalized street names or numbers, so shopkeepers's signs served as their location addresses.

Calling Cards

Since the beginnings of social interaction among individuals, it has been customary for a person to announce their coming in one form or another. Some cultures sent signals, like smoke signals or drum patterns; others, such as the ancient Israelites, sent a servant ahead to announce their coming. Even in modern times, a person usually telephones or sends a note before planning a visit.

In the late seventeenth and early eighteenth centuries, the social practice of using cards, referred to as visiting or calling cards, developed. Calling cards were originally used by nobility in European countries, such as France and Italy, and later in Great Britain. These cards were handed to footmen when paying calls to announce the arrival of a visiting party. If the person being called upon was not present, the card was then left at the home so that the recipient would know of the visit. Their use was popularized during the reign of Louis XVI, when the custom developed in France to use cards when paying New Year's calls. With the abundance of visitors during that time of year, calling cards gave record of those who had stopped by with well wishes.

Calligraphers made the early calling cards, which included the name of the individual and his or her hereditary titles. Cards were embellished further with ornamentations and designs, including flowery borders and other illustrations. In better circles, cards were done on the best quality, cream-white paper with the name written in plain script.

Part of the reason that settlers came to America was to rid themselves of the social structure and class distinctions of Europe. So it seems ironic how eagerly early Americans adopted the social ritual of the calling card.[2] American ladies pursued the ritual according to the rules spelled out in etiquette books of the time, such as *Godey's Lady's Book*. One's visiting card was a subtle indication of his or her breeding. According to Godey's: "[A calling card's] texture should be fine; its engraving, a plain script, its size not too large or small to attract attention either way."[3] According to Hechtlinger and Cross, the typical dimensions of one's calling card or *carte de visite,* was 2" x 4".

Calling cards filled a real need of early Americans, especially after the Civil War. Visits to another's household were not taken lightly, considering the conditions associated with travel.[4] Without the luxury of paved roads or modern transportation, visiting usually entailed a dusty, rough ride across dirt trails and rocky terrain. In its true form, calling was a lady's principal preoccupation. Most days, one was paying calls on others, and then one afternoon per week was set aside to receive visits. Upper-class matrons typically made two or three visits an afternoon, each lasting from 20 to 30 minutes. Any and every event provided for a visit. And for each visit given, a visit equal in length was returned. Teas and cakes would be served during visits, and the main function of the call would take place—gossip.[5]

Visiting and card exchanging were very serious business for nineteenth century socialites. One did not call upon those outside of a person's own social class. Small silver trays were placed in the entrance hallways of homes to collect visiting cards. The number of cards on these trays, as well as the names on them, usually provided a good reflection of an individual's social standing.

Since it was possible to miss the person being called on, either because they were out, resting or ill, a practice of "turning cards" evolved. By turning particular corners of one's card, messages could be sent, even in the absence of the receiver. There were four statements that one could make simply by folding down the corners of a card. They are, with their French names: *visite, felicitation, conge,* and *condolence.* Visite entailed turning the upper left corner of one's card. It meant that the visitor had come in person and a call should be returned when the recipient had a chance. Felicitation sent a message of congratulations to the recipient, for events such as weddings and births. In that case, the upper right corner was turned. Turning the lower right corner for condolence expressed sympathy for the recipient on a death or ill-fated event. Finally, a

Figure 1: Calling cards varied in price from 30 for 10 cents to 12 for 20 cents. A rate card from around 1895 distributed by the Crown Card Company in Cadiz, Ohio, gives a sample of the kinds of cards available and their respective prices.

turn of the lower left corner meant conge. Conge announced that one was leaving town and, hence, no visits were required until his or her return.[6]

Calling card cases brought an extra sense of elegance to this formalized event. These cases were tucked into a young lady's reticule before a social visit.[7] They were made of a variety of materials, from gold and silver, to carved ivory, mother-of-pearl, wood, silk, velvet, leather and hand-embroidered wrist bags. A person's calling card case was just as much a status symbol as the cards it held.

The term "calling cards" includes several slightly varied kinds of cards that were used during the time period from the late seventeenth century to the mid-eighteenth century. Friendship, mourning, and hidden name cards usually fall under the catch-all term of calling cards, although they each served distinct purposes. Friendship cards were exchanged among close acquaintances. Some of them had warm wishes or loving sentiments printed on them in addition to one's name. Formal mourning cards were given out upon the death of a friend or loved one. They usually had phrases such as "with sympathy" or "in loving memory" printed on them.

Some individuals chose to use hidden name cards for their visiting card (Figure 2). These cards were made of pasteboard with a cutout decorative flap on the front. When the flap was lifted it revealed the name of the person who gave it.

Figure 2: The hidden name card (top) opened to reveal a name (bottom).

Advertising Trade Cards

The industrial revolution of the eighteenth and nineteenth centuries transformed society from agrarian to industrial. Advances in technology led to the mass production of goods. Society was entering a production era when goods were being produced in large quantities. The problem early manufacturers faced was the public's lack of awareness about the wide variety of goods and services available. Advertising was the answer. A related problem resulted from strict governmental rules regarding where advertising could or could not be placed. A partial remedy was found with the emergence of the advertising trade card. Similar to the early tradesmen's cards, advertising trade cards sought to inform consumers of the availability and location of goods and services. According to a pamphlet distributed by The Trade Card Collector's Club, as industry boomed, businesses discovered that their success or failure hinged upon their ability to capture the public's attention and draw people into new patterns of spending.

Ranging from wallet size to postcard size and larger, trade cards surfaced in the early 1800s as lithographers began printing cards for nearly every product being manufactured. (Lithography was a flat-plate printing process in which printed and non-printed surfaces existed on the same plate, allowing for detailed color printing.) It was a less expensive method of printing than the other methods available. By the 1890s, lithographed cards had almost completely supplanted all other forms of printed cards.

Advertising trade cards were given to the purchasers of many assorted items, including shoes, thread and other household items, especially during the Victorian era.[8] Large and small companies alike used trade cards to advertise their products and services. These cards were left on counters for customers to take, handed out by traveling salesmen, or mailed to prospective clients.

Trade cards were usually illustrated, relying on visual appeal and wit to attract the attention of customers.[9] Advertising trade cards were designed to be flashy, clever and durable, in the advertiser's hope that the miniature prints would be passed around and saved, constantly reminding consumers of goods and services being offered.[10] Advertisers were successful in one respect: their cards were kept by consumers. Families would paste these cards into albums, like they kept photographs. Entire scrapbooks were put together that incorporated trade cards, visiting cards, post cards, love letters, pressed flowers, scraps of lace, buttons, product labels and wrappers, bits of wrapping paper and other small tokens. In fact, the public's interest in saving these cards led companies to tailor their cards to the popular images and themes of the time. Some companies even went so far as to run a series of cards carrying a continuous theme. In any case, advertising trade cards served as reflections of the attitudes and opinions of the American people.

Some of the major themes that can be found in the trade cards of nineteenth century America are: patriotic images, contrasts between city life and country life, racial stereotypes, women (and the home), and children.[11] With the Civil War just behind them, Americans were in the process of rebuilding their country. National "mascots" such as Uncle Sam (and his predecessors, Brother Jonathan, Columbia and Lady Liberty) became popular, and appeared frequently on trade cards.

The contrast between city and country life was a second popular theme in American trade cards. Cities were pictured as magnificent monuments to industry, with cityscapes and warehouses being two of the more prominent images used in advertising. By contrast, the country was portrayed as very idyllic. Since most of the printers of trade cared were from the city, they had little knowledge of what country living was really like, so instead, they painted a picture of what they *thought* it was like. Scenes of large rolling hills, manors and plantations represented an idealistic image of what country life was supposed to be. The truth was that, although some families were fortunate enough to have the luxury of a large farm estate, the majority of rural dwellers lived in smaller, much simpler conditions.

A third, and very important, theme that ran in advertising trade cards was the portrayal of racial stereotypes. Some of the major non-Caucasian races that were addressed were blacks, Indians, Chinese and Japanese[12] [the section on the various racial stereotypes omitted].

Figure 3: Trade card for the Hektograph Co. in New York.

The fourth major theme in advertising trade cards related to women. Reflecting the view of her position in nineteenth-century society, the image of women was almost invariably represented as a dutiful wife and a loving mother.[13] Since many of the items advertised on trade cards were household items, it is only natural that these cards would speak to women and their role in society. Many such advertisements emphasized the qualities of products or services that would allow a woman to improve her role as mother and wife. For example, a trade card for Scourene shows the lady of the house saying, "I need not depend on anyone, for housecleaning is my only pastime since I procured Scourene." It emphasized the ease in using the product, and suggested that cleaning could be more efficiently done with it. Other cards show women in groups, (sometimes with children) going about their chores, such as washing, sewing or ironing together.

Children were the last major theme used in advertising trade cards. Children were considered the most prized possession of Victorian parents. With the growing wealth and advancing technologies of the nineteenth century, parents had more time and money to spend on and with their children. Often, children were treated as miniature adults. They were dressed up in the finest clothes and were often given parties, sometimes with as many as fifty children attending. Children appear frequently in trade cards for items varying from clothing to medicines, soaps to silverware.

Figure 4: Advertising trade card for L.H. Yeager & Co., sellers of china, glass and silverware.

It is important to remember that advertising trade cards were just that—advertisements. Many times the illustrations on these cards had nothing to do with the product or service being offered. Essentially, these cards were designed to be collected and kept as reminders. If they promoted sales for a company, that was an added bonus.

Business Cards

Around 1880, the term "business card" was coined to describe a newer, more simplified form of card communication. The purpose of these cards, according to an etiquette book of the time, was to be a valuable form of advertising, as well as an introduction to business acquaintances.[14] Business cards were predominantly black and white, unlike the brightly colored trade cards. They contained basic contact information, company name, and address. Instead of being handed out indiscriminately, these cards were exchanged between business contacts. Essentially, business cards provided the same function as early tradesmen's cards.

The use of business cards continued throughout the end of the nineteenth century, and these cards are still used in business today. Nearly every country in the world uses business cards for formal business interaction, although their importance varies. In American business, cards are distributed casually in day-to-day routines. Cards are left behind after meeting with a client, inserted into brochures, posted on community boards, handed out to acquaintances, and so on. In other countries, cards are used in different ways. The country where business cards serve the utmost of importance, however is Japan. [Most of the section on Japan is omitted, since similar information is found in Chapter 14 on international uses of business cards.]

When doing business in Japan, both sides of one's business card should be imprinted—one with the business person's regular card and the opposite side with a Japanese translation. The Japanese business person will also have a double-sided card with the appropriate translation for the receiver. When presenting cards, it is important that the side with the proper translation for the recipient is facing up.

PacRim
MARKETING GROUP INC.

DAVE ERDMAN
President

2758 S. King St., Suite 206 ☐ Honolulu, HI USA 96826-3345
Phone (808) 949-4592 ☐ Fax (808) 942-5251
Toll Free 1-800-338-4502 U.S. ☐ eMail: erdman@eworld.com

DIRECT MARKETING • SALES PROMOTION • JAPAN/U.S.A. ENTRY PROGRAMS

Figure 5: On the top, the regular business card with the Japanese translation on the back (bottom).

パックリム
マーケティング・グループ

出 武　亜土万
取締役社長

ハワイ州ホノルル市サウス・キング通り2758　206号室
郵便番号96826-3345
Tel:(808) 949-4592　米国内無料電話:(800) 338-4502
Fax:(808) 942-5251

Cards are passed with the thumb and forefinger. Giving or receiving a card with both hands shows greater humility toward the other person.[15] The photograph below depicts a Japanese business card exchange.

Figure 6: Card exchange between Japanese and American businessmen.

Business Card Design

Not so long ago, business cards were printed on plain white card stock. The provided a concise summary of contact information: name, company, title, department, address and telephone number. They were considered part of a business person's stationery, along with envelopes and letterhead. Usually, each of the pieces was coordinated, exhibiting the same logos and typestyles. This new format was developed during the sales era, which followed the production era of the industrial revolution. During the sales era, manufacturers produced goods which, in turn, company representatives sold to the population at large. The focus during this period was on selling. If a salesperson did not make a sale with one customer, they simply pressed on to the next prospect.

During the mid-1950s, a shift occurred in the economy at large, from being sales oriented to being more market driven. The focus shifted to the customer. Companies realized that they could not rely on sales alone to be profitable; instead, they had to address the needs of their market. By producing goods and services that the public demanded, sales of these items would come naturally. As this new, marketing era ensued, companies learned that the relationship between producer and consumer was dynamic, and interaction between these two groups worked both ways. As more companies adopted a marketing concept, they realized that they needed to develop a method to attract customers, much like the trade cards did in the nineteenth century.

'Business cards became the equivalent of miniature billboards, representing on a 3 1/2" x 2" piece of paper different products and services. Design became a more important aspect of one's business card. The objective was to present as much information about a company as was needed in the most effective way. Note the emphasis on the amount of information to be put onto one's card. With such a small area to work with, too much information listed on one's card could product clutter, thereby, making the card ineffective. According to Murray Raphel, an award-winning advertising and marketing consultant, business cards tell people who you are, what you do, and how to contact you in as few words as possible.

The difference between a good business card and a great one lies in its design. The function of design is to get a point across, not just to decorate one's card. Through the thoughtful use of format, size, color, typography and typeface, logomark and illustration, one can express an endless variety of messages.[16]

The term business "card" [as in cardstock] is very limiting. More companies and individuals are choosing to imprint their business cards on a wide variety of materials including: metal, wood, plastic, leather, glass, china, vinyl and paper. They are also employing different printing methods. Some of these imprinting methods are raised-letter thermography, hot foil stamping, embossing, debossing, four-color process, screen printing and engraving. Although the standard business card tends to be printed horizontally on a piece of 2" x 3 1/2" cardstock, cards of larger and smaller sizes are available, as well as die-cut cards, which are printed and then cut into custom shapes. Vertical cards, cards with printed backs, fold-over cards, and photo cards are among the design styles encountered.

Some modern-day companies have gone so far as to incorporate products they manufacture into their business cards. For example, there are cards printed on emery boards, circuit boards, cardboard, seed packets, fabric samples, wallpaper pieces, mouse pad materials, china plates, ceramic mugs, gold and silver coins, templates, rulers and mini-menus.

Business cards are a reflection of the person handing them out. The elements and design of a business card should convey the same message as the company or individual would convey in person. Therefore, with a profession such as a lawyer, a card with a clean layout and subdued graphics is appropriate. On the other hand, an advertising consultant may choose a card with bright, vivid colors and bold type that would immediately catch the receiver's attention. Each card reflects the nature of the business and the presenter.

There is no limit to the possibilities for business card design. However, when designing one's business card, it is important to include certain fundamental elements. Contact information is an obvious element of information. The name, location and telephone number of a company or individual should certainly be included. With the changing technologies in communications, modern business persons are including e-mail addresses, World Wide Web sites, and so on. Another important piece to incorporate into a business card is a brief explanation of the products or services available. Unless a company name or job title is descriptive enough in itself, (for example, The Acme Nut and Bolt Manufacturing Company), a receiver may not be able to tell what a company does. The description of services can be expressed in a line of type or illustrated through a clever graphic.

Business cards are the most personal form of advertising in business. It is critical that the messages conveyed by these cards are an accurate reflection of the company or individual distributing them. Business card design helps to create these messages and present them in an effective manner.

Technology and Business Cards

Recently, there has been a shift in the major forms of communication worldwide. The Internet and electronic mail, along with other forms of digitized communications have changed the face of business and effected the ways in which business is conducted. Business cards have been swept along in this wave of change. Machines have been invented that scan business cards into computer data bases, and more recently, they have been put into disk format. Who is to say how much longer business cards will remain an integral part of business relations? But one thing remains certain—business cards hold their own place in the history of business.

The Business Card Museum

Erdenheim, Pennsylvania, (215) 836-0555

Chapter **16**

Decode Our Culture and History through Business Cards— The Business Card Archives & The Business Card Museum

Fifty Million!

Fifty Million—that's a mighty large number. In fact, it's an almost unbelievable number. Try to visualize 50,000,000 anything—even if it's something as small as a business card. It makes a really big pile, whatever you're talking about.

The mind doesn't know how to grasp such large quantities. I certainly couldn't. So the first time I heard of the Business Card Archives, or the fact that there was a man who had that many cards, I though it was either an exaggeration or a misprint. The first few times I talked about it, my mind had already tried to make it manageable by referring to "the man with five (sic) million cards." But it's true, I've seen them, sort of. I've been to the Business Card Archives and met the highly enthusiastic caretaker. I've heard his philosophy that cards have historic and cultural value. And I've heard the amazing (yes, in this case it's not an exaggeration) story of how the Archives came to have over fifty million cards.

All of the cards shown in this chapter are from the Business Card Archives, as well as others shown throughout the book.

Walter Day Is the Guardian of the Archives

I'm willing to bet that before you finish this page, you'll be saying, "I've heard of that guy." Walter Day is the spirit, heck, the whole moving force, behind the Business Card Archives, located in Fairfield, Iowa (which is itself a most unusual community). He is a collector of interesting things, and in the process, he finds ways to make us interested in them as well. He has done it several times, and in each case he made his interests become highly visible to the media.

In the last twenty years, there have been more than one thousand articles on Walter and his various projects, and he has been on nearly as many radio and TV shows. You probably don't remember his name, but you'll remember having heard about what he's talked about. His high visibility on behalf of an array of causes has led a media insider to refer to him as "the most famous non-famous person." He has generated so much media exposure for his successive projects that he keeps showing up in the news time and again.

His adventures over the last twenty years have included:

□ Newspapers—Selling (and reproducing) historical newspapers as collectibles and historical teaching materials

□ Yearbooks—Collecting yearbooks, particularly of famous people; if you've seen any celebrity's high-school picture, it's probably because of Walter's collection

□ Video and Pinball Scores—By creating the "World's Most Famous Arcade" in Ottumwa, Iowa, he became the Official Scorekeeper for that sport and determines the "official" record holders. He has been regularly contacted and quoted by everyone from Guinness Book of Records to all the national wire services.*

□ Business Cards—Known as "The Business Card Detective"

---

* Walter Day has released *Twin Galaxies' Official Videogame & Pinball Book of World Records* (984 pages, the "Bible of Games"). It is available for $19.95 from your local bookstore.

Photograph of Walter Day at the Business Card Archives

Walter becomes downright eloquent and quotable when he talks about business cards, because he considers them a reflection of the culture that produced them. Here are a few of his quotes:

- "If you would take all the cards carried by a man over his lifetime, you would see a tapestry of his entire life."
- "Business cards are like little footprints that show a man's trajectory through life."
- "Business cards give us a rare glimpse into secret nooks and crannies of our culture, that we may not otherwise see."
- Business cards let you "see the unusual things people do for a living, that fill such narrow niches: so obscure, so unusual, so fine tuned."
- "Think of cards as fingerprints, that have captured the world culture at its funniest, its strongest, and its most thought-provoking moments."

OWEN R. MURTAGH
COLLECTOR

SHERLOCK HOLMES

ALL TYPES   **371-9644**

MEMORABILIA

Brown print on cream stock; notice it was printed prior to area codes

---

THE
SMOTHERS
BROTHERS

MARCY CARRIKER

SMOBRO PRODUCTIONS
8489 W. THIRD STREET • SUITE 1078 • LOS ANGELES, CA • 90048
(213) 651-5718 • FAX (213) 651-3503

Black ink on off-white stock

A Trip to Fairfield, Iowa

My trip to the Business Card Archives was like going to "where business cards go to die," rather like the "elephant graveyard." They have been lovingly gathered by Walter Day in his large Victorian house; but the boxes of cards completely fill it. There are boxes stacked floor to ceiling in room after room, and the basement, and the out-buildings, and some have been stored elsewhere as well. Cards are packed everywhere!

Visualize, if you will, a box large enough to hold a refrigerator, filled to the top with business cards. Now multiply that by fourteen such boxes, and that's about a million cards. So now multiply that quantity by fifty and you start to sense the immensity of the enterprise. Most of the cards are still uncataloged. Walter said he spent two years organizing just over a million of them—and just that smallish portion that I viewed was still impressive.

Once I got over being overwhelmed, I was struck first by the beauty and the infinite variety obvious in such an array of cards. I was also caught by the vision. Here was a microcosm of businesses that revealed the changing tastes and styles over the entire 20th century. Just in the two days I spent immersed in the cards, I became much more discerning.

Walter had already established himself as an inveterate business card collector, and by 1990 had amassed approximately one million cards. It was then that his story and the Craig Shergold story intersected; for most of Walter's collection exists because of the unprecedented responses to Craig's wish.

A STORY THAT TOUCHED THE WORLD'S HEART
Craig Shergold's Wish

Nearly ten years ago, a nine-year-old boy in England named Craig Shergold was diagnosed with an incurable brain tumor. While he was in the hospital undergoing treatment, he received many get well messages from friends and family. When it was noted that he was getting so many cards, it turned into a challenge to see how many cards he could get. Initially, requests were spread by hospital staff and family friends, but Craig, too, began to request more greeting cards.

The local newspapers shared the tear-jerking story—which was spread by radio, TV and print media all over the world. This deeply moving story became a media event, which had unanticipated consequences. Soon, the wish became a desire to get into the Guinness Book of World Records for having the largest greeting-card collection. Word spread. Craig Shergold received all kinds of help to fulfill his last wish. Somehow, along the way, that request got distorted into requests for postcards or business cards, as well. Those variations were mistakes, for in truth, he had only wanted get well-cards.

The public was touched in a very real way by whichever version of the story they heard. It was about that time that fax machines were becoming standard office equipment. Caring people kept their fax machines worked overtime, transmitting the story and requesting a display of concern for the dying child. The phenomenal outpouring of response is itself a major story of caring, and provides dramatic evidence against the public's indifference to another's suffering. This story has touched many people deeply, so they will be interested to know the next chapter of the story.

For Craig the end of the story is happy. He was brought to the United States where state-of-the-art surgical techniques successfully removed the tumor. Craig recovered and has not suffered any further symptoms. For everyone else affected by this story, there has been no end as yet.

At some point, the request was turned into something akin to a chain letter, that keeps generating wave after wave of additional mail. More recently, the request keeps reappearing on the Internet. There are many different versions that continue to stir the emotions, but they share a very specific call to action—send cards.

The little town in England where Craig lived was inundated. "But with Craig now well into his teens, his dream has turned into a nightmare for the post office in the small town outside London where he lives. Like Craig himself, his request for cards just refuses to die, inundating the post office with millions of cards every year. Just when it seems like the flow is slowing, along comes somebody else who starts up a whole new slew of requests for people to send Craig post cards (or greeting cards or business cards—Craig's letters have truly taken on a life of their own and begun to mutate)."[1] Since the Children's Wish Foundation of Atlanta, Georgia, has been listed as the address to collect and count cards, most of the outpouring of cards, of any type, has been sent there.

Craig Shergold Time Sequence

February, 1989	Diagnosed with brain tumor (age 9)
	Made an appeal for greeting cards
September, 1989	Media (*Daily Mirror* and *Sun,* England) launched card appeals for Craig, which were picked up and transmitted by all the wire services
May, 1990	Craig made Guinness Book of Records with over 16 million cards
March, 1991	Tumor successfully removed; no recurrence to date
1992	Craig listed in Guinness as receiving over 33 million cards
Since 1992	Ongoing and constant appeals to stop cards

Confusion Between Children's Wish Foundation and Make a Wish Foundation

Fulfilling Craig's wish had been undertaken by the Children's Wish Foundation (headquartered in Georgia). Its goal is "to fulfill the favorite wish of a terminally ill child. It also helps provide the family with some special memories—not just final images of hospitals, doctors, and intravenous equipment."[2] The Children's Wish Foundation is easily confused with the Make a Wish Foundation (based in Arizona). Both organizations provide a special wish to terminally ill children, but they operate very differently. For example, Children's Wish Foundation provides wishes to children in other countries, while the other does not. Since Craig was from England, he would not have been involved with the Make a Wish Foundation. However, because the two organizations often tend to be lumped together in the minds of the public, both have felt the outpouring of cards and well wishes generated by Craig's wish.

Although the Make a Wish Foundation (Phoenix) was **never involved**, they, too, have tried valiantly to stem the flood with press releases and a hotline for queries regarding Craig. It has not helped; cards continue to pour in.

CHILDREN'S WISH
FOUNDATION
INTERNATIONAL ®

CHILDREN'S WISH FOUNDATION OVERWHELMED BY MAIL FOR MIRACLE WISH KID

ATLANTA (May 20, 1997) Thousands of cards continue to pour into Children's Wish Foundation International, Inc. each day even though Craig Shergold's wish to be in the Guiness Book of World Records was fulfilled over seven years ago.

WHO:
Craig Shergold, the Miracle Wish Kid who, at age 9, was diagnosed with a brain tumor in 1989 and was not expected to survive more than a few months.

Today, Craig is 17 years old and lives with his family in Carshalton, England. He underwent surgery in May 1991 at the University of Virginia Hospital and 85-90 % of the tumor was removed. Craig's doctors are hopeful that the rest of the tumor is benign.

WHAT:
Craig's wish was to be in the Guiness Book of World Records for receiving the most get-well cards. A group of volunteers in England contacted Children's Wish Foundation International. The Foundation immediately began soliciting get well cards. Craig's wish was fulfilled in May 1990 when he was listed in the 1991 Guiness Book with a new world record: over 16, 250,000 get well cards. Cards continued to pour in, earning Craig a listing in the 1992 Guiness Book for receiving 33 million cards. To date, Craig has received over 100 million cards.

WHERE:
Craig's mail fills up whole rooms of Children's Wish Foundation's warehouse. The Foundation relies on a staff of volunteers to sort through the mail, sending it off to recycling at the Shergold's request.

WHY:
Children's Wish Foundation International, Inc., is a nonprofit organization that seeks to fulfill the wishes of seriously ill children throughout the world.

PHOTO OPPORTUNITY:
Warehouse rooms full of mail at Children's Wish Foundation International in Atlanta, Georgia.

# # # #

Headquarters: 3615 Roswell Road, Atlanta, GA 30350-7526, 770-393-WISH (9474), 1-800-323-WISH (9474), Fax 770-393-068
Correspondence Address: Post Office Box 28785, Atlanta, Georgia 30358
United Kingdom: 48 Curzon Street, Mayfair, London W1Y 7RE, 071-493-1356, Fax 071-493-1308

CRAIG'S BOUNTY TO THE ARCHIVES
How Millions of Cards Came to Iowa

It was apparent by 1990 that the scale of the card contribution was unprecedented. When Walter contacted Children's Wish Foundation in Georgia, he asked if he could have some of the unused cards for his collection. They were pleased to transfer the bounty, if he would come and get them. Walter arranged to have them shipped to Fairfield, Iowa. One day, a 46-foot semi-truck pulled up in front of his house. Three days later, despite two people working full time, it was still being unloaded when yet another 46-foot truck arrived. Walter and the Archives are still adjusting to the scale of that delivery. No contributions to the Business Card Archives have occurred since. The house became severely impacted, and determined progress toward organization has barely made a dent.

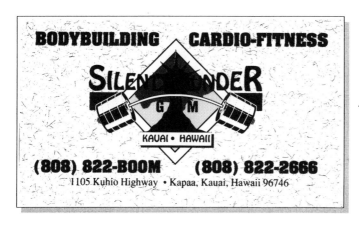

Turquoise and salmon in logo; black print on gray-flecked stock

The Avalanche of Cards Continues Today

The scale of contributions is beyond anything that could have been predicted. To this day, there have been over 330 million cards received at the Children's Wish Foundation. Many of them come in parcels which include small presents, as well. A high volume of additional responses come by fax machine, but these have never been tallied.

According to director, Arthur Stein, at the height of the response, the Children's Wish Foundation was in a donated location in a prestigious office complex. The traffic jams created by the delivery trucks and postal vehicles were so constant that they interfered with the other tenants, and they eventually lost their lease.

Like *The Miracle on 34th Street*

We all grew up with the 1939 movie about the old man who worked at Macy's and claimed to be Santa Claus. The movie's drama rested on the fact that the US Postal Service is obligated by law to deliver the mail to the proper person. In that movie, the post office delivered all the letters addressed to Santa Claus to the old man—proving to all the world that he must be who he claimed to be.

The Craig Shergold story is like the story of that Santa. Almost any variation of his name, with or without the address will reach the Children's Wish Foundation. When the mail was at its highest, it was dispatched by the truckload. Now, the postal volume has dwindled to four or five trays of mail a day (a tray is nearly 3 feet long, and holds 50 to 60 letters per foot). That translates to over 700 letters a day still coming in. The Foundation has about 75 volunteers that do nothing but process the "Craig correspondence."

Not all the mail arrives by the US mails. Federal Express and United Parcel Service also continue to make large and constant deliveries. To this day, packages are even sent overnight or with rush handling instructions, since the senders are hoping to get their offerings to the boy in time. Considering that forty percent of the volume comes from foreign countries, there is a lot of money involved.

Forest green and dark red on greenish stock

Odd-sized card; black and gray on off-white stock(2.5")

What Happens to What Arrives?

Every letter and package is opened and tallied. The cards themselves are not kept, but for some years have been sent to a landfill. The gifts or trinkets are passed to appropriate recipients. While these letters increased public awareness of the Foundation and help bring additional wishes by dying children to its attention, it has brought little in the way of monetary donations. Mrs. Shergold had authorized the Children's Wish to apply any contributions received in Craig's name toward helping other children achieve their wishes. To date, that amount hasn't exceeded $18,000. That is a noble sum, but small when considered against the massive amounts spent on postage and shipping.

Pleas to Stop the Cards Have Failed

Since Craig reached his goal to set a world record with his card collection in 1991, he has had no further interest in more cards. The pleas to stop the flow of cards and sympathy started soon thereafter. They have included media heavies like Dear Abby and The Today Show. The story has already entered the realm of legend—to be whispered from mouth to mouth. But it's about many real, ordinary people doing a little something in an effort to "make a difference." Mr. Erdman, the founder of The Business Card Museum (latter part of this chapter) said every week brings multiple requests from people asking the Museum to send any extra cards to the "dying boy."

The force of goodness which is behind all these interminable responses is very real and sincere. It shows that people are eager to do good, if they know what is needed. Unfortunately, most of the effort is misplaced and does minimal good. The energy should be redirected to other more worthwhile activities. **STOP SENDING CARDS.**

It also shows that that momentum is hard to extinguish, once it starts to build. Imagine what could be accomplished if so many caring people could put the same level of energy behind another worthwhile effort. Think what could be achieved if that amount of concern were directed toward other beneficiaries!

Walter's Dream and the Business Card Archives

What started as an interesting story about the Archives has grown as surely as Walter's collection. This has given me a sense of perspective as to the larger importance of cards, far beyond their impact on individual businesses. Each card is a tiny piece of a larger context. Further, the human interest angle is, itself, the hero of this story. It is undaunted and unflagging. All those people who responded did so as an expression of their innate goodness. That deserves applause because it speaks to the human soul rather than to material reward.

The Business Card Archives can provide only a partial means to preserve a collection that has historic and cultural significance. Walter Day feels that it should be placed in the hands of a broader non-profit organization that can further organize it, expand it, and assure the cards' continued survival. My involvement with this project has influenced me to care that cards receive a heightened appreciation. In that spirit, and to sustain efforts to protect and catalog those cards already held by the Business Card Archives, I will donate a portion of the sale of each book to such an organization for that purpose.

For more information

The Business Card Archives
P.O. Box 1556, Fairfield, Iowa 52556

THE BUSINESS CARD MUSEUM
Visit the Business Card Museum

No treatise on business cards would be complete without a reference to the Business Card Museum in suburban Philadelphia, Pennsylvania, founded by Ken Erdman, a writer, speaker, and advertising executive. He is Chairman of the Three Marketeers, Inc, a promotional products supplier. It sells, among other promotional products, unusual business cards and products imprinted with business cards.

Over the years, he threw unusual business cars he received into a box on his desk, a collection that eventually grew to exceed 300,000 cards. In 1989, Erdman received an assignment to write a cover story on the importance of business cards for *The Rotarian*[3] (the official magazine for Rotary International, with a circulation of over 500,000). That article included a sidebar wherein the editor suggested that readers send Erdman unusual cards. The flood gates soon opened!

Now Ken pursued his hobby with real vigor and he let his large network of friends and business associates know he was collecting. And the cards kept coming. As his interest grew, he discovered that there was no museum devoted to business cards. Recognizing the artistic and historical importance of business cards as collectibles, he established the Business Card Museum as a not-for-profit corporation in Pennsylvania.

The goal of the museum was to collect interesting and unusual cards, antique cards (dating back to the mid 1800s), cards with interesting graphics, cards of celebrities, cards with unusual personal and business names, humorous cards, cards made of unusual materials, die-cut cards, magnetic cards, and special collections such as cards of Rotarians, cards from people connected with the United Nations, cards from diners across the country—all special interests of Ken's. For cards to be included in the Museum's collection, they had to contain graphics or meet one of the criteria mentioned above. Cards with only plain type are relegated to storage boxes for trading with other collectors.

In addition to the hundreds of drawers that organize the cards according to numerous criteria, the Museum has emphasized displaying cards. It has glass shelving along one wall, an old refrigerator door to display magnetic business cards, and racks of poster panels with cards attached. The Museum also has most of the books written on business cards (not many), hundreds of magazine and newspaper articles about cards, and relevant audio and video tapes on the topic.

Additionally, it has made slides of the best examples to be used in Ken's many speaking engagements. Currently, he and his helpers are putting together a traveling exhibit for schools and libraries. There is also a Business Card Museum newsletter.

Ken is ever-ready to talk about his hobby, which has certainly grown into a monumental activity and resource.

- ❑ "The business card is a direct reflection of either the person or the business."
- ❑ "Over the years, in studying and reviewing cards of the late 19th century and thereafter, you can see the evolution of print, type, design, graphics and photography, which gives you an overview of advertising and marketing."
- ❑ "Your card, properly designed, establishes credibility in the mind of the receiver."
- ❑ "The business card creates an image of the giver, whether delivered in person or any other way."

Networking Leads to Unexpected Results

Ken is an avid networker and wrote one of the first books on the topic: *Network Your Way to Success* (Ken Erdman and Tom Sullivan, Philadelphia, PA, Marketers Bookshelf, 1992). So it is fitting that the growth of the Business Card Museum is so tightly connected with networking. At a local Tourist Bureau annual meeting, Ken exchanged cards with a newspaper reporter and told him that his card would now be in the Business Card Museum. The reporter chuckled after hearing the story of the museum and mentioned it some weeks later in a conversation with another reporter who was looking for an "off the wall" story for the Sunday edition. The result was that the second reporter spent half a day at the museum and featured it in the Chicago Tribune. The Tribune hired an Associated Press photographer to come to take pictures for the story. He was so impressed, he arranged for the Associated Press to do a similar story. The story appeared with a color picture that appeared in cities around the country—and more cards rolled in.

And still the story didn't end. Another interview was picked up by the Knight Rider chain of papers, leading to yet another round of publicity. TV and radio interviews followed, as well as news in the foreign press. The exciting part of the story is that all the positive publicity that brought the Business Card Museum to the world came from the simple act of exchanging business cards between two people who had just met. It truly was the "handshake left behind."

Support for the nonprofit Business Card Museum comes from memberships in the museum and items sold in the museum store. It is open by appointment Monday Through Friday, and Saturday or Sunday for people coming from long distances.

For more information

Business Card Museum
402 Bethlehem Pike, Erdenheim, Pennsylvania 19038
(a north-western suburb of Philadelphia)
(215) 836-0555

Your Card Is Your Cover

Think of yourself as a book and your business card as your book cover. Would people want to see what is inside? People can and do tell a book by its cover (the part they see first), and that is what induces them to want more. It is not that different with you. Your business card creates an expectation of what is to come. Make sure you have one that shows how good you *really* are.

Walter Day's comment in Chapter 16 reminds us that it may be possible to view a man's life by seeing his developing series of business cards. What new "chapters" are you likely to create, now that you've given your business card its much-deserved attention?

And In Conclusion...

The word "Conclusion" is a bit misleading. In this instance, it merely serves to say there are no more chapters—now the "ball is in your court." You can create your own personalized chapters by the way you use the information to craft your business image with just the right touch. There is no such thing as "till death do us part" when it comes to a business card. You should constantly re-invent your card because that process encourages you to stay fresh and receptive. Your card should reflect the changes so necessary to survive in business.

A business card is powerful, with influence out of proportion to its size. That's why having a dramatic and noteworthy card does so much good. It creates interest in you and what you do. It communicates on several levels—a silent ambassador that is not so silent. It is the embodiment of all you are and do, and as such, deserves serious consideration.

Let Your Card Grow Along With You

A business card should be a central part of your strategy for building interest in your business. You want to lead people to buy what you offer, and be glad they did. The messages that accompany your card are not invisible, but some are close to being so. Many messages are direct, and while others may be subtle, they are nonetheless registered. The information you have gathered in your reading of this book will help you understand the intentional and unintentional messages you send. Your new-found knowledge of business cards will not only enable you to intelligently craft your own card, but will also help you read the telltale messages sent by others.

Print some modified cards. As you give them away, watch for reactions. Make a point of giving them to everyone, even those who have your old cards (especially those people) and say, "Here's my new card; what do you think?" As you continue to solicit reactions and notice features shown on other people's cards, you will begin to think of other modifications you can make. Here is a shocking and novel idea: **You don't have to be down to the end of the box before you print your next improvement**.

As your business "changes" so should your card. Let your even-better, ever-evolving card start working for you right away! Would you get a new outfit and leave it in the closet until the old one wears out?!! Of course not. Put your new marketing image and identity to work without delay.

Greater Awareness Yields Better Choices

By now you've probably noticed that there is much more information in this book than that which pertains solely to business cards. You have become aware of the ways your business choices effect the way customers respond to you. Nothing occurs in isolation. The card reflects the priorities of the business and its management. It personifies the company. Attention to business card "body language" makes one notice what the customers see, and provides the advantage of a new and different perspective that is so essential. The mere decision to improve the messages on the card often changes the way a businessman sees himself, his business, and his involvement in his industry.

Never consider a detail minor. The purpose of this book is to show you that communication occurs with or without your control. How well you know your customers or clients is reflected by how well you communicate with them. If you are not careful about the subtle messages you and your business are sending, why should they think you'll be careful about the things you promise to do for them? There is no mystery here—no fancy decoding tricks. Anyone can find the hidden messages on a business card—and many people do. They simply don't bother to tell you why they find you desirable or not.

A Strong Card Builds a Stronger Business

If this book does nothing more than make you take a more perceptive look at business cards, your time has been well spent. If, however, you take its lessons to heart, you have gathered information that will provide benefits throughout your life. The steps taken to develop a business card can be applied in many situations. Your card is but a sample of how you handle more complex demands. Look for signs of coherence and consistency. Praise and reward it when you find it.

Pride in your business is reflected in your card and is part of its body language. When your card sends a message of competence and quality, you may rest assured that you've created something to be proud of. If your card makes the right connections and creates favorable impressions, you will begin to open doors that may otherwise have been closed. Customers, sales, profits—all can be enhanced by the little business card—your hard-working, silent ambassador.

Section IV

References, Resources and Other Notes of Interest

To Those in College or Business School

Taking classes in business is preparation for a life in the world of commerce. Although your course work may be informative and challenging, it is far from complete. Of equal weight is the application of all that newly-acquired knowledge in the work world. Your ability to weave the "book larnin" to business practicalities will determine your value to your employer, and ultimately the amount you can earn.

Your course preparation deals with the *facts* of business, but without the politics, the human interactions, the frustrations and the daily pressures which are an inevitable part of business life. Your prosperity demands that you learn how to function within the corporate culture, learn to "read" situations quickly and accurately. Each company will be different, but all of them require that you adjust to their prevailing corporate milieu.

Every business is being buffeted by massive forces for change within its industry, as well as from foreign countries. Couple those pressures with major demographic and social shifts, government intervention, altered consumer expectations, and the impact of competitors, and you see why businesses are being challenged to change in unprecedented ways. You, too, must learn how to swim in those turbulent waters so that your years of preparation can be productive.

You are planning either to be an employee or self-employed. During your work life you are likely to be both. Either road brings different rewards, different risks, different trade-offs. Though you don't know what's ahead, you need to know that **the ability to survive and flourish most often goes to the nimble**. Being nimble combines alert, timely perceptions with the ability to act decisively. The capacity to "read the signals," then respond appropriately was necessary for the caveman, but is no less important today. They are different signals—but no less vital.

How this Book Can Help

Woven throughout this book is a steady discussion of the *logic that is behind various business decisions*. As you read any of this information, look *behind it to the mindframe involved* in the various choices. Greater awareness of your own mindset improves the quality of decisions that *you* are capable of making. Sharpened perception makes you ever more capable of discerning the quality of choices made by those around you.

A business card reflects the quality of decisions that a business has made. As you become more skilled at decoding the subtle messages on business cards, you will also see more of the assumptions that exist within the organization (and you're less likely to be deceived). You will more quickly recognize the implicit cues of the corporate culture. Your abilities to send and read all sorts of subtle forms of communication will be stronger.

- If you are job hunting, remember that **you are selecting the employer**, rather than the other way around. Evaluate the cards of companies you consider. Also pay attention to the section in Chapter 12 on using resume cards to package yourself.
- As an employee, you will be in a position to influence the messages being sent by your company. Inevitably, you will

avoid various blunders and sway others to communicate (as well as function) more productively.

☐ If you set out to be an entrepreneur, self-employed and committed to living by your wits, you will need every resource you can muster. This book's advice should strengthen your position, for you will find yourself (and your venture) constantly being tested on issues great and minor. Start by signaling that you are not a wannabe, but a serious player.

This book is devoted to increasing your awareness of those things which are often overlooked. Cards are simply a vehicle for focusing your attention. Don't stop there; look for and attend to the unstated messages that give you a potent advantage, wherever they are encountered. Push past the obvious. **Be nimble**. The more willingly and capably you can do so, the more proficient you become in your chosen profession. As more people operate in that way, the better the quality of business practices. I'm persuaded that such receptive thinking will lead to a more ethical and value-oriented business climate. That bodes well for each of you personally, your employers, your industries, and our entire country.

Never doubt that the little choices can and do have a decisive, long-range impact. Do your part to improve the quality of decisions being made at work and at home. You have incredible power to influence the directions that you and your employers decide to take—and that will effect us all.

Address

The place where business in conducted (Chapter 5); can involve a variety of locations:

- Store or retail outlet
- Warehouse
- Office or home office
- Billing address
- Sales office
- Mailing address
- Company headquarters
- Virtual office location
- Wholesale facility
- Shipping address

Business Card

A highly-condensed form of communication that provides useful contact information about you. The parts found on most cards are:

- Business name
- Logo or visual image of the business
- Name of the person using the card
- That person's title
- Address; may be mailing, administrative, shipping, retail, etc.
- Telephone, fax and other contact numbers like e-mail, Web site, pager, extension
- Tag line or slogan

Business Image

Every business has an image, whether or not there has been any attempt to create one. Signs of a good business image:

- Gets noticed immediately
- Creates a positive impression
- Makes an impression that is remembered
- Distinguishes and sets the business apart

- Sends a clear message
- Leads to sales or some benefit for the business
- Attracts interest and catches the eye
- Has relevance to the receiver

Color Impact (Chapter 6)

- Grabs attention—stands out
- Spotlights material—gives it importance
- Looks (and is) more expensive
- Adds more beauty and is visually interesting
- Organizes information
- Adds emotional impact, more recognizable
- Reveals mood and personality
- Assists comprehension
- Sends subliminal communication; emotion-laden messages

Color Printing

Use of inks to add additional colors to a design (Chapters 6 and 11) by means of:

- Spot color, whether one or more shades
- PANTONE MATCHING SYSTEM® shade(s)
- Four-color process; cyan (medium greenish blue), magenta (hot pink), yellow, and black
- Photographic process

Credibility and Credentials

Your card should strengthen confidence-building perceptions by its good taste and attractiveness (Chapter 4). Indicate that you are capable and hassle free by explicitly stating your credentials and any business policies that reassure those the company serves. Establish your credentials regarding:

- Yourself and your own capabilities
- The business itself—its products and services
- The business location
- Convenience and all the ways you make it easy to do business
- Payment options—credit cards and other appropriate terms
- The many ways you make the buyer's life easier

Decoding Information (body language) on Cards

Reading the messages that are "between the lines." Decoding actually involves developing a method for interpreting what you *already* see (Chapter 2). Kinds of information that can be revealed by a business card:

- Coherent marketing strategy
- Customer orientation or lack of one
- Level of professionalism and care
- Whether well established or positioned
- Approximate size of the business
- Evidence of competence and reliability
- Stage of the business
- Signs of success
- Credibility cues
- Philosophy or goals of the business

Design

Design is like good taste—it's hard to say what it is, but you sure can tell when it's missing (Chapter 8). It always considers *how* information is presented, not just whether it is appropriate. Good design is usually simple; to do more overwhelms the card and looks cluttered and busy.

Designer Agreement

The client and designer should clearly determine the following, in writing, *before* the job begins:
- The project and its scope
- Who is responsible for what; define what the client and what the designer does
- What services will be performed: logo, image, card design only, etc.
- Time frames for each stage of performance and deadlines
- Rights and responsibilities of each party
- Budget—costs, deposits, payments
- Breakdown of costs for services or other types of costs (color separations, photographs, etc.)
- How approvals will be handled
- Role of subcontractors regarding supervision and payment
- Form of input and output (electronic or camera-ready art)
- Copyright ownership explicitly discussed and stated
- How to deal with extra work, corrections, dissatisfaction, termination or new ideas and changes

Electronic Business Cards—Personal Data Interchange (PDI)

Methods of providing basic contact information electronically or on-line. The alternatives are (Chapter 10):
- Business cards on disk
- The *sig* on e-mail; requires an e-mail address

- Virtual business cards; vCards®
- Plan files
- Web address, whether a page or site

International Business Cards

When doing business abroad, be sensitive to cultural differences in the way that cards are treated (Chapter 14). Cards are taken very seriously in other countries; follow the local customs:

- Show the same respect for a person's card that you would show toward that person
- It could be taken as an insult if you don't handle their cards carefully
- Don't give cards casually or to everyone you meet; be selective
- Keep enough cards with you so you're prepared, whatever happens
- If it is not an English-speak country, translate your card into their language and offer a two-sided or second card

Logo

A logo is a particular graphic image that is identified with a business (Chapter 7). It symbolizes the business and provides additional cues about its personality. Images should be:

- Easy to remember, recognize and relate to
- Triggers for the senses or affect emotions in a positive way
- Representative of related things—as a rattle symbolizes a baby
- Unique and distinctive
- Balanced, with the right size and proportion
- Good looking and feels good
- Recognizable after being photocopied or faxed
- Compatible with the rest of the card and the primary business message
- Consistently used on all communications
- Timeless not dated or over-done

Name of the Business

Identifies the organization (Chapter 4); should have the following characteristics

- Distinctive and unique
- Memorable
- Able to communicate an image or emotional connection
- Appealing to the customer
- Protectable
- Can be easily pronounced or spelled

- Free of unintended or negative messages
- Unlikely to be confused with other businesses
- Can be translated without meaning anything offensive or inappropriate
- Compatible with the business image

Networking

Method of building business and referrals through people you know or whom you encounter in social and business settings; depends on establishing and sustaining on-going relationships (Chapter 12); often conducted at:
- Organizational meetings
- Social (non-business) situations
- Conferences, trade shows, and conventions
- Corporate (in-house) events
- One-on-one discussions or in groups

Photographs (Chapter 7)

When used on a card, they can be:
- Mug shot; head shot
- Photograph which bleeds to the edge; text in reverse print or on back
- Photograph showing the services or products of the business
- Photographs arranged as a montage of images
- Photoprocess business cards; full color, generated from the computer

Printers and printing

The way your concept is turned into a tangible card; includes steps (Chapter 11):
- Determining the specifications
- Bidding; deciding on the costs and options
- Getting the project "camera ready"
- Checking the proof for accuracy
- Press runs and doing any special effects

Shapes and Sizes of Cards (Chapter 6)

- Standard sized, horizontal or vertical
- Two-sided cards
- Folded cards
- Odd-sized cards, either larger or smaller
- Odd-shaped cards; die-cut cards

Tag Lines and Slogans

A short phrase about the business which conjures up a strong mental image (Chapter 4); choose one that people will relate to and remember. Kinds of tag lines:

- Statement of purpose, philosophy, or mission statement
- Motto or slogan
- Pledge
- Policy
- Guarantee
- Jingle
- Pun, joke, or play on words
- Relevant quote or aphorism—or a takeoff on one

Telephone Numbers (Chapter 5)

- Business telephone numbers
- Emergency or after-hours contact number
- Home telephone number
- Fax number and fax-on-demand number
- Voice messaging number
- E-mail address
- Web site or web page
- Pager, digital, or voice
- Cellular phone number
- 800 or 888 numbers
- 900 numbers
- Extension number or voice mailbox, within a large organization

Type Styles

Chose a type or combination of styles that reflects the business identity; each type family comes in a variety of forms, like italic and compressed (Chapter 7). The combination of fonts, sizes of type, upper- and lower- case letters, etc. permit an infinite array of choices. Avoid using too many styles or sizes on your card; always consider readability.

Appendix A

The Difference Between Employee and Independent Contractor[*]

Here are some basic questions which can help you determine if a person working for you is an employee or an independent contractor. These questions are based on the "Twenty Factor Test"[1]. It is easy to see that not all these rules apply to all jobs equally. Time has also changed business relationships and therefore the relevance of some of the factors discussed below. Still these questions are an excellent starting point for keeping for employers out of trouble.

1. Who gives the person instructions?

Employee

The employer either gives or reserves the right to control the following: when, where and how the work is to be performed. Attention: Depending on the type of work no such instructions actually have to be given in order to make the person an employee. In the case of many professionals, such as sales, professional or a minister generally, no actual directions are given.

Independent Contractor

Has the right to follow his own judgment as to when, where and how to perform the work.

2. What kind of training must be provided for the person to perform the work?

Employee

The company trains the employee to perform the work in a particular manner (or reserves the right to do so).

Independent Contractor

Does not require any company-specific training to perform the work.

---

* Information provided by Dr. Inge Casey, (602) 952-8328
Note: This information is relative to the issues in Chapter 8 about who owns the trademark developed for a business—the employer (business) or the designer/artist.

3. How integrated into the business is the work performed?

Employee

Services are necessary, and integrated into the operations of a business. The success of the business depends significantly on these services.

Independent Contractor

The services are not personally or substantially integrated into the business.

4. Who must render the services?

Employee

Must perform the services personally.

Independent Contractor

Not require to render the services personally. Can have employees or subcontractor do them.

5. Who hires, supervises and pays the person?

Employee

Hired and supervised directly by the employer.

Independent Contractor

Can hire, supervise and pay his or her own assistants. The method of accomplishing the result is not relevant, only the result itself.

6. What is the continuity of the relationship?

Employee

Maintains a continuing relationship, which may include instances where work is performed at recurring but irregular intervals.

Independent Contractor

A continuing relationship is not assumed to exist.

7. Who sets the working hours?

Employee

Required to perform the work within set hours established by the employer.

Independent Contractor

Hours of work established by the worker.

8. What is the total commitment required?

Employee

Usually expected to devote full time to the business, implying that the worker is restricted from performing services for other businesses.

Independent Contractor

Free to work when and where and for whom he or she chooses

9. Where is the work performed?

Employee

Word is generally performed at the employer's premises.

Independent Contractor

Work is performed wherever the worker chooses, e.g., at the worker's office.

10. **Who controls the sequence of work?**

Employee	Independent Contractor
Required to follow the routines and schedules established by the employer	Free to develop and follow own pattern of work.

11. **What kind of reports are required?**

Employee	Independent Contractor
Regular written or oral reports are required.	Not necessarily required to submit reports of any kind,

12. **How is the Person paid?**

Employee	Independent Contractor
Receives payment by the hour, week or month.	Receives payment by the job or on a commission basis.

13. **How are business and travel expenses paid?**

Employee	Independent Contractor
Business and travel expenses are ordinarily paid by the employer, indicating that the employer reserves the right to control these activities.	Generally pays for his or her own expenses.

14. **Who provides the tools and materials to accomplish the task?**

Employee	Independent Contractor
Tools and materials provided by the employer.	Generally furnishes his or her own tools and materials.

15. **Who pays for the investment in basic production facilities?**

Employee	Independent Contractor
Has no investment in the facilities of the workplace, indicating the worker's dependence on the employer for such facilities in order to perform the work.	Invests in facilities and tools in order to perform the work, such as an office rented from an unrelated party.

16. **Who carries the risk of profit and loss?**

Employee	Independent Contractor
Cannot directly realize a profit or suffer a loss as a result of his or her services.	Subject to a real risk of economic loss due to investments, or liabilities, such as salaries to unrelated employees.

17. For how many entities are the services performed?

Employee	Independent Contractor
Performs services for one person or simultaneously for more than one person, if such persons are part of the same service arrangement.	Performs services for a multiple of unrelated persons or businesses simultaneously.

18. Are the services available to the general public?

Employee	Independent Contractor
Services are available only to one employer at a time.	Services are made available to the general public on a regular and consistent basis.

19. Is there a right to fire?

Employee	Independent Contractor
Employer has the right to discharge the worker and can exercise control on how the worker performs the work through the threat of discharge.[2]	Cannot be fired so long as he or she produces a result that meets contractual specifications.

20. Is there a right to quit?

Employee	Independent Contractor
Has the right to terminate his or her relationship at any time without incurring liabilities.	Can terminate services but only at the risk of, for example, financial loss or breach of contract litigation.

Evaluate a person's status for each of the 20 questions. This way you will see which of these two classification applies to that person. If the majority is clearly on one side or the other you know how this person should be classified. Sometimes you can restructure the job in one way or the other to make the classification unambiguous.

Trap: Some jobs are covered by statutes which make them employees, regardless of how you might answer the above questions. Most full-time salespersons fall into this group, but real estate salespersons do not.

Self defense. If the result is still ambiguous, talk to your lawyer or accountant. These are professionals who have to support you in case of a dispute with the IRA.

Either independent contractors or employees are a valid and appropriate business choice. The important question is how the relationship is structured.

[1] Rev. Ruling 87-41 1987-1 C.B. 296
[2] See also AZ SB 1386, 1996 for related information

Appendix B

The American Institute of Graphic Arts (AIGA)*
Standard Form of Agreement for Graphic Design Services

General Edition This document is intended to be used as a basis of agreement between designers and their clients. It has important legal consequences. Consultation with an attorney is encouraged with regard to its completion or modification.

The Client and Designer agree as follows:

Agreement made as of date

Between the Client

And the Designer

For the Project referred to as

1.   THE PROJECT

1.1   *Description of the Project*
       The Project that is the subject of this agreement shall consist of:

2.   SERVICES
       The Designer shall provide the Basic and Supplementary Services specified below.

2.1 *Basic Services*
The Designer shall provide Basic Services for the Project consisting of consultants, research design, checking quality of Implementation, and coordination of the Project and its Execution. In connection with performing the Basic

---

*   This document (1988 edition) was provided by the American Institute of Graphic Designers (AIGA, 1059 Third Avenue, New York NY, 10021 (212) 752-0813), and is used with permission. It has only been re-formatted to fit the page size of this book.

Services, the Designer shall prepare and present materials to the Client that demonstrate or describe the Designer's intentions and shall prepare various materials, such as artwork, drawings, and specifications, to enable the design to be printed, fabricated, installed, or otherwise implemented.

2.2 *Supplementary Services*
In addition to the Basic Services described above, the Designer's fee may also include the provisions of certain specialized Supplementary Services, but only to the extent described below. Such supplementary Services might include: Creative services including copy development, writing, editing, photography, and illustrations. Preparation of special artwork including drawing of logotype, nonstandard typeface, maps, diagrams and charts and preparation of existing materials for reproduction such as partial or complete redrawing, line conversion, retouching, captioning within an illustration, diagram, or map, and making camera-ready color separation overlays. Production services including typesetting and proofreading. Preparation of special presentation materials including detailed renderings, models, mockups, and slide presentation. If any of these other services are required, but are not to be provided by the Designer as Supplementary Services, they will be coordinated by the Designer, provided by others, and billed to the client as reimbursable expenses.

The Supplementary Services to be provided by the Designer with respect to the Project shall consist of:

2.3 *Implementation*
The Designer's services under this Agreement do not include Implementation such as printing, fabrication and installation of the Project design. The Client and Designer agree that any such Implementation is to be provided by others, and the Designer's services with respect to such Implementation shall be restricted to providing specifications, coordination, and quality-checking. Unless otherwise specified in its Agreement, the Designer shall have no responsibility to the providers of such Implementation, and charges therefor shall be billed directly to the Client. While not responsible for Implementation, in a supervisory capacity the Designer may assume responsibility for paying such charges, and the Designer shall be entitled to reimbursement from the Client for implementation costs plus such handling charges as is specified in Section 3.7.

3. COMPENSATION

3.1 *Fees*
The Client shall pay the Designer for the services described in this Contract as follows:

3.2 *Hourly Rates*
Where specified in this contract, the Client shall pay the Designer at the Designer's standard rates as in effect at this time.

The Designer's standard rates currently in effect are as follows:

No change shall be made in the Designer's standard rates prior to

3.3 *Initial Payment*
Upon signing this Agreement, the Client shall make a payment of

This initial payment shall be credited against the amounts due hereunder as follows:

3.4 *Payment Schedule*
After receipt of an invoice, the Client shall make payments within

The Designer may render invoices according to the following schedule:

3.5 *Revisions and Additions*
A fixed fee or fee estimated not to exceed a specified amount is based upon the time estimated to complete the services specified in this Agreement during normal working hours. Any revisions or additions to the services described in this Agreement shall be billed as additional services not included in any fixed fee or estimated fee specified above.

Such additional services shall include, but shall not be limited to, changes in the extent of work, changes in the complexity of any elements of the Project, and any changes made after approval has been given for a specific stage of design, documentation or preparation of artwork.

The Designer shall keep the Client informed of additional services that are required and shall request the Client's approval for any additional services which cause the total fees, exclusive of any surcharge for rush work, to exceed the fixed or estimated fees set forth in section 3.2 by more than the following amount:

3.6 *Rush Work*
The Client shall pay a surcharge for any services requiring work to be performed outside of normal working hours by reason of unusual deadlines or as a consequence of the Client not meeting scheduled times for delivery of information, materials or approvals.

The surcharge for rush work shall be at the standard rates plus

Normal working hours for this Project are as follows:

3.7 The client shall reimburse the Designer for all out-of-pocket expenses incurred by the Designer with respect to the Project including, but not limited to expenditures for: Implementation, typesetting, photostats, photoprints, photography, film and processing, acetate color overlays, transfer proofs, presentation and artwork materials, electrostatic (xerographic) copies, Fax and long-distance telephone charges, postage, and local deliveries, including messengers, out-of-town travel, and shipping.

Automobile travel will be charged at a standard rate per mile of

Reimbursable Expenses will be billed at a cost plus a surcharge of

3.8 *Reimbursable and Implementation Budgets*
Any budget figures or estimates for Reimbursable Expenses or Implementation charges such as printing, fabrication, or installation are for planning purposes only. The Designer shall use his or her best efforts to work within stated budgets but shall not be liable if such expenses exceed budgets.

3.9 *Records*
The Designer shall maintain records of hours and reimbursable expenses and shall make such records available to the Client for inspection on request.

3.10 *Late Payment*
The Client shall pay a service charge for all overdue amounts of

4. CLIENT'S OBLIGATIONS

4.1 *Client's Representations*
The Client shall appoint a sole Representative with full authority to provide or obtain any necessary information and approvals and may be required by the Designer. The Client's Representative shall be responsible for coordination of briefing, review, and the decision-making process with respect to persons and parties other than the Designer and its sub-contractors. If, after the Client's Representative has approved a design, the Client or any other authorized person requires changes that require additional services from the Designer, the Client shall pay all fees and expenses arising from such changes as additional services.

4.2 *Materials to be Provided by the Client*
The Client shall provide accurate and complete information and materials to the Designer and shall be responsible for the accuracy and completeness of all information and materials so provided. The Client guarantees that all materials supplied to the Designer are owned by the Client or that the Client has all necessary rights in such materials to permit the Designer to use them for the Project.

The Client shall indemnify, defend, and hold the Designer harmless from and against any claim, suit, damages and expense, including attorney fees, arising from or out of any claim by any party that its rights have been or are being violated or infringed upon with respect to any materials provided by the Client.

All copy provided by the Client shall be in a form suitable for typesetting. Where photographs, illustrations, or other visual materials are provided by the Client, they shall be of professional quality and in a form suitable for reproduction without further preparation or alteration. The Client shall pay all fees and expenses arising from its providing of materials that do not meet such standards. The Designer shall return all materials provided by the Client with 30 days after completion of the project and payment of amounts due. The client shall provide the following materials and services for the project:

4.3 Liability of Designer
The Designer shall take reasonable precautions to safeguard original or other materials provided by the Client. The Designer shall, however, not be liable for any damage to, or loss of any material provided by the Client, including artwork, photographs, or manuscripts, other than or on account of willful neglect or gross negligence of the Designer.

4.4 Approval of Typesetting and final Artwork
The Client shall proofread and approve all final type before the production of artwork. The signature of the Client's Representative shall be conclusive as to the approval of all artwork drawings and other items prior to their release for printing, fabrication, or installation.

4.5 Instructions to Third Parties
The Client specifically grants to the Designer the right to act on the Client's behalf to give instructions on behalf of the Client to any person or entity involves in the Project, such as photographers, illustrators, writers, printers, and fabricators.

Any such instructions or approvals by the Client may only be made through the Designer. The Client shall be bound by all such instructions given by the Designer with the scope of this Agreement.

5. RIGHTS AND OWNERSHIP

5.1 Rights
All services provided by the Designer under this Agreement shall be for the exclusive use of the Client other than for the promotional use of the Designer. Upon payment of all fees and expenses, the following reproduction rights

for all approved final designs created by the Designer for this project shall be granted:

5.2 Ownership
All drawings, artwork, specifications, and other visual representation materials remain the property of the Designer. The client shall be entitled to temporary possession of such materials only for the purposes of reproduction after which all materials shall be returned, unaltered, to the Designer.

All preliminary concepts and visual representations produced by the Designer remain the property of the Designer and may not be used by the Client without the written permission of the Designer.

The Designer shall retain all artwork, drawings, and specification, for which reproductions rights have been granted for a specified period from the date of the signing of this Agreement. Upon expiration of this period, all such materials may be destroyed unless the Client has requested, in writing, that they be retained and agrees to pay reasonable storage charges. The Client shall have reasonable access to all such materials for the purpose of review.

The specified time for the Designer to retain such materials shall be

5.3 *Third Party Contracts*
The Designer may contract with others to provide creative services such as writing, photography, and illustration. The Client agrees to be bound by any terms and conditions, including required credits, with respect to reproduction of such material as may be imposed on the Designer by such third parties.

The Designer will endeavor to obtain for the Client the same reproduction rights with respect to materials resulting from such services as the Designer is providing the Client under this Agreement except as specified below:

6. MISCELLANEOUS

6.1 *Code of Ethics*
The Designer's services shall be performed in accordance with the AIGA Code of Ethics and Professional Conduct for Graphic Designers.

6.2 *Credit*
The Designer shall have the right to include a credit line on the completed designs or any visual representations such as drawings, models, or photographs and this same credit shall be included in any publication of the design by the Client. The Client shall not, without written approval, use the Designer's name for promotional or any other purpose with respect to these designs. The Designer's credit line shall read as follows:

6.3 *Samples and Photographs*
The Client shall provide the Designer with samples of each printed or manufactured design. Such samples shall be representative of the highest quality of work produced. The Designer may use such copies and samples for publication, exhibition, or other promotional purposes.

The number of samples to be provided to the Designer shall be

The Designer shall have the right to photograph all completed designs or installations and shall have the right to use such photographs for publication, exhibition, or other promotional purposes.

6.4 *Confidentiality*
The Client shall inform the Designer in writing if any portion of any material or information provided by the Client or if any portion of the Project is confidential.

6.5 *Sales Tax*
The Client shall pay any sales, use, or other transfer taxes that may be applicable to the services provided under this Agreement, including any tax that may be assessed on audit or the Designer's tax returns.

6.6 *Applicable Law*
This Agreement shall be governed by the law of the principal place of business of the Designer.

6.7 *Assignment*
Neither the Client or the Designer may assign or transfer their interest in this Agreement without the written consent of the other.

6.8 Either party may terminate this Agreement upon giving written notice to the other as specified below. Upon termination of this Agreement by the Client or by the Designer for cause, the Designer may retain any initial payment and the Client shall pay the Designer for all hours expended on the Project, up to the date of termination, at the Designer's standard rates, together with all other amounts due hereunder. Any initial payment that has been received shall be credited against any such amounts due. All indemnities shall continue even after any such termination.

The amount of written notice to be given by either party shall be

6.9 *Arbitration*
Either party may request that any dispute arising out of this Agreement shall be submitted to binding arbitration before a mutually agreed upon arbitrator pursuant to the rules of the American Arbitration Association.

The arbitrator's award shall be final and judgment may be entered upon it in any court having jurisdiction thereof.

6.10 *Entire Agreement*
This Agreement represents the entire agreement between the Client and the Designer and may be changed or modified only in writing.

6.11 The Client represents that it has full power and authority to enter into this Agreement and that it is binding upon the Client and enforceable in accordance with its terms.

The Designer represents that it has full power and authority to enter into this Agreement and that is binding upon the Designer and enforceable in accordance with its terms.

7. TIME SCHEDULE
The Designer and Client agree that the work shall be completed according to the following schedule:

The Designer reserves the right to adjust the schedule in the event that the Client fails to meet agreed deadlines for submission of materials or granting approvals and to allow for changes in the scope or complexity of services from those contemplated by this Agreement.

8. CONTINUATIONS AND OTHER CONDITIONS

9. DEFINED TERMS

Basic Services	As described in Section 2.1.
Client	As defined on page 1.
Designer	As defined on page 1.
Implementation	As defined in Section 2.3.
Project	As described in Section 1.
Reimbursable Expenses	As described in Section 3.7.
Supplementary Services	As described in Section 2.2.

10. SIGNATURES
This Agreement was entered into between the Designer and the Client of the day and date set forth on page 1.

Designer

Client

Endnotes

Chapter 1

[1] Qubein, Nido R., "If I Were in the Market to Buy what You Sell, would I Buy It from You?, *Professional Speaker*, September, 1994, p 4.

[2] Qubein., p 5.

Chapter 5

[1] Mackay, Harvey, *Arizona Republic*, Phoenix, AZ, April 6, 1997.

Section II

[1] *Print Magazine's Book of Contest Winners*, 1996, Preface, p 4.

Chapter 6

[1] Soden, Garrett, *Looking Good on Paper: How to Create Eye-Catching Reports, Proposals Memos and Other Business Documents*, AMACOM (American Management Assn.), New York, NY, 1995, p 18.

[2] White, Jan V., promotional information for White, "Color in Business Documents," 1992.

[3] White.

[4] "Pantone® Color Tidbits", promotional materials, Pantone, no date.

[5] White, Jan V., *Color for Impact*, Strathmoor Press, 2250 Ninth St. #1040, Berkeley CA, (800) 217-7377, 1994, p 28.

[6] Wheildon, Colin, *Type & Layout; How Typography and Design Can Get Your Message Across—or Get in the Way*, Strathmoor Press, 2250 Ninth St. #1040, Berkeley CA, (800) 217-7377, 1995, p 80.

[7] Wheildon, p 81.

Chapter 7

[1] Adler, Elizabeth W., *Print that Works; The First Step-by Step Guide that Integrates Writing, Design and Marketing*, Bull Publishing Company, Palo Alto CA, 1991, p 259.

[2] Parker, Roger, *The Makeover Book,* Chapel Hill NC, Ventana Press, 1989. p 143.

[3] Prudential Insurance, Newark NJ.

[4] Betty Crocker, Minneapolis MN.

[5] Wheildon, p 30.

[6] Wheildon., p 32.

Chapter 8

[1] Thomas Hine, "The Images that Tell Who We Are," *The New York Times*, September 8, 1996, p 72.

[2] Adler, p 173.

[3] Parker, *One Minute Designer*, QUE Corp., Indianapolis, IN, 1993, p xvi.

[4] Adler, p 179.

[5] Graphic Artists Guild of Albany, "A Practical Guide to Working with Graphic Designers," Albany, NY, 1997, p 7.

[6] Adler, p 174.

[7] Strauss, Linda; Unpublished manuscript (untitled); Linda Strauss Advertising, 2114 W. Marlette Ave., Phoenix AZ 85015 (602) 249-3333.

[8] Gotimer, Jeffrey, from Sales Moves syndicated column by Jeffrey Gotimer, author of *The Sales Bible*.

Chapter 9

[1] Yankelovich Clancy Shulman, "Corporate Identity: Image Impact Analysis; A Quantitative Research Study Measuring the Impact of Corporate Identity Materials," 1992, p 8.

[2] Altman Weil Pensa, Inc., "Comparative Study of Law Firm Identity Systems," 1994.

Chapter 10

[1] Feinberg, Steven L., Editor, *Crane's Blue Book of Stationery*, New York, Doubleday, 1989, p 209.

[2] Ubinas, Helen, "It's in the cards again: A way to meet is revived," *Hartford Courant*, June, 1996.

[3] Emery, Vince, *How to Grow Your Business on the Internet*, Second Edition, Scottsdale, AZ, Coriolis Group Books, p 244.

[4] Wichner, David, *Arizona Republic*, Phoenix AZ, January 10, 1997, p A-1.

[5] Internet Mail Consortium, promotional information, http://www.imc.org/pdi/.

Chapter 12

[1] Jordan, Claudia, *Jobfinder: How to Find a Better Job Faster*, Phoenix AZ, WorkLife Publishing, 1997, p 47.

[2] Jordan. p 48.

[3] Jordan, p 48.

[4] Convention Liason Council, Washington D.C.

[5] Center for Exhibition Industry Research, Bethesda MD.

[6] Smith, Mark S.A., Guerrilla Trade Show Selling, New York, John Wiley, 1997. pp 119-120.

[7] Konopacki, Allen, "More Out of Trade Shows," Chicago IL, Incomm Center for Research and Sales Training, Miscellaneous training materials, copyright dates and page numbers unknown.

[8] Konopacki.

[9] Konopacki.

[10] Konopacki.

Chapter 14

[1] Betts-Johnson, Marie, "Internationally Speaking," *Professional Speaker*, June 4, 1997, p 12.

[2] Betts-Johnson, p 13.

[3] Crane & Co., "Crane's Global Guide," Dalton, MA, 1994.

[4] Chu, Henry, *Arizona Republic*, July 11, 1997 (originally in Los Angeles Times), p A23.

[5] Chu.

Chapter 15

[1] Jay, Robert, *The Trade Card in Nineteenth-Century America*, Missouri, University of Missouri Press, 1987, p 4.

[2] Galley, Dorothy C., "When Social Calling Had Grace—Calling Cards," *The Antiques Journal*, December, 1979, p 18

[3] Dunhill, Priscilla, A Victorian Scrapbook, New York, Workman Publishing, 1989, p 115.

[4] Galley, Dorothy C., "When Social Calling Had Grace—Calling Cards," *The Antiques Journal*, December, 1979, p 18.

[5] Dunhill, p 118.

[6] Martin, Judith, *Miss Manners' Guide to Excruciatingly Correct Behavior*, New York, Athenum, 1982, p 509.

[7] Rivera, Betty, "Calling Card Cases," *Country Living*, January, 1991, p 20.

[8] Kern-Foxworth, Marilyn, *Aunt Jemima, Uncle Ben and Rastus: Blacks in Advertising, Yesterday, Today and Tomorrow*, Connecticut, Praeger Publishers, 1994, p.33.

[9] Jay.

[10] Trade Card Collectors Association pamphlet, 1987.

[11] Jay, p 61.

[12] Jay, p 70.

[13] Jay, p 84.

[14] Gurner, p 1.

[15] Rowland, Diana, *Japanese Business Etiquette*, New York, Warner Books, 1985, p 14.

[16] P•I•E Books, *Business Card Graphics 2*, Tokyo, Japan, P•I•E Books, 1992, p 11.

Chapter 16

[1] Source unknown; downloaded from the Internet.

[2] Promotional literature, Children's Wish Foundation, no publication date.

[3] Erdman, Ken, "Does Your Business Card Really Mean Business?" *The Rotarian*, August, 1989, Vol. 155, #2, pp 12-17.

Resources

Places to Get Unusual Cards Made

Braille Business Cards (See pages 119–120)

Can put Braille impressions on your existing printed cards or prepare them from scratch
Access USA (800) 263-2750
P. O. Drawer 160, 242 James Street, Clayton NY 13624

Engraved Business Cards and Stationery (See pages 267–269)

Engraved cards and stationery, variety of colors and special effects, like foiling and embossing
The Ligature (213) 585-2152 (800) 944-5440
3223 E. 46th Street, Los Angeles, CA 90058-2474

Ponte Engraving Company (602) 258-1687
1546 E. McKinley Street, Phoenix AZ 85006

Superior Engraving (973) 429-7155
P.O. Box 151, Bloomfield NJ 07003

Holographic Business Cards

Custom or stock holograms; or cards printed on stock showing crystals, glitter or hyperplaid
Krystal Holographics (801) 753-5775
365 North 600 West, Logan UT 84321

AD 2000 (203) 624-6405
780 State Street, New Haven CT 06511

Jot/a/CARD® (as shown on pages 229–330)

3" x 6" Perforated cardstock used to write notes which are then torn off, leaving a note and a business card
Business Cards Plus (616) 327-7727, (800) 875-7727
8939 Shaver Road, Kalamazoo, MI 49002

Leather Business Cards

Can be printed and embossed (like a brand), one or two colors; minimum order 100 cards
Torel (512) 293-2341
P.O. Box 592, Yoakum TX 77995

Metal Business Cards

Brass, gold, silver, aluminum; can also be printed in rotary style
Hirschhorn Company (203) 562-5830
2 Academy Street, New Haven CT 06511

Photoprocess Business Cards (See pages 207–8)

Full color business cards (See page and)
Future Imaging Systems (800) 974-8881
5327 Jacuzzi Street, Suite 3B, Richmond CA 94804

Plastic Business Cards

Clear, translucent, matte or white plastic stock, various shapes
Flexcorp (704) 344-0424, (800) FLEXCORP
500 East Boulevard, Charlotte NC 28203

Pop-Up or 3-D Business Cards

Variety of customized shapes that are held in place with rubber bands, 3-D and moving parts
Perrygraf (818) 993-1000 (800) 423-5329
19365 Business Center Drive, Northridge CA 91324-3552

American Slide-Chart Corporation (630) 665-3333 (800) 323-4433
P. O. Box 111 Wheaton IL 60189-0111

Talking or Blinking Cards (See page 329)

Variety of customized cards that flash and blink; also talking cards
Call for a distributor in your area
Clegg (310) 225-3800 ext 122
19220 S. Normandie Avenue, Torrance CA 90502

Two-tone Backgrounds

Split fountain technique, also called rainbow cards; backgrounds are printed with two different shades of ink at the same time (no two cards are exactly alike); then text printed in black; also neon stock
Custom Printed Products (903) 764-2356 (800) 200-1883
Rt. 2, Box 2660., Elkhart TX 75839

Wooden Business Cards (as shown on page 261)

120 varieties of wood (species printed on the back of each card) two ply, thin and flexible; can be printed 1 or 2 colors; minimum order 100; blank cards are available for your own printing
Cards of Wood (616) 887-8257
1267 House Road, Belmont MI 49306

Helpful and Unusual Card-Related Resources

Any item marked with a * is available through Off the Page Press. Consult our Fax on Demand at (888) 206-3506 or Web site at Quick-and-Painless.com for current selection and prices

*Card-It® (See page 327)

Machine that cuts perfectly aligned mounting slots to easily attach your business card to any size paper, brochure or folder; eliminates need for staples, paper clips, tape or glue and won't injure your card
Available from Off the Page Press (602) 874-0050, or see ordering information on last page of book

Personal Font

Send personalized notes. Create a custom font which accurately reproduces your own handwriting (for use on your computer keyboard); or select other hand-lettering styles; selection of unique products that combine the distinctiveness and personality of your handwriting with the convenience of a word processor
Signature Software (800) 925-8840
489 North 8th Street
Hood River OR 97031

Busicards® (as shown on pages 328–9)

Cardholders with cartoons by Walt Hendrickson to hold standard business cards or prepaid phone cards; comes in various designs;
Busicards
P. O. Box 4065, Rockford IL 61110-0945 or (815) 965-0936 or fax (815) 965-0945

NetCards® (See page 348)

Double folded resume card; format permits you to print a resume in brief on your printer; combination business card and brochure; pre-printed and perforated NetCards are available in 100 card packs in various metallic colors; can be printed with or without the NetCard Printing Software
PM Resource (800) 842-6558
P.O. Box 357, Oconomowoc WI 53066

*PANTONE® Color Formula Guide 1000

(solid color, not process color); Fan deck of 1,000 PANTONE MATCHING SYSTEM colors, specifying the shade and composition of each shade; also available, a variety of color products, including software programs that assist in color matching and selection

Promotional Products

Supplier of unusual business cards and promotional products incorporating business card formats
The Three Marketeers (215) 836-6000
402 Bethlehem Pike
Erdenheim PA 19038

Recommended Resources—Books, Tapes, Videos

Any item marked with a * is available through Off the Page Press. Consult our Fax on Demand at (888) 206-3506 or Web site at Quick-and-Painless.com for current selection and prices

Books

Adler, Elizabeth W. *Print that Works; The First Step-by-Step Guide that Integrates Writing, Design and Marketing*, Peachpit Press, Berkeley CA, 1991.

———— *Everyone's Guide to Successful Publications: How to Produce Powerful Brochures, Newsletters, Flyers, and Business Communications, Start of Finish*, Peachpit Press, Berkeley CA, 1993.

The Best of Business Card Design, Rockport MA, Rockport Publishers, 1994.

Susan Friedmann, *Exhibiting at Tradeshows: Tips & Techniques for Success*;

—————— *Secrets of Successful Exhibiting*; Trade Show Success; P.O. Box 1850, Lake Placid NY 12946-5850 (518) 523-1320

Lanier, Terri. *Working Solo*, 1994. All available from Portico Press, P. O. Box 190, New Paltz NY 12561-0190 (800) 222-SOLO

—————— *Working Solo Sourcebook,* 1995.

—————— The Frugal Entrepreneur, 1996.

*Martin, Diana and Cropper, Mary. *Fresh Ideas in Letterhead and Business Card Design,* Cincinnati OH, North Light Books, 1993.

Miller, Steve and Bowden, Charmel, *Over 88 Tips & Ideas to Supercharge Your Exhibit Sales,* HiKelly Productions, 32706 39th Avenue SW, Federal Way WA 98023; (253) 974-9665, 1997.

*Morrison, Terri, Conaway, Wayne A., and Borden, George A. *Kiss, Bow, or Shake Hands, How to Do Business in Sixty Countries*, Holbrook MA, Adams Media Corporation, 1994.

Smith, Mark S.A, Wilson, Orvel Ray, Levinson, Jay Conrad. *Guerrilla Trade Show Selling*, New York, John Wiley, New York, NY, 1997 (See video in next section)

Sodem, Garrett. *Looking Good on Paper: How to Create Eye-Catching Reports, Proposals, Memos and other Business Documents*, New York, American Management Association, (AMACOM), 1995.

*Wheildon, Colin. *Type & Layout; How Typography and Design can Get Your Message Across—or Get in the Way*, Strathmoor Press, 2550 Ninth Street, Suite 1140, Berkeley CA 94710-2516, (800) 217-7377, 1995.

*White, Jan V. *Color for Impact*, Strathmoor Press, 2550 Ninth Street, Suite 1040, Berkeley CA 94710-2516, 1994.

—————— *Color for the Electronic Age: What Every Desktop Publisher Needs to Know about Using Color Effectively in Charts, Graphs, Typography, and Pictures,* New York NY, Xerox Press, 1990.

Audio Tapes

All these sources have additional products available

Susan Friedmann, P.O. Box 1850, Lake Placid NY 12946-5850 (518) 523-1320
- Power Exhibiting

Konopacki, Allen, INCOMM Center for Research & Sales Training, 1005 North LaSalle Drive, Chicago IL 60610; (312) 642-9377
- Seven Tips for Successful Trade Show Selling
- Also offers a free quarterly newsletter

Petrina, Bernard H., Executive-Management Renewal Programs, P.O. Box 6309, Harrisburg, PA 17112 (717) 652-8773, (800) 535-3633
- How to Sell at a Trade Show (3 tape set: before the show, at the show, after the show)
- Trade Show Tips

Smith, Mark S.A., The following audio tapes are available from The Valence Group, (800) 488-0780
- 10 Things Most Companies Do at Trade Shows that Don't Work and How You Can Fix Them (audio)
- Trade Show Secrets: Making Them Pay Off for Your Business
- 7 Steps to Trade Show Success
- 5 Ways to Make Your Trade Show Pay Off Big

Video Tapes

*Cossman, E. Joseph. *How to Start and Build a Business of Your Own* 60 min, ($29.95) (07-4250)

Franchise Fever: How to Buy and Franchise a Business Opportunity 45 min, ($19.95) (07-5949)

*Prescott Group. *Business Networking Made Easy*, 20 min ($29.95) (07-4007)

Smith, Mark S.A., *Guerrilla Trade Show Selling: The Ten Things Most Companies Do at Trade Shows that Don't Work and How You Can Fix Them* 45 min.

*Tom Kat Productions. *Marketing Where Your Competition is NOT!* 35 min. ($39.95) (07-4052)

Buying a Business 75 min. ($59.95) (07-4019)

Selling a Business 48 min. ($59.95) (07-4039)

Make Quick & Painless® Choices

Decisions require knowledge, but acquiring enough knowledge to make an informed decision is usually time-consuming. Too often we have to make choices **before we feel that we're ready**, before we've learned enough. So we postpone making them, or decide, yet feel dissatisfied with what we chose because it was based on insufficient information. As a consequence, we frequently experience a lack of confidence about our own decisions. Further, we know that there is probably a logical, systematic way to deal with the choice and get the desired outcome, if we only had the energy to find it. So instead of feeling satisfied, we wonder what we've missed or what will come back and haunt us later.

Intelligent decisions occur after experiencing a learning curve. Yet, we seldom can find the time to sort out sufficient information to go through the process. Even those who like to figure things out find that today's pace of life forces us to leap, leap, leap without the opportunity to look, look, look. Decisions clamor at us on all sides, leaving us to feel besieged and dispirited.

Off the Page Press is pleased to announce a new line of books called **Quick & Painless,**® designed to supply the learning curve so a person makes effective and confident business and personal decisions. *The Business Card Book* is the first in the series and considerably more complete than most of them. (A brief condensed version will soon be published.) Except for the few comprehensive guides, books in the series will be short enough to be read in an hour or two. Most of the upcoming titles will be carefully targeted to address specific questions. New titles will be released regularly and often. You can count on Off the Page Press to provide reliable useful answers without aggravation. These guides will walk you through what you need to consider to gain the best answer possible. In fact, you can trust the assistance to be both *quick and painless*!

Our Web site (**Quick-and-Painless.com**) and fax on demand system (**1-888-206-3056**) will always have our most current listings.

Who can use the Quick & Painless® line of books? Classroom teachers, emergency-room clerks, real-estate sales people, construction workers, retired businessmen, entrepreneurs, city councilmen and college students about to embark upon a new career. Everyone from the professional to the homemaker will benefit from the straight-forward and condensed format of this series.

Examples of forthcoming topics:
- Locate elder care with confidence
- Select promotional products (premiums) that stretch your advertising dollars
- Communication so people listen and remember
- Understand your internal clocks to make you more productive
- Conduct faster, yet much more effective meetings
- Increase available energy and become more productive with less effort
- Beat stress by replacing it with something you enjoy
- Purchase a variety of products and services economically and fearlessly
- Hire and get the best value from service providers economically and fearlessly like attorneys, accountants, and brokers
- Build "War Rooms" to deliver more revenue and productivity

Contests

Enter *any* or *all* of these contests

Valuable prizes will be awarded for the most useful and unique responses. Your entry should be your own creation or idea; originality and humor are encouraged. Winners will be announced the week of Thanksgiving each year that entries are received. Deadline for entries October 31; entries postmarked after that date will be included in the following year's competition. All entries become the property of Off the Page Press and will not be returned. Enter as often as you wish. In the event that a duplicate entry wins, the prize will be awarded to the first submitted. Send a SASE for list of winners.

Every entry should show your name, address, phone number, and date of submission. Submit all entries in writing and with any relevant examples to: Business Card Contest (1, 2, or 3), Off the Page Press, P.O. Box 1269, Scottsdale AZ 85252 OR Enter on our Web site: Quick-and-Painless.com

Contest 1 WILD AND WONDERFUL WAYS TO USE BUSINESS CARDS

- Clever or unusual uses for business cards
- Ways your card has helped to make your money
- Unusual ways to distribute cards
- Effective strategies and benefits from the use of cards
- Tell an interesting story or experience related to your business card

Contest 2 MAKE-OVER OF YOUR BUSINESS CARD

Send in a Before and After; initial version and a modified version. Provide the actual cards themselves. **OR** Tell an experience or success story that occurred because you changed your card.

Contest 3 THE FAX NUMBER DILEMMA

Have you solved the problem of fax numbers being called unintentionally? (See Chapter 5) Tell us how to distinguish the fax number so that it is only called for faxing information.

BUSINESS CARD BINGO

Organizational Mixer

At a gathering, network among those present until you find someone whose card has each of the characteristics shown. You must have a different person for each box. Have the person sign in the box that relates to his or her card. The first person with all the boxes filled wins, although all the completed cards qualify for door prizes.

C	A	R	D
Has the person's photograph	Has gold foil or printing	Has an e-mail address	Has a bird or an animal
Is NOT printed in black ink	Is a non-standard shape or size	Is a folded card	Has a cartoon or joke
Is printed on two sides	Has bullets	Shows more than one location	Shows the person's degrees
Does NOT have an address	Shows a coupon or offer	Is embossed	Has a border

Modify this format to include some business card features specific to your members; for example, including the club logo on their cards.

Sick Card?
Send it to the Business Card Clinic®

The Clinic specializes in diagnosis of business cards. It evaluates your:

- Readability
- Suitability of image or mood
- Layout
- Copy precision
- Color choices
- Completeness
- Unintended messages

The Clinic diagnoses your existing card, explaining what it needs to make it healthier. The evaluation reveals where your card is most effective and those areas where it needs "treatment." Think of this service like the lab work which is performed prior to medical treatment. Your customized diagnosis costs a flat $49.95.

Use your Clinic diagnosis to secure maximum benefit from this book or as a starting point for working with your own designer or printer. Modifications and improvements are always easier when you have a clear idea about which corrections are most needed.

Preparing for the Card Evaluation

1. Get a copy of the diagnostic questionnaire; see the box. The information you provide will be used to customize the analysis of your card.

2. Complete the questionnaire, and attach your present or proposed card.

3. Send it along with a check for $49.95 (payable to Off the Page Press) or pay by credit card, stating: Card number, expiration date, name and address of card holder.

4. Send the above materials to: Clinic, c/o Off the Page Press, P. O. Box 1269, Scottsdale, AZ 85252.

Additional follow-up (treatment) by Business Card Clinic is available, with scope of services and fees to be established on an individual basis.

❑ I want the Business Card Clinic Questionnaire (no charge)

   ❑ Fax it to me at (_____)_____

   ❑ e-mail it to me at _____

   ❑ Mail it to me at _____

_____

To receive your questionnaire, fax your request to (602) 970-3925 or call (602) 874-0050.

A copy is also available immediately through our Web site (quick-and-painless.com) or by calling our Fax on Demand system (888) 206-3056.

Glossary

A

Acronym—The first letter in a number of words

Advance—An amount paid prior to the start of work or during the work; may be payment of expenses or partial payment of the fee

Alignment—In layout, lining elements up exactly such as type, borders and artwork relative to each other and the edge of the paper; all parts of a page become related to each other, aids reading and comprehension

Art Work—All forms of illustrations, including drawings, photographs, maps, etc.

B

Bleed—Printing where ink runs to the edge of the paper; also called trim; ink is printed on paper larger than the final size, which is then trimmed (cut) back to the final size

Blind Embossing—Pressing a metal die into the surface of paper to raise an image in the shape of the die. When a surface is blind embossed, the image appears without ink

Body Language
Communication with gestures and without words

Bold; Boldface—Type letters with a normal form, but heavier strokes like **this**; used for emphasis

Brightness—Characteristic of paper or ink referring to how much light it reflects

Bullets—Typographic characters used to set off units of type; usually circles like this (•); used for emphasis

C

CMYK—See Four-color Process

Calligraphy—Artistic handwriting, lettering, and flourishes

Camera-Ready Material
Artwork that is fully ready to be converted to separations and printing; also called a mechanical

Center—To line up text or graphics to the center of the page, can be horizontal or vertical

Character—Any letter, numeral, punctuation mark or other alphanumeric symbol

Chroma—The intensity or purity of a color

Clip Art—Copyright-free drawings, illustrations and photographs purchased in books or computer programs

Coated Paper or Stock
Paper coated to create a smooth printing surface; usually glossy

Color Separation—Division of colors of a continuous tone multicolored original by photographic filtration into separate printing plates for different colors

Condensed—Typestyles which have been redrawn to require less horizontal space; has increased x-height; effect is tall and tightly spaced; contrasted with expanded typestyles

Continuous Tone—The gray shades of a photograph before it has been prepared for printing

Contractor—See Independent Contractor, also Appendix A

Contrast—Gradation of tones from highlights through middle tones to shadows

Copyright—Provides the owner, usually the creator (artist, composer, writer, designer) of the work, unless a work-for-hire with exclusive rights to the copyrighted work for a limited period of time. Registered with the U.S. Copyright Office Even without registration, the creator holds a copyright by a notice like: © Joe Blow, 1995; the right to copy a creative work

Copyright Notice—See Copyright

Corporate Identity or Image
Elements of design by which a company establishes a consistently recognizable image

Crop or Cropping—To cut away a portion of a work of art or photograph for aesthetics or to fit into a layout

Cyan—One of the four inks in four-color process printing; also called process blue (it is actually turquoise in color) yellow, magenta and black are the other three

D

DPI or Dots Per Inch—The more DPI, the sharper the image, also called having a higher resolution

Debossing—Impression made by pressing an image into paper to make depressed effect; opposite of embossing; requires a die

Decorative Type—Type faces used to attract attention, so used sparingly since they are harder to read

Design—To create a visual impression; that which is created

Designer—Person who decides the graphic arrangement, type and placement of the visual and verbal elements

Die Cut—A shape cut out of paper, usually with metal dies

Dull Finish—Flat finish on coated paper, slightly smoother than matte; also called suede finish, velour finish and velvet finish; contrasted with glossy

Duotone—Using two colors to print a photograph; one ink color reproduces the shadows and highlights, and the second ink reproduces the middle tones

E

Element—One part of an image or page

Em—Measure of type width equal to the width of the letter m; varies for different typefaces

Embossed Finish—Surface pattern made by pressing paper against an engraved roll to create a textured look

Embossing—Pressing an image into paper to create a raised surface; requires a die; can be two or three dimensional

Employee—Person hired to perform services on an ongoing basis, usually salaried; contrasted with independent contractor

En—Measure of type width equal to the width of the letter n; varies for different typeface

Engraving—Method of printing with etched plate; considered high quality; permits very clear small letters

Estimate—Price that states what a job will probably cost; also called bid, quotation; based on specifications provided by customer

Exhibition—Public exhibit; trade show

Expanded or Extended Type Typeface that has been redrawn to cover more horizontal space; appears wide in proportion to its height, thus seems fat; compared with condensed

F

Fair Use—Concept of copyright law allowing without permission from copyright holder use of short quotations from a copyrighted work, usually for reviewing or teaching

Family of Type—All sizes and weights and variations of the same type design

Finish—Surface characteristics of paper

Flip—To reposition graphic elements

Flop—To change the orientation of an image so it is the mirror image of its original

Flush Left or Flush Right
Aligning text so that either the left side or the right side is even and the other side is uneven

Foil and Foil Stamping
Colored metallic material stamped on paper, instead of ink

Font—A collection of type of one face containing all its characters; a typeface

Format—Overall design of a printed piece; decisions include size, layout, type, printing instructions, etc.

Four Color Process/Process Color—Means of achieving full color with four inks: yellow, magenta (pink-purplish red), cyan (turquoise blue) and black. Each color is separated into its own negative. The full-color effect is created by overlapping dots made of these four transparent ink colors

Frankenstein Cards—A collection of card parts that are put together but don't fit into a harmonious card

Freelance; Freelancer
Professional such as artist or photographer who is self-employed; also called contract artist; see also Independent Contractor

G

Gloss—Paper, ink or varnish that has a shiny appearance

Graphics—Visual communications; supplements type

Graphic Designer—Design professional whose work is usually printed; tasks include designing of layout and specifying size, type, art, colors and paper, etc.

H

Halftone—Results from preparing a continuous-tone photograph for printing; changing it into a pattern of small black and white dots

Halftone Screen—Engraved glass through which photographs or other shaded images are reduced to a series of dots

Hierarchy of Attention—The orderly arrangement of the visual components of a layout; involves size, contrast, position, form and content

High Chroma—Chroma indicates the brightness of an ink color; high chroma colors are very bright

Hot Stamping—See Foil

Hue—The color itself, i.e., red, green, purple

I

Italic—Type that slants to the right; used for emphasis

Independent Contractor Person who is self-employed and works for others on a per-project basis; contrasted with employee; determined in accordance with IRS guidelines (See Appendix B.)

J

Justify or Justified—To set the left, right or both margins so they are perfectly even

K

Kern or Kerning—To adjust the space between characters in words and letters so it reads better

L

Laminate—To protect paper by giving it a glossy surface by applying a transparent plastic coating

Laid—Paper with a tiny parallel line pattern through it in the same color

Layout—A sketch or drawing of a design for a printed piece

Leading—The amount of space between lines of type, expressed in points

Left Justified—Flush left alignment

Letterspace—Amount of space between letters; measured in points

Line—A solid black image that can be reproduced without using a halftone screens; also called a rule

Line Space—Amount of space between lines of type; measured in points

Lithography—Form of printing; permits colors and raised or flat letters

Logo or Logotype—Artistic mark or graphic created to be a symbol for an individual or business; also called an emblem

Low Chroma—Chroma indicates the brightness of an ink color; low chroma colors are not bright

Lower Case—Little letters; compared to upper case; easier to read than upper case

M

M—In printing used to indicate a quantity of 1,000

Make-ready—The work done at the print show to prepare a piece for printing

Magenta—A bright pink-pur-plish red, one of the four process colors (yellow, cyan and black are the other three)

Matte Finish—A paper surface with no gloss or shine

Mechanical—Camera-ready art consisting of type, graphics and line art showing the exact placement of every element

N

Network or Networking The ability to do business through your contacts and the contacts of your contacts

O

One-Time Rights—The right to reproduce an artwork once for a specified purpose

Opacity—The degree to which ink shows through to the back of the page

Overlays—Transparent sheets prepared by the past-up person for camera-ready art, showing one color per overlay. Each layer must be perfectly registered to the one below; instructions are also written on overlays

Overrun—Additional copies beyond the number originally specified

P

PANTONE MATCHING SYSTEM—System designed for uniform color production in printing; standardized colors, not made from four-color process

Paste-up—The process of pre-paring camera-ready art involves organizing all the elements for a printed piece and gluing them perfectly into their final position

Pica—A unit of measure in printing; there are 6 picas to an inch, and one pica has 12 points

Plate—A thin sheet of metal on a printing press that transfers the image to the paper; treated so that only the part that is to print receives the ink

Point—A unit of measurement used in measuring type; there are 12 points per pica and 72 points to an inch

Positioning—Establishing your identity in the mind of the public

Prepress—Camera work, color separating, stripping, plate mak-ing and other functions per-formed by the printer prior to printing; also called preparation

Press O.K.—The approval by the client of a press proof sheet before the print run begins

Process Blue—see Cyan

Process Color—See Four-Color Process

Proof or Press Proof
Preliminary copy of the printed piece used for checking accuracy before an entire job is printed; corrections are written on the proof

Q

Quotation or Quote
Printer's estimate of the cost of doing a specific job

R

Rag Content—In paper, contains at least 25% rag or cotton fiber; the more rag content, the more elegant and expensive the paper

Ragged Right or Edge
Column of type that does not line up evenly on the right; contrasted to justified

Register or Registration
To place printing properly with regard to the edges of paper and other printing on the same sheet; such printing is said to be in register

Resolution—The level of refinement of an image, depending on how many dots there are per inch (DPI) images with higher resolution have more dots per inch and reproduce better

Reverse—Type or an image is usually printed in ink and appears in the foreground; when reversed, the ink makes up the background and surrounds the type or image, which are the color of the paper beneath them

Rough Layout or Rough
Sketch giving a general idea of size and placement of text and graphics

Rule—Lines, can be in various widths

S

Sans Serif—Type designed without finishing strokes (feet and trim); looks like this, not this

Satin Finish—Paper with a smooth, satin-like finish

Scaling—Calculating the amount a picture must be reduced or enlarged to fit a specified area; indicated as a percentage of the original

Scanner—Electronic device for putting visual images into the computer

Screen—Dots in patterns or rows used to create halftones; also called linecount

Separation—See Color Separation

Serif—Type designed with finishing strokes (feet and trim); easier to read than sans serif type

Shade—A color value achieved by adding black to a color; compared to tint

Slogan—A sentence or phrase used consistently to express a central message; also called tag line

Small Caps—Small capital letters about the height of lower case letters (x-height)

Sole Proprietorship—A business that is owned by one person or couple

Solid—Area completely and solidly covered with ink; 100% of the specified color

Specifications—Complete and precise written description of features of a printing job; abbreviated "specs"

Spot Color—A single color used as a display accent

Stamping—Pressing an image into paper with a metal die; embossing; may be combined with foils or ink to give the image color; when no color, it is called blind embossing

Stock—The paper or other surface to be printed

T

Tag Line—A sentence or phrase used consistently to express a central message; also called slogan

Target Market—An occupational, demographic or psychological group of consumers designated as the prospects for sales; group towards which the promotional efforts are directed

Thermography—A method of producing business cards where the inks are heated; results in raised lettering

Tight Register—Nearly exact register; elements on a page closely lined up in printing

Tint—A shade of color, often black, created by using a small dot pattern and expressed in a percentage; 10% tint is light and 80% tint is quite dark; a color value achieved by adding white to a color; compared to shade

Trade Customs—Business terms and policies codified by trade associations such as in printing and the graphic arts

Trademark—Unique words or images that have been registered with the Federal Trademark Office (and or state) so that the holder has the exclusive rights to the symbols; designated by either or ® on the design or words

Tradeshow—Exhibition for members of a profession or organization; usually with booths or displays

Typeface—A set of characters with design features making them similar to one another and different from all other typefaces

Type Family—All styles of a particular typeface

Typography—The art and science of composing type to make it legible, readable and pleasing; the arrangement of type on a page

U

Uncoated Paper—Paper on which the printing surface consists of the stock itself

Unjustified—Not aligned to the edge of the page, also called ragged edge

Upper Case Letters
Alternate term for capital letters; compared with lower case letters

V

Vanilla Pudding—Adjective to describe something that is dull or uninteresting

Varnish—A thin protective coating applied to a printed sheet for beauty and protection; can be either gloss or dull

Vellum—A good quality paper; uncoated and relatively absorbent with a slightly rough surface

W

White Space—Area of a printed piece that does not contain images or type; used for guiding the eye and organizing the layout also called negative

Wove—Paper surface with a soft smooth finish

Work For Hire—A relationship in which all rights, title and interest in a creative work, including the copyright, is owned by the party who commissions the work (employer) and not the creator (employee)

X

x-Height—Measure of height of the lower case letters of a typeface; the greater the x-height, the greater the height of the lower case letters and the greater its legibility

Index